FIX YOUR

CHEVROLET

ALL MODELS

1972 to 1960

By

BILL TOBOLDT

Member Society of Automotive Engineers
Associate Member Automotive Engine Rebuilders Association

SOUTH HOLLAND, ILLINOIS
THE GOODHEART-WILLCOX CO., INC.
Publishers

INTRODUCTION

FIX YOUR CHEVROLET is a handbook of time and money-saving information for Chevrolet, Chevy II, Camaro, and Vega owners, and mechanics.

It describes simplified tune-up procedures; tells how to locate trouble and make many adjustments and repairs without the use of expensive equipment.

FIX YOUR CHEVROLET covers shortcut methods of removing parts and replacing defective parts; tells you how to make emergency repairs if your car "conks out," and how to get better than normal Speed, Power, and Economy. It also covers the use of Special Speed Equipment.

In this book, when discussing service procedures, the various engines are usually identified by displacement--390 cu. in., 223 cu. in., etc., rather than by names such as the Impala, Bel Air, Nova. The names identify the complete chassis, which in most cases, is available with a choice of engines. For this reason, it is necessary to determine the displacement of the engine to be repaired, in order to select the repair procedure which is applicable.

FIX YOUR CHEVROLET is based on material obtained from many sources, particularly from topflight Chevrolet mechanics throughout the country, from the Chevrolet Motor Division, General Motors Corporation, and from many tool and equipment manufacturers.

Bill Toboldt

1972 Chevrolet Caprice Coupe.

CONTENTS

TUNE-UP
TIPS

To get maximum performance and best fuel mileage, special care must be taken when doing a tune-up job. While accuracy and precision are required, doing a good tune-up job on a Chevrolet, Chevelle, Chevy II, Camaro, Corvette, Monte Carlo and Nova is not difficult.

WHEN TO DO A TUNE-UP JOB

In general, a tune-up job is needed after about 10,000 miles of operation. However, a much better gauge of when such work is necessary will be indicated when the fuel mileage and performance drop below normal. Because fuel consumption is so dependent on the type of driving, it is impossible to state what fuel mileage can be expected from various

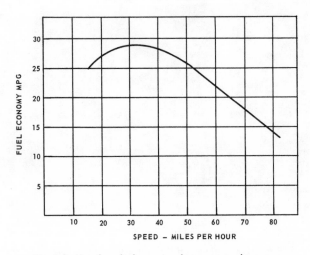

Fig. A-1. Note how fuel economy drops as speed increases.

Chevrolet built cars. Naturally the driver who maintains a steady, conservative speed, will get many more miles per gallon than will the driver who is always driving as fast as possible, regardless of conditions. Fig. A-1 is typical and shows how fuel economy drops as the speed increases.

7

It will be found that cars used mostly in city stop-and-go driving will have lower fuel economy and require a tune-up job more frequently than cars used mostly on trips of ten miles or more. The reason is that on trips of short duration, the engine does not reach full operating temperature. Consequently, valves will tend to stick, compression will drop, and operation of the engine will be rough and more fuel will be required.

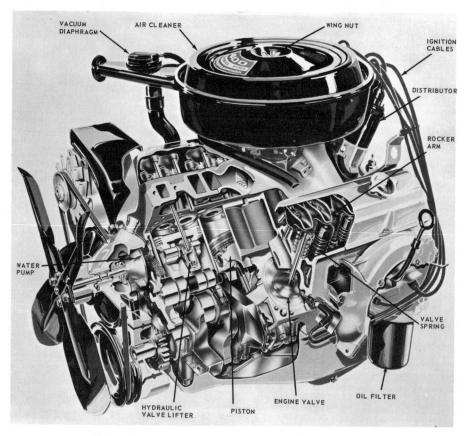

Fig. A-1. Sectional view of V-8 engine 1970–1972. Typical.

In many cases a tune-up job is advisable every 10,000 miles, or possibly sooner, if maximum performance and economy are desired.

Leaving the tune-up go for a longer period will invariably result in hard starting, poor fuel economy, and possibility of roadside failure.

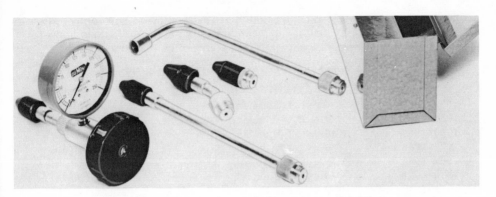

Fig. A-3. Typical compression gauge with special adapters for use with different type engines.

FIRST STEP IN TUNE-UP

The first step in a tune-up job is to make sure the valves are not sticking. Then check compression.

A good way to make sure the valves are free and are not sticking is to take advantage of one of the special oils that are available and designed to free sticking valves.

While instructions with different brands of such lubricants vary somewhat, the usual procedure is to bring the engine up to operating temperature. Then remove the air cleaner from the carburetor and with the engine running at a fast idle, the contents of a can of a tune-up oil is poured slowly and steadily into the air intake of the carburetor. As this is done the engine speed should be increased. Huge clouds of smoke will come from the exhaust, so this operation must be done out-of-doors. It is usually advisable to use the tune-up oil when it will not be necessary to use the car for several hours. In that way the tune-up oil will have ample time to dissolve any gum on the valve stems, and in that way sticking will be eliminated.

When the car is started after using the tune-up oil, it will be found that the engine will idle more smoothly and stepped-up performance will result. A compression test can now be made. It will be safe to assume that there will be no compression loss due to sticking valves.

HOW TO MAKE A COMPRESSION TEST

The first step is to remove the air cleaner, Fig. A-2, and this is held to the carburetor by means of the wing nut. After removing the wing nut, the air cleaner can be lifted from the carburetor. Then block the throttle and choke in the wide-open position. Remove all the spark plugs and then insert the compression gauge, Fig. A-3, into each of the spark plug holes in turn, Fig. A-4. Crank the engine through at least four compression strokes to obtain highest possible reading.

Check and record the compression of each cylinder. The compression should read as indicated in the accompanying table. Variations between the highest and lowest reading cylinders should be less than 20 lbs.

Compression Pressure at Cranking Speed

Year	Model	Compression Pressure
1969-1962	4 cyl. 153 cu. in.	130 lb.
1968-1962	6 cyl. 194 cu. in.	130 lb.
1969-1963	6 cyl. 230 cu. in.	130 lb.
1972-1966	6 cyl. 250 cu. in.	130 lb.
1967-1963	V-8 cyl. 283 cu. in.	150 lb.
1970-1968	V-8 cyl. 302 cu. in.	190 lb.
1972-1968	V-8 cyl. 307 cu. in.	150 lb.
1969-1963	V-8 cyl. 327 cu. in.	160 lb.
1968-1966	V-8 cyl. 327 cu. in. (350 hp)	150 lb.
1971-1968	V-8 cyl. 350 cu. in.	160 lb.
1970-1969	V-8 cyl. 350 cu. in. (370 hp)	190 lb.
1971	Chevrolet 350 cu. in. (245, 270 hp)	160 lb.
1971	Chevrolet 350 cu. in. (330 hp)	150 lb.
1972	V-8 cyl. 350 cu. in. (155, 165, 175 hp)	160 lb.
1972	V-8 cyl. 350 cu. in. (255 hp)	155 lb.
1970-1966	V-8 cyl. 396 cu. in.	160 lb.
1972-1970	Chevrolet 400 cu. in.	160 lb.
1972	Chevrolet 402 cu. in.	160 lb.
1970-1966	V-8 cyl. 427 cu. in.	160 lb.
1970-1969	V-8 cyl. 427 cu. in. (425, 430, 435 hp)	150 lb.
1972	Chevrolet 454 cu. in. (270 hp)	160 lb.
1971-1970	Chevrolet 454 cu. in. (345, 360 hp)	160 lb.
1971	Chevrolet 454 cu. in. (425 hp)	150 lb.
1970	Chevrolet 454 cu. in. (450 hp)	150 lb.
1965-1963	Chevrolet 409 cu. in. V-8	150 lb.
1965-1963	Corvette 327 cu. in. V-8	160 lb.
1962	Chevrolet 235 cu. in. Six	130 lb.
1962	Chevrolet 283 cu. in. V-8	150 lb.
1962	Chevrolet 327 cu. in. V-8	150 lb.
1962	Chevrolet 409 cu. in. V-8	150 lb.
1962	Corvette 327 cu. in. V-8	160 lb.
1961	Chevrolet 235 cu. in. Six	130 lb.
1961	Chevrolet 283 cu. in. V-8	150 lb.
1961	Chevrolet 348 cu. in. V-8	150 lb.
1960-1953	Chevrolet 235 cu. in. Six	130 lb.
1960-1957	Chevrolet 283 cu. in. V-8	150 lb.
1960-1958	Chevrolet 348 cu. in. V-8	150 lb.

If one or more cylinders read low or uneven, pour about a tablespoonful of engine oil on top of each piston in each low reading cylinder. This oil is poured into the spark plug hole. Crank the engine several times and recheck the compression. If the compression comes up but does not reach

Fig. A-4. Checking compression on a V-8 engine.

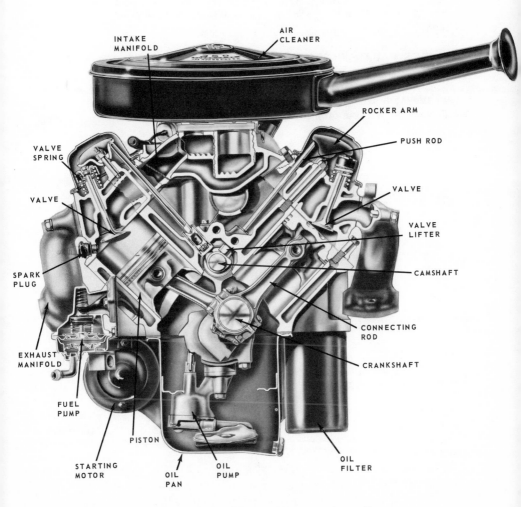

INTAKE MANIFOLD

AIR CLEANER

ROCKER ARM

PUSH ROD

VALVE SPRING

VALVE

VALVE LIFTER

VALVE

CAMSHAFT

SPARK PLUG

CONNECTING ROD

CRANKSHAFT

EXHAUST MANIFOLD

FUEL PUMP

PISTON

STARTING MOTOR

OIL PAN

OIL PUMP

OIL FILTER

Sectional view of Camaro 350 cu. in. V-8 engine. (Typical) normal, the rings and pistons are probably worn and reconditioning would be needed. If the compression does not improve, the valves are sticking or are seating poorly.

If two adjacent cylinders indicate low compression and injecting oil does not increase the compression, the cause may be a head gasket leak between the cylinders. Engine coolant and/or oil in cylinders could result in case of such a defect.

The compression check is important because an engine with low or uneven compression cannot be tuned successfully to give peak performance. Therefore, it is essential that improper compression be corrected before proceeding with an engine tune-up. If a weak cylinder cannot be located with the compression test, it is desirable to make a cylinder balance test.

CYLINDER BALANCE TEST

To make a cylinder balance test, the engine is operated on a few cylinders at a time while the remaining spark plugs are grounded. The usual method of grounding the spark plugs is by means of a special wiring

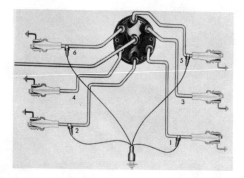

Fig. A-5. Method of shorting out cylinders when making a cylinder balance test.

harness, but if such a harness is not available the wires can be disconnected from the spark plugs and held against any convenient point on the engine by means of a familiar spring-type clothespin. Fig. A-5 shows the test being made by means of the wiring harness. In addition, a vacuum gauge, Fig. A-6 can be used to accurately determine the performance of the cylinders which are operating. If a vacuum gauge is not available, it is then necessary to estimate the speed of the engine as the spark plugs are shorted out.

The procedure is to connect a vacuum gauge to the intake manifold of the engine. Then start the engine and operate it at a fast idle. By means of the wiring harness, or other means, ground all the cylinders except the two being tested.

Tune-up Tips

Fig. A-6. Type of vacuum gauge used to check engine performance.

Divide the firing order in half and arrange one half over the other. The cylinders to be tested together appear one over the other. For example, V-8 firing order 1-8-4-3-6-5-7-2 should be arranged as follows:

$$\frac{1\text{-}8\text{-}4\text{-}3}{6\text{-}5\text{-}7\text{-}2} = 1\text{-}6,\ 8\text{-}5,\ 4\text{-}7,\ 3\text{-}2.$$

The L-Six firing order would be arranged:

$$1\text{-}5\text{-}3\text{-}6\text{-}2\text{-}4 = \frac{1\text{-}5\text{-}3}{6\text{-}2\text{-}4} = 1\text{-}6,\ 5\text{-}2,\ 3\text{-}4.$$

The firing order of the Chevy II Four would be arranged:

$$1\text{-}3\text{-}4\text{-}2 = \frac{1\text{-}3}{4\text{-}2} = 1\text{-}4,\ 3\text{-}2.$$

1972 Chevrolet Monte Carlo Coupe.

IGNITION
TUNE-UP

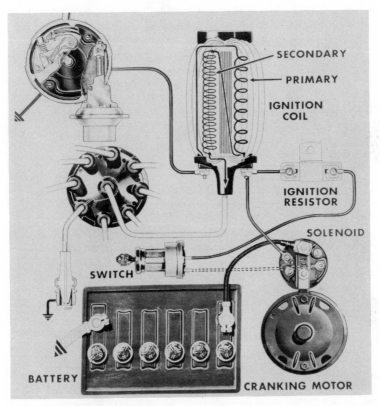

Fig. B-1. Typical wiring diagram of Chevrolet ignition system. Note block type ignition resistor. On recent models this is replaced with a single resistor wire.

The ignition system, Fig. B-1, is designed to supply the spark that ignites the combustible mixture in the combustion chamber. The ignition system is easily serviced.

QUICK TEST OF SPARK

There are many types of expensive equipment available for testing the spark. However, a satisfactory method requiring no equipment, is to disconnect the high tension cable at one of the spark plugs. Then, with the engine operating, hold the end of the spark plug wire about one-quarter inch away from some metal portion of the engine, such as the exhaust manifold, or the cylinder block. A strong, spark should jump from the end of the wire to the engine. If the spark will not jump that distance, or is weak or intermittent, the ignition system requires servicing. Before disconnecting the wire at the spark plug, be sure to observe the precaution given in the paragraph "Checks and Care of Ignition Cable." Also make sure that there are no leaks from the fuel system which might be ignited by the jumping spark.

WHAT TO DO ABOUT SPARK PLUGS

Spark plugs should give at least 10,000 miles of satisfactory service. But it must be remembered that the continued use of old spark plugs results in hard starting and increased fuel consumption, Fig. B-2. Also

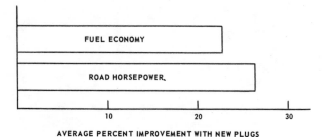

AVERAGE PERCENT IMPROVEMENT WITH NEW PLUGS

Fig. B-2. Note improvement in fuel economy and road horsepower when new spark plugs are installed.

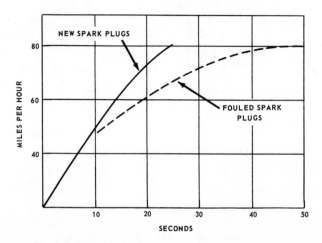

Fig. B-3. When spark plugs are fouled, acceleration drops off.

under wide open throttle conditions, maximum power will not be developed, Fig. B-3. Spark plugs that have a sooty insulator can be easily cleaned and put back into service, but plugs on which the electrodes are worn should be replaced with new ones.

When spark plug insulators are covered with soot, it is an indication that the engine requires servicing of some sort, or the wrong kind of spark plug is being used. The correct type of spark plug for use on Chevrolet engines is given in the accompanying table.

Spark Plug Type
Original Equipment

Car Model	Displacement	Spark Plug Model	Spark Plug Gap	Distributor Gap +
1959-1961	235 cu. in. Six	AC 44	.035 in. ·	.016 in.
1959-1961	283 cu. in. V-8	AC 44	.035 in.	*
1959-1961	348 cu. in. V-8	AC 44N	.035 in.	*
1962	235 cu. in. Six	AC 46	.035 in.	.016 in.
1962	283 cu. in. V-8	AC 46	.035 in.	.016 in.
1962	409 cu. in. V-8	AC 43N	.035 in.	*
1962-1968	153 cu. in. Four	AC 46N	.035 in.	.016 in.
1962-1968	194 cu. in. Six	AC 46N	.035 in.	.016 in.
1963-1969	230 cu. in. Six	AC 46N	.035 in.	.016 in.
1966-1969	250 cu. in. Six	AC 46N	.035 in.	.016 in.
1963-1967	283 cu. in. V-8	AC 45	.035 in.	.016 in.
1968	302 cu. in. V-8	AC 43	.035 in.	.016 in.
1968	307 cu. in. V-8	AC 45S	.035 in.	.016 in.
1963-1968	327 cu. in. V-8	AC 44	.035 in.	.016 in.
1968	327 cu. in. V-8 250 hp	AC 44S	.035 in.	.016 in.
1968	327 cu. in. V-8 others	AC 44	.035 in.	.016 in.
1967	350 cu. in. V-8	AC 44	.035 in.	.016 in.
1966-1967	396 cu. in. V-8	AC 43N	.035 in.	.016 in.
1963-1965	409 cu. in. V-8	AC 43N	.035 in.	.016 in.
1966-1967	427 cu. in. V-8	AC 43N	.035 in.	.016 in.
1968	427 cu. in. V-8 430 hp	AC 43XL	.035 in.	.016 in.
1968	427 cu. in. V-8 others	AC 43N	.035 in.	.016 in.
1969-1971	153 cu. in. Four	AC R46N	.035 in.	.016 in.
1970	153 cu. in. Four	AC R46Y	.035 in.	.016 in.
1970	230, 250 cu. in.	AC R46T	.035 in.	.016 in.
1971	230, 250 cu. in.	AC R46TS	.035 in.	.016 in.
1969-1970	302 cu. in. V-8	AC R43	.035 in.	.016 in.
1969-1970	307 cu. in. V-8	AC R43S	.035 in.	.016 in.

Car Model	Displacement	Spark Plug Model	Spark Plug Gap	Distributor Gap +
1971	307 cu. in.	AC R45TS	.035 in.	.016 in.
1969	327 cu. in. V-8 210 hp	AC R45S	.035 in.	.016 in.
1969	327 cu. in. V-8 235 hp	AC 45S	.035 in.	.016 in.
1969-1970	350 cu. in. V-8 255, 300, 350 hp	AC R44	.035 in.	.016 in.
1969-1970	350 cu. in. V-8 370 hp	AC R43	.035 in.	.016 in.
1971	350 cu. in. 245 hp	AC R45TS	.035 in.	.016 in.
1971	350 cu. in. 270, 330 hp	AC R44YS	.035 in.	.016 in.
1969-1970	396 cu. in. V-8 265, 325 hp	AC R44N	.035 in.	.016 in.
1969-1970	396 cu. in. V-8 350, 375 hp	AC R43N	.035 in.	.016 in.
1971	400 cu. in. 255 hp	AC R44TS	.035 in.	.016 in.
1971	402 cu. in. 300 hp	AC R44TS	.035 in.	.016 in.
1969	427 cu. in. V-8 335 hp	AC R44N	.035 in.	.016 in.
1969-1970	427 cu. in. V-8 390, 400, 425 hp	AC R43N	.035 in.	.016 in.
1969-1970	427 cu. in. V-8 430 hp	AC R43XL	.035 in.	.016 in.
1969-1970	427 cu. in. V-8 435 hp	AC RC42N	.035 in.	.016 in.
1970	454 cu. in. V-8 345 hp	AC R44T	.035 in.	.016 in.
1970	454 cu. in. V-8 360 hp	AC R43T	.035 in.	.016 in.
1970	454 cu. in. V-8 390, 450 hp	AC R43T	.035 in.	.016 in.
1971	454 cu. in.	AC R42TS	.035 in.	.016 in.
1972	250 cu. in.	AC R46T	.035 in.	.016 in.
1972	307 cu. in.	AC R44T	.035 in.	.016 in.
1972	350 cu. in.	AC R44T	.035 in.	.016 in.
1972	400 cu. in.	AC R44T	.035 in.	.016 in.
1972	402 cu. in.	AC R44T	.035 in.	.016 in.
1972	454 cu. in.	AC R44T	.035 in.	.016 in.

+ When specified, gap refers to used points; when new points are installed, set gap to .019 in.

* When setting gap on these engines, set dwell angle to 28 to 32 deg. If dwell meter is not available, connect a test lamp to primary lead at distributor. Rotate shaft until one of the circuit breaker cam lobes is under the center of the rubbing block on the breaker lever. Turn adjusting screw, Fig. B-18, until the lamp lights, then back off one-half turn.

Careful examination of the spark plugs will usually disclose whether the plug is the correct type for the kind of service in which the car is being used and also the general condition of the engine will be revealed. Typical conditions are shown in Figs. B-4, B-5, B-6 and B-7.

The terms "hot" and "cold" as applied to spark plugs, indicate that

Fig. B-4. Left. Spark plug fouled by excessive oil. Fig. B-5. Right. When spark plug insulator is covered with dry soot, an excessively rich fuel mixture is indicated.

the temperature of a certain plug is hotter than another plug. The higher the temperature of a spark plug, the less tendency there is for soot to collect on the insulator. The spark plugs listed in the table are for normal driving. If the car is driven at high speeds for prolonged periods, a "colder" type spark plug should be used. Or if the car is used exclusively in slow speed stop-and-go city driving, a warmer type plug may be more satisfactory.

Fig. B-6. Left. When spark plug insulator has burned appearance, the plug is too "hot" for that particular engine and a "cooler" running plug should be installed. Fig. B-7. Right. When the spark plug gap is worn as shown, new plugs should be installed.

The plug shown in Fig. B-7 is definitely worn out, as indicated by the eroded condition of the firing point or gap. The center electrode should be flat with sharp edges, and the side electrodes should not have a groove or show other signs of spark wear. In an emergency, a plug with worn electrodes can be put back into service by filing the end of the center electrode so that it is perfectly flat. If there is a groove worn in the side electrode, it should be removed with a file.

When the spark plug insulator has a rusty, brown or greyish powder deposit, or when the insulator is light brown around the tip, the plug has the correct heat range and is operating satisfactorily.

Fig. B-8. To effectively clean spark plugs, specialized equipment is advisable.

CLEANING AND CHECKING SPARK PLUGS

The best way to clean spark plugs is by means of special equipment, as shown in Fig. B-8. If this is not available, the soot should be scraped from the insulator and from the interior of the metal body of the spark plug as much as possible. After the spark plug is cleaned, it should be carefully examined to make sure that the insulator is not cracked at any point, or has other defects. In addition, it is important to check the condition of the firing point or gap, as an excessively worn gap, Fig. B-7, will reduce the effectiveness of the plug and it is usually advisable to install a new one. A gap is worn when the end of the center electrode is rounded and when the side electrode has a groove worn in it.

ADJUSTING THE SPARK PLUG GAP

When adjusting the spark plug gap, never attempt to bend the center electrode as this invariably results in breaking the insulator. Only the side electrode should be bent when adjusting a spark plug gap. Combination gauges and adjusters are available at nominal cost. Fig. B-9 shows one type of tool which also includes a file for filing the electrodes, as well as a gauge to use in adjusting the gap and a hook with which to bend the side electrode. It should be pointed out that by the time the electrodes

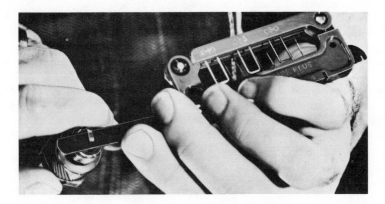

Fig. B-9. One type of spark plug gap gauge which includes a file used to true plug gap and a tool for bending the side electrode.

are worn to a degree that filing is needed, it is better to install new plugs. Higher voltages are needed to jump the gap of worn electrodes and consequently misfiring and hard starting will result.

The gap should be adjusted to specified amount, .035 in., and care should be exercised that this adjustment is made with accuracy. Either a round wire type gauge, Fig. B-9, or a flat sealer type gauge can be used. However the round wire type is preferred when measuring the gap of worn firing points.

REMOVING AND INSTALLING SPARK PLUGS

Before removing a spark plug it is first necessary to disconnect the spark plug wire. Do not pull on the wire itself because the wire connection may be damaged. Instead grasp, twist and pull the molded cap only in order to disconnect the wire. Then carefully blow all the dust and dirt which may be surrounding the spark plug. If this dirt is not removed it will drop into the combustion chamber and eventually damage the engine valves. The spark plug can then be unscrewed from the cylinder head. A 13/16 in., (some plugs 5/8 in.) "deep" socket wrench is used to remove the spark plugs. Special deep sockets with sponge rubber lining in the upper end designed to grip the plug insulator and also reduce the possibility of cracking the insulators are available.

Before installing the spark plugs make sure that the spark plug threads and surface contacting the head are clean. This is particularly important as any dirt may result in compression leakage, but also make the spark plug operate at higher than normal temperatures with attendant misfiring and short life.

When tightening the spark plugs, the factory specifies 20 to 25 ft. lb. torque. That is 20 to 25 lb. exerted at the end of a one foot wrench, or 40 to 50 lb. at the end of a six inch wrench.

REMOVING THE DISTRIBUTOR CAP

In order to replace ignition breaker points, the condenser or rotor, it is first necessary to remove the distributor cap.

There are three different methods used to hold the distributor cap in place on the Chevrolet cars. The design shown in Fig. B-10 is used primarily on the Chevrolet V-8 engine. To remove this type of cap all that is necessary is to press down on the latch and give it a half turn with a screwdriver, as shown in Fig. B-10.

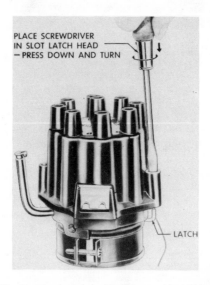

PLACE SCREWDRIVER IN SLOT LATCH HEAD — PRESS DOWN AND TURN

LATCH

Fig. B-10. Removing cap from distributor used on V-8 engines.

Fig. B-11 shows the distributor cap clip used on the 1962 and earlier six cylinder models. Two clips are provided, one on each side of the distributor cap. They are released by prying them away from the cap.

The cap used on the 1963-1969 four and six cylinder distributors is held by two conventional screws, Fig. B-12. Removing these screws permits removal of the cap.

After removing the distributor cap on any distributor it should be cleaned carefully and then thoroughly inspected. Check to be sure that it

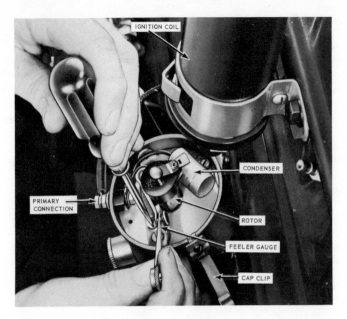

Fig. B-11. Method of adjusting breaker point gap on distributor used on 1962 and earlier Chevrolet Six. Note clips used to hold cap in place.

Fig. B-12. Typical of distributors used on 1963–1972 four and six cylinder engines.

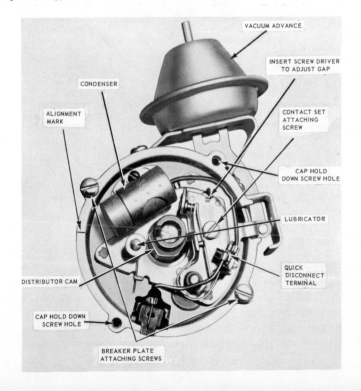

is not cracked at any point. Particular attention should be paid to any evidence of charring between the firing points on the interior of the cap. Such a condition results from arcing of the spark. Also make sure the interior of the towers are clean and are not corroded. Any evidence of corrosion should be removed. The easiest way to do this is to roll some fine grain abrasive paper around a pencil and use this as a hone to remove the corrosion, Fig. B-13.

If the cap is cracked, or if there has been any arcing between the points in the interior of the cap, or if the interior of the towers cannot be cleaned, a new cap should be installed.

Fig. B-13. Using a piece of fine emery cloth on a pencil to clean towers of distributor cap.

REMOVING THE DISTRIBUTOR ROTOR

With the cap removed, the rotor can then be removed. On the type distributor used on the V-8 engines, Fig. B-14, the rotor is held in place by two screws which enter the centrifugal advance mechanism. Removing these screws permits lifting the rotor from its position. On other distributors, Fig. B-11, the rotor is pulled vertically from the top of the distributor shaft. On this latter type of construction, if the spring contact on top of the rotor is defective, a new rotor should be obtained. Also if the firing end of the rotor is badly erroded, the rotor should be replaced.

REPLACING THE CONDENSER

The condenser, Figs. B-11, B-12 and B-14, is replaced at the same time that the regular points are replaced. To remove a condenser, all that is necessary is to remove the attaching screw and disconnect the short wire which connects the condenser to the breaker points.

Specialized equipment is needed to test a condenser, but as the cost of a new condenser is relatively low, they are usually discarded without

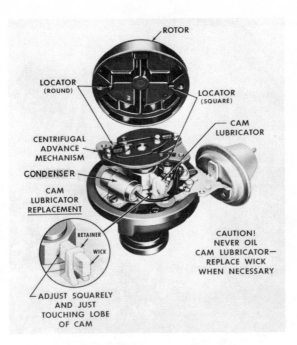

ROTOR

LOCATOR (ROUND)

LOCATOR (SQUARE)

CAM LUBRICATOR

CENTRIFUGAL ADVANCE MECHANISM

CONDENSER

CAM LUBRICATOR REPLACEMENT

RETAINER

WICK

ADJUST SQUARELY AND JUST TOUCHING LOBE OF CAM

CAUTION! NEVER OIL CAM LUBRICATOR— REPLACE WICK WHEN NECESSARY

Fig. B-14. Details of V-8 distributor. Cam lubricator on 1972 distributor has been changed to the round type as used on six cylinder distributors.

testing whenever ignition breaker points are replaced. A defective condenser will cause severe arcing of the breaker points, resulting in a scorched or smoky appearance of the points, accompanied with misfiring.

REPLACING BREAKER POINTS

Ignition breaker points should be replaced when the contacts are badly burned, Fig. B-15, or when there is excessive metal transfer from one point to the other. Metal transfer is considered excessive when it equals or exceeds the gap width or approximately 0.015 in.

Fig. B-15. Note pitted condition of these ignition breaker points.

Fix Your Chevrolet

Burned points are generally the result of a defective condenser or the result of an accumulation of oil and dirt on the points. This is usually caused by oil bleeding from the distributor base bushing onto the points, by excessive or improper cam lubricant being thrown on the points, or neglecting to clean the points periodically.

Excessive metal transfer from one point to the other is generally caused by incorrect point alignment, incorrect voltage regulator setting, wrong type of condenser, or a radio condenser installed to the distributor side of the coil, or extended operation at speeds other than normal.

Chevrolet 307 cu. in. V-8 engine equipped with 2-barrel carburetor and fitted with Controlled Combustion System.

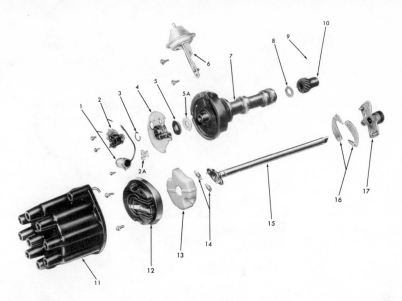

Fig. B-16. View of typical V-8 distributor. 1–Condenser. 2–Contact point assembly. 2A–Cam lubricator. 3–Retaining ring. 4–Breaker plate. 5–Felt washer. 5A–Plastic seal. 6–Vacuum advance unit. 7–Housing. 8–Shim washer. 9–Drive gear pin. 10–Drive gear. 11–Cap. 12–Rotor. 13–Radio shield. 14–Weight springs. 15–Main shaft. 16–Advance weights. 17–Cam weight base assembly.

Breaker points which have a smooth gray surface are still serviceable and will make contact over the entire contacting area.

On the six cylinder and four cylinder models, the distributors are readily accessible and the breaker points may be replaced without removing the distributor from the engine. On the V-8 engines, the distributors are not so accessible. Consequently, most mechanics prefer to remove the distributor from the engine, as this will permit a more careful examination of the condition of the breaker points, and also simplify the adjustment of the breaker point gap.

Naturally, if the distributor is to be overhauled or tested on a distributor test bench, it will be necessary to remove the unit from the engine.

HOW TO REPLACE BREAKER POINTS

Eight Cylinder Engine Distributor: The contact point set is replaced as one complete assembly and only the dwell angle (breaker point gap) requires adjustment after replacement. The breaker lever spring tension and point alignment are set at the factory and require no further adjustment.

Remove the distributor cap by placing a screwdriver in the slot head of the latch, press down and turn 1/4 turn in either direction. Remove the radio shield 13, Fig. B-16. Remove the attaching screws which hold the base of the contact assembly in place. Remove the primary and condenser leads from the nylon connection, in the contact set, Fig. B-17. Contact set can then be lifted from the distributor.

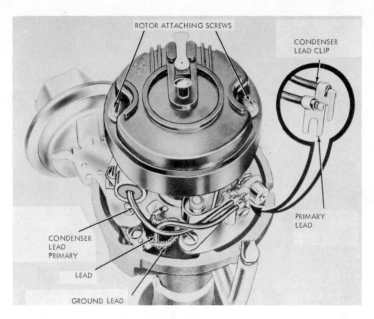

Fig. B-17. Note rotor attaching screws and leads on this V-8 distributor.

To install a new set reverse this procedure. When installing the primary and condenser leads, be sure they are installed as shown in Fig. B-17. Improper installation will cause lead interference between the cap, weight base and breaker advance plate.

If the car has approximately 20,000 miles, or sooner if desired, the cam lubricator wick, Figs. B-14 and B-16, should be changed. Using long nosed pliers, squeeze assembly together at base and lift out. Remove all lubricant from cam surface and replace in same manner. The end of the cam lubricant wick should be adjusted to just touch cam lobes. Over-lubricating of cam, resulting in grease on contact points, can be caused by cam lubrication wick bearing too hard against the cam surface. A correctly adjusted cam lubricator wick will provide adequate lubrication of cam. Do not apply additional grease to the cam surface.

Crank the engine and observe action of the points to be sure that they open and close as the engine is cranked. Then after installing the distributor cap, operate the engine at idle speed and adjust the points accurately as follows: Using a hex type wrench, turn the adjusting screw, Fig. B-18, in a clockwise direction until the engine begins to misfire, then turn the screw one-half turn in the opposite direction. This will give the approximate dwell angle of 30 deg. which is preferred. If a dwell meter is available, that should be used for adjusting the breaker point gap.

Four and Six Cylinder Distributor 1962-1972: To replace the ignition breaker points on this type of distributor, first release the distributor cap holddown screws, remove cap and rotor. Pull primary and condenser lead wires from contact point quick disconnect terminal, Fig. B-12.

Ignition Tune-up

Remove contact set attaching screw, lift contact point set from breaker plate. Clean breaker plate of oil sludge and dirt, and place new contact point assembly in position on the breaker plate, and install attaching screw. Be careful to wipe protective film from set prior to installation. Note that the pilot on the contact set must engage matching hole in breaker

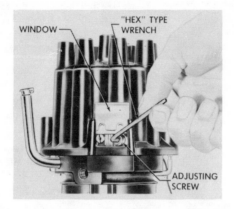

Fig. B-18. Method of adjusting breaker point gap on V-8 distributor.

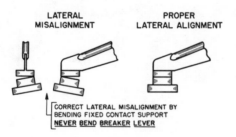

Fig. B-19. Ignition breaker points must be accurately aligned.

plate. Connect primary or condenser lead wires to quick disconnect terminal on contact point set. Check and adjust points for proper alignment and breaker arm spring tension, Fig. B-19. If points require alignment, bend the stationary contact support. The contact spring pressure should be 20 to 23 oz., as measured with a spring balance. Weak spring tension will cause chatter, resulting in arcing and burning of the points and an ignition miss at high speed. Excessive tension will cause undue wear of the contact points. When checking the spring pressure, the scale should be hooked to the breaker lever and the pull exerted at 90 deg. to the breaker lever. The reading should be taken just as the points separate. Pressure can be adjusted by bending the breaker lever spring.

The point opening of new points can be checked with a feeler gauge, but the use of a feeler gauge on rough or uncleaned breaker points is not recommended as the reading would be inaccurate. Correct point setting for both four and six cylinder distributors is .019 in. for new points and .016 for used points. To adjust the contact point opening, first turn or crank the engine until the breaker arm rubbing block is on the high point of the cam lobe. This will provide maximum point opening. Loosen the contact support block screw, Fig. B-12. Use a screwdriver to move the point support to obtain the correct opening of .019 in. for new points and .016 in. for used points, Fig. B-20. Then tighten the contact support lock screw and recheck the point opening. If available, check the adjustment with a cam angle or swell gauge.

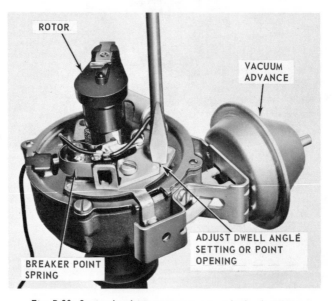

Fig. B-20. Setting breaker point gap on six cylinder distributor.

An exploded view of the distributor used on six cylinder Chevrolet built cars from 1962-1972 is shown in Fig. B-21. The four cylinder distributor is similar in detail.

235 cu. in. 1962-1954 Six Distributor: To replace the ignition breaker points, first remove the distributor cap and rotor, Fig. B-11. Remove the primary wire. Loosen the primary outside spanner nut, and unhook the breaker arm spring from the terminal. Remove contact point lock screw and remove the assembly. Carefully wipe the protective oil film from the contact point of the new set. Place the contact point and support assembly in position over pivot post and adjusting screw, and install lock screw loosely. Place breaker arm over pivot post and hook arm spring over terminal stud. Tighten terminal stud nut securely, and assemble

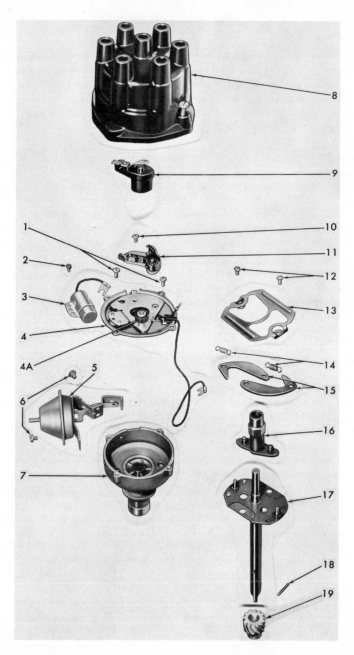

Fig. B-21. Exploded view of typical six cylinder distributor. 1–Breaker plate attaching screws.
2–Condenser attaching screws. 3–Condenser. 4–Breaker plate assembly. 4A–Cam lubricator. 5–
Vacuum control assembly. 6–Vacuum assembly attaching screws. 7–Housing. 8–Distributor cap.
9–Rotor. 10–Contact point screws. 11–Contact point assembly. 12–Weight cover screws. 13–
Weight cover. 14–Weight springs. 15–Advance weights. 16–Cam assembly. 17–Main shaft assembly. 18–Roll pin. 19–Drive gear.

primary wire, lock clip and nut to terminal. Set point opening and align points. Point opening on new points should be .019 in. and used points .016 in. Breaker arm spring tension should be 19 to 23 oz. Replacing rotor and cap completes the operation.

REPLACING THE DISTRIBUTOR

When it is decided to overhaul the distributor, or to check the advance on a distributor test bench, it is necessary to remove the distributor from the engine, and the procedure is as follows: On radio equipped Corvettes, remove ignition shield from over distributor and coil. One bolt is accessible from top of shield, the other two are at rear of shield facing the fire wall. On all models release the distributor cap hold down screws or clips, remove the cap and place it clear of the work area. If necessary, remove the secondary leads from the distributor cap after first marking the cap tower from the lead to No. 1 cylinder. This will aid in the reinstallation of the leads and the cap. Disconnect the primary lead from the coil terminal. Scribe a realignment mark on the distributor bowl and engine in line with the rotor segment. Disconnect the vacuum line to distributor. On the Corvette, also disconnect the tachometer drive cable. Remove the distributor hold down bolt and clamp, Fig. B-22. The distributor can then be lifted from the engine. Note the position of the vacuum advance mechanism relative to the engine, so the distributor can be reinstalled in its original position.

Avoid rotating the engine with distributor removed, as that would necessitate complete retiming of the ignition.

To reinstall the distributor when the engine has not been cranked while the distributor was removed, proceed as follows: Turn the rotor about 1/8 turn in a clockwise direction past the mark previously placed on the distributor housing to locate the rotor. Push the distributor down into position in the cylinder block with the housing in the normal installed position, Fig. B-22.

It may be necessary to remove the rotor slightly to start the gear into mesh with the camshaft gear, but rotor should line up with the mark when the distributor is down in place. Then tighten the distributor clamp bolt snugly and connect the vacuum line. Connect primary wire to coil terminal and install cap. Also install spark plug and high tension wires if they were removed.

If the engine was cranked while the distributor was removed, it will be necessary to position the number one piston in firing position. To do this, remove number one spark plug and with the finger on the plug hole, crank the engine until compression is felt in the number one cylinder. Continue cranking until timing mark on crankshaft pulley lines up with timing tab attached to the engine front cover. An alternate method is to remove the rocker cover (left bank on V-8 engines) and crank engine until number one intake valve closes. Then continue to crank slowly about one-third turn until the timing mark on pulley lines up with timing tab.

Install distributor in block in normal position, Fig. B-22, noting position of vacuum control unit. Position rotor to point toward front of engine with the distributor housing held in installed position. Then turn rotor counterclockwise approximately one-eighth turn more toward left cylinder bank and push the distributor down to engine camshaft. It may be necessary to rotate rotor slightly until camshaft engagement is felt.

While pressing firmly down on distributor housing, kick starter over a few times to make sure oil pump shaft is engaged. Install hold down clamp and bolt and snug down bolt. Turn distributor body slightly until points just open and tighten distributor clamp bolt. Place distributor cap in position and check to see if rotor lines up with terminal for number one spark plug.

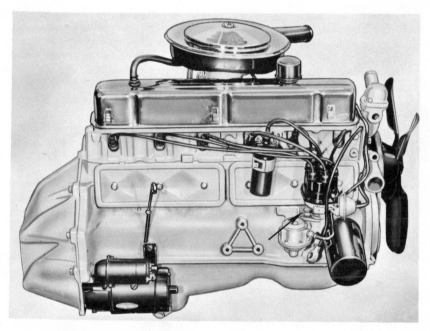

Fig. B-22. Arrow points to distributor clamp screw. Also typical of V-8 construction.

Install distributor cap, check all high tension wire connections and connect spark plug wires, if they have been removed. It is important that wires be installed in their location in the supports. The brackets are numbered to show the correct installation. Wires must be installed as indicated to prevent cross firing. Fig. B-22 shows the location of the wires on the six cylinder model. On V-8 engines follow the numbering on the brackets. Connect vacuum line to distributor and distributor primary wire to coil terminal. The engine can then be started and the timing set.

Fig. B-23. Typical timing marks.

TIMING THE IGNITION

In order to get maximum performance and economy from any of the Chevrolet engines, it is necessary that the ignition timing be set with a high degree of accuracy. If the timing is too far advanced, there is danger of burning holes in the pistons, and if the spark is too far retarded, maximum power will not be attained, and in addition fuel economy will drop.

Ignition timing marks on a 235 cu. in. Six are located on the flywheel and can be seen through an opening in the left side of the flywheel housing. Other engines, four, six and V-8, have the timing marks on the crankshaft pulley or on the vibration damper at the front end of the crankshaft, Fig.. B-23, which is typical of the timing markings at the front end of the engine.

Note the markings on the pads are in 2 deg. increments, with the greatest number of markings on the "A" side of the "O." The "O" marking indicates top dead center of number one cylinder and all before top dead center settings fall on the "A" (advance) side of the "O."

Before attempting to time the engine, the marks should be wiped clean so they are clearly visible. If necessary, chalk the proper mark so it can be clearly seen. The engine is correctly timed when the breaker points

Fig. B-24. One type of timing light.

34

just start to open when the piston is on its compression stroke and the correct degree mark is in alignment with the index mark.

The actual timing is usually done with the aid of a timing light, Fig. B-24. Another method which does not use any special equipment will be described later. Connect the timing light to number one spark plug and to the battery, or follow the instructions accompanying the timing light. Disconnect spark advance hose and plug the vacuum source opening. Start the engine and operate at specified idle speed. Aim timing light at timing marks. Adjust the timing by loosening the distributor clamp and rotating the distributor body as required until correct timing mark is in alignment with pointer. Tighten clamp to hold distributor in position. Stop engine and reconnect vacuum.

OCTANE SELECTOR

Fig. B-25. Octane selector on 1962 and earlier Chevrolet Six.

On the 1962 and earlier 235 cu. in. six cylinder engines, set the octane selector at zero, Fig. B-25. Start the engine and run at idling speed. Aim the timing light at flywheel housing opening on 1962 and earlier Six's. The timing mark should align with correct degree mark as listed in the specifications. If the marks do not align, loosen distributor clamp bolt and rotate the distributor until the marks do align.

After the timing has been correctly set, the distributor clamp bolt should be tightened. Also be sure to reconnect the vacuum line.

If a timing light is not available, a method can be used which requires no special equipment. Crank the engine until number one piston is coming up on the compression stroke. Remove the spark plugs. Compression will be felt by holding your thumb over the spark plug hole when the piston is coming up on the compression stroke. In addition, both intake and exhaust valves will be closed. Continue cranking until the desired timing mark lines up with the index mark. With the ignition cable connected to number one spark plug, place the plug on some metal part of the engine, such as the exhaust manifold. Then loosen the distributor hold down clamp and rotate the distributor body. At the same time, observe the spark plug. Tighten the distributor in position when a spark jumps at the plug gap. The timing will now be set at the correct position.

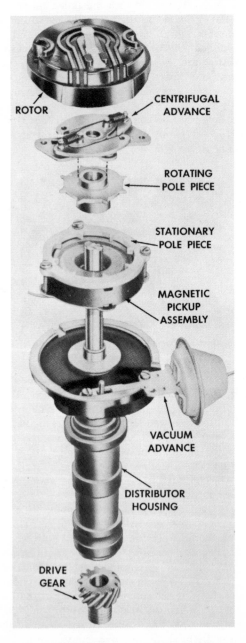

Fig. B-26. Magnetic pulse distributor components.

Ignition Tune-up

DISTRIBUTOR SHAFT ROTATION

The distributor shaft on all Chevrolet, Chevy II, Nova, Chevelle, Camaro, Corvette and Monte Carlo engines rotates in a clockwise direction.

FIRING ORDER

The firing order on all V-8 engines is 1-8-4-3-6-5-7-2. On the in-line six cylinder engines it is 1-5-3-6-2-4, and on the four cylinder engine it is 1-3-4-2.

On the V-8 engines, the numbering from front to rear is left bank 1-3-5-7 and the right bank 2-4-6-8. On six and four cylinder engines, the front cylinder is number one and the remaining cylinders are in normal numerical order.

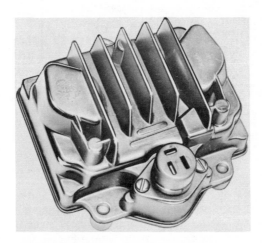

Fig. B-27. Ignition pulse amplifier unit used with transistor ignition.

TRANSISTOR IGNITION

The transistor ignition system available as optional equipment features a specially designed distributor, Fig. B-26, pulse amplifier unit, Fig. B-27, and a special coil. A wiring diagram of the transistor ignition system is shown in Fig. B-28. Two resistance wires are also used in the circuit; one as a ballast between the coil negative terminal and ground, while the other resistance wire provides a voltage drop for the engine run circuit, and is bypassed at cranking. The other units in the transistor system (the ignition switch, spark plugs and battery) are of standard design.

Although the external appearance of the distributor resembles a standard distributor, the internal construction is quite different. As

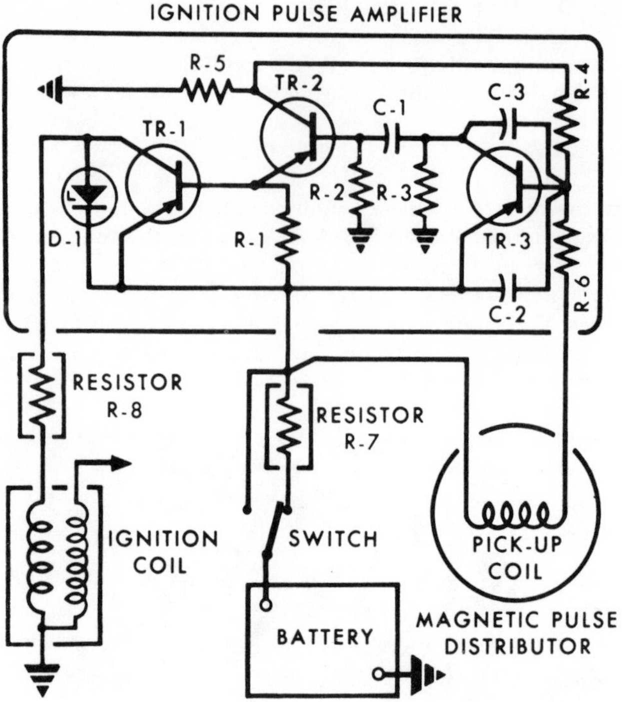

IGNITION PULSE AMPLIFIER

Fig. B-28. Wiring diagram of ignition pulse amplifier.

shown in Fig. B-26, an iron timer core, or rotating pole piece, replaces the conventional breaker cam. The timer core has the same number of equally spaced projections, or vanes, as the engine has cylinders.

The pole piece rotates inside a magnetic pickup assembly, which replaces the conventional breaker plate, contact point set and condenser assembly. The magnetic pickup assembly consists of a ceramic permanent magnet, a pole piece and a pickup coil. The pole piece is a steel plate having equally spaced internal teeth, one tooth for each cylinder of the engine.

The magnetic pickup assembly is mounted over the main bearing of the distributor housing, and is made to rotate by the vacuum control unit, thus providing vacuum advance. The timer core is made to rotate about the shaft by conventional advance weights, thus providing centrifugal advance.

Since there are no moving parts in the ignition pulse amplifier unit mounted forward of the radiator bulkhead, and the distributor shaft and bushings have permanent type lubrication, no periodic maintenance is required for the transistor ignition system. At time of overhaul, the upper bushing may be lubricated by removing the plastic seal and then adding

Ignition Tune-up

SAE 20 oil to the packing in the cavity. A new plastic seal will be required since the old one will be damaged during removal. The distributor lower bushing is lubricated by engine through a splash hole in the distributor housing.

Tachometer readings for test purposes can be made on the primary circuit of the breakerless ignition system in the same manner as on the conventional ignition system. However before attempting to connect a test tachometer into the primary circuit, make sure that the system will not be damaged by the tachometer that is to be used.

The ignition coil primary can be checked for an open circuit by connecting an ohmmeter across the two primary terminals with the battery disconnected. Primary resistance at 75 deg. F. should be between .35 and .55 ohm. An infinite reading on the meter indicates that the primary is open. For the engine to run but miss at times, the primary open may be of the intermittent type.

The coil secondary winding can be checked for an open circuit by connecting an ohmmeter from the high tension center tower to either primary terminal. To obtain a reliable reading, a scale on the ohmmeter having the 20,000 ohm value within, or nearly within, the middle third of the scale should be used. Secondary resistance at 75 deg. F. should be between 8,000 and 12,500 ohms. If the reading is infinite, the coil secondary winding is open.

A dwell reading cannot be obtained on this type of system.

CHECKS AND CARE OF IGNITION CABLE

Whenever ignition cables are disconnected from spark plugs, or from the distributor, special care must be taken not to pull on the wires, but on the molded cap only. This applies particularly to radio resistor wire which has been used on all Chevrolet cars since 1958. These wires can be identified by the letters TVRS or the word Radio stamped on the covering of each cable. The conductors of these cables are made of fabric which has been impregnated with graphite or other material to make it a conductor of high tension current. Pulling on the cable may separate the conductor from the connector at one end, or the weather seal may be damaged. Arcing within the cable would then occur and misfiring and hard starting result. The resistance of each cable is approximately 24,000 ohms. When checking the ignition, these wires should not be punctured with a probe, as the probe may cause damage to the conductor.

If there is any doubt as to the condition of the radio type ignition cable, and there is no ohmmeter available for checking its resistance, it is always a safe plan to install a new wire, or have the wire tested in a shop which has the necessary equipment.

It is very important that the insulation on the cable from the distributor to the spark plugs and from the coil to the distributor be examined carefully, for if this insulation has deteriorated, current will leak and misfiring will result. If the insulation becomes dry so that it is cracked on the surface or is oil soaked, new cables should be installed. A simple

Fig. B-29. If insulation on ignition cable cracks when bent into a sharp arc, cable should be replaced.

test is to bend the cable into a sharp arc, as shown in Fig. B-29. If cracks appear in the surface, a new cable should be installed.

When high tension cables are removed or disconnected, special care must be taken to replace them in their original position. That applies not only to the actual connections from the distributor to the spark plugs, but also to their position in their brackets. If they are placed in the wrong position in the bracket, cross firing from one cable to another will occur and attendant misfiring, Fig. B-30.

IGNITION RESISTOR

Prior to 1959, a block type resistor was used in the primary circuit of the ignition system, Fig. B-1. This is connected between the ignition and the coil. Since that time a resistance wire is used in place of the block type unit. This primary resistance is cut out of the circuit while the engine is being cranked, but as soon as the engine starts, all the current for the ignition coil passes through the resistor. In that way a full 12V current is supplied to the coils for easy starting.

Should this resistance, either the block type or the wire type, become defective, engine misfiring and eventual complete failure of the engine will result. Be sure to check the resistance when an illusive misfiring occurs. The resistance of the ignition resistor on four and six cylinder cars is 1.8 ohms and on V-8 engines with conventional ignition the resistance is 1.35 ohms, and in the case of transistor ignition systems the resistance of a resistor is .43 and .68 ohms.

CHECKING PRIMARY IGNITION CIRCUIT

Except for defective resistors in the line from the ignition switch to the coil, trouble in the primary ignition circuits is usually confined to loose or dirty connections. Pay particular attention to battery and battery ground connections, making sure they are tight and show no evidence of corrosion.

REPLACING THE IGNITION COIL

When replacing the ignition coil, care must be exercised that it is correctly connected to the circuit. The center tower is, of course, the high tension connection and is connected to the center tower of the distributor. The other two terminals of the ignition coil are the primary connections. One terminal is marked "+" and the other "-". The negative terminal should be connected to the primary connection of the distributor, and the other or "+" terminal, to the R terminal of the starter solenoid. From the solenoid the connection goes to the starting switch and then to the "+" terminal of the starting battery. The positive terminal of the coil will have two wires connected to it, and the negative terminal will have only one.

While the coil will operate if the primary connections are reversed, full power will not be developed and missing will occur at high engine speeds.

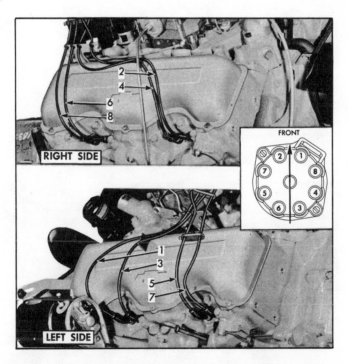

Fig. B-30. Firing order and spark plug wire installation on 348 cu. in. V-8 engine.

TROUBLE SHOOTING

See also Starting, Engine and Fuel System Troubles.

ENGINE WILL NOT START

Weak battery. Excessive moisture on high tension wiring and spark plugs. Cracked distributor cap. Defective coil or condenser. Worn ignition breaker points. Coil to distributor high tension cable not in place. Loose connections or broken wire in low tension circuit. Incorrect ignition breaker point gap. Defective spark plugs.

HARD STARTING

Faulty or improperly adjusted spark plugs. Defective or incorrectly adjusted ignition breaker points. Loose connections in primary circuit. Worn or oil soaked high tension wiring. Low capacity condenser. Defective ignition coil. Defective distributor cap. Defective rotor.

ENGINE MISFIRES

Worn or dirty spark plugs. Defective insulation on high tension cables. Defective distributor cap. Poor cylinder compression. Defective or incorrectly adjusted breaker points. Defective coil. Lack of power. Incorrect ignition timing. Defective spark plugs. Defective ignition breaker points.

POPPING, SPITTING, PREIGNITION

Loose wiring connections. Faulty spark plugs. Spark timing advance too far.

Showing location of temperature switch as installed on 1972 Chevrolet small V-8.

CARBURETOR AND
FUEL SYSTEM SERVICE

The carburetor and fuel system, as a rule, cause every little trouble and require a minimum of attention. A basic fuel system includes:

Fuel Tank	Fuel Pump	Fuel Filter	Intake Manifold
Fuel Line	Carburetor	Air Cleaner	Fuel Gauge

In addition to the foregoing, the fuel system on late model cars includes an emission control system and an evaporative control system. The carburetors on such cars (except those with mechanical cams) are equipped with idle mixture limiter caps. These caps must not be removed and no attempt should be made to adjust the fuel mixture. However, the idle speed must be adjusted to specifications.

Several different types and makes of carburetors are used on the various Chevrolet built cars. Many of these carburetors are illustrated in this chapter, Figs. C-1, C-2 and C-3, for example. In each case the adjustment and other parts are indicated. It will be found that carburetors of Rochester, Holley and Carter are all represented.

Before attempting to do any other work on a carburetor, be sure the ignition system is in good condition and is correctly timed. Engine compression must be up to standard and at full operating temperature before attempting to adjust the carburetor. It is best to drive the engine for fifteen to twenty minutes before adjusting the carburetor to be sure the temperature has stabilized.

In general, poor performance usually results from weak compression, or defective ignition, rather than troubles in the carburetor. Be sure that there are no leaks in the intake manifold or vacuum operated accessories.

PRELIMINARY ADJUSTMENT PROCEDURE

After stabilizing the temperature of the engine by operating for at least fifteen minutes, check torque of carburetor to intake manifold bolts to exclude possibility of air leaks. Similarly, check bolts securing intake manifold to engine block. Also check vacuum lines to any vacuum operated accessories for leaks.

Inspect manifold heat control valve (if used) for freedom of action and correct spring tension.

IDLE SPEED AND MIXTURE ADJUSTMENT

The location of the idle mixture and speed controls is shown in Figs. C-1 and C-2. All carburetor adjustments must be made with the engine at operating temperature and with the distributor vacuum line discon-

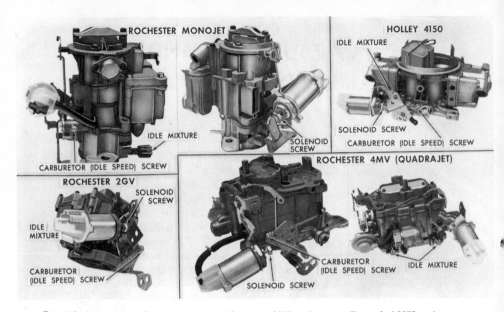

Fig. C-1. Location of idle mixture and speed screws, 1971 carburetors. Typical of 1972 carburetors.

nected and plugged.

The procedure for adjusting the idle speed and mixture on single barrel carburetors on cars built prior to 1970 is as follows:

Remove air cleaner, Fig. A-2. If available, connect tachometer and vacuum gauge to engine. Set hand brake and shift transmission into neutral. As a preliminary adjustment, turn idle mixture adjustment lightly to seat and then back out one and one-half turns, Figs. C-1 and C-2. Be careful not to turn idle mixture screws firmly against seat as damage may result.

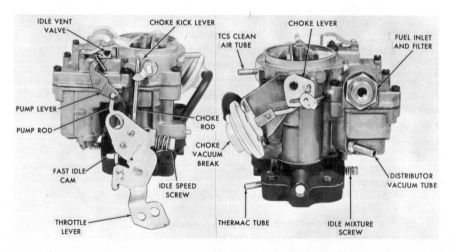

Details of 1970 model Rochester 2GV carburetor.

Carburetor, Fuel System Service

With the engine operating and choke wide open, adjust idle speed screw to specified idle speed. Then adjust idle mixture screw to obtain high vacuum reading. If vacuum gauge is not available, turn idle mixture adjustment in until engine misfires and operates roughly. Then turn idle mixture screw out until the engine lopes due to rich mixture. Then turn in until engine operates smoothly.

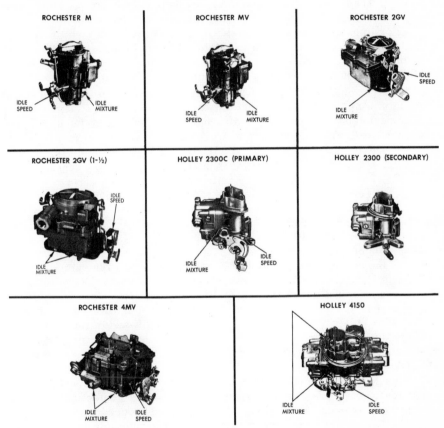

Fig. C-2. Location of idle mixture and idle speed adjustment on additional Rochester and Holley carburetors. See also Fig. C-1.

On air conditioned vehicles, turn air conditioner "off" except on L4 and L6 engines with automatic transmission and 325 and 350 hp 327 cu. in. engines (manual trans.) where idle speed is set with the air conditioner on.

Recent instructions for idle speed adjustment for engines with idle solenoids is as follows: Adjust idle speed to 500 rpm by adjusting solenoid plunger hex only, Fig. C-3. Disconnect wire at solenoid and observe idle speed. De-energizing the solenoids allows the throttle lever to seat against the carburetor idle screw. Adjust the carburetor idle screw as necessary to obtain 400 rpm. Then adjust mixture screw in to obtain a 20 rpm drop (lean roll). Then adjust mixture out one-quarter turn.

Dual and four barrel carburetors: On dual and four barrel carburetors there are two idle mixture adjustments. The adjusting procedure is similar to that just described. First turn both needles until they lightly touch the seat. Then back out approximately one and one-half turns. Adjust first one needle and then the other to obtain maximum reading on the vacuum gauge or to obtain maximum idle speed for that particular throttle setting. Then adjust mixture screw in to obtain a 20 rpm drop (lean roll). Adjust mixture screw out one-quarter turn. Repeat for second mixture screw and then readjust the speed screw to obtain the specified idle speed.

1971 carburetor adjustments: No attempt should be made to adjust idle mixture on carburetors with idle mixture limiter caps. The only adjustment is for idle speed. On all engines, disconnect distributor spark advance hose and plug vacuum source opening. Disconnect fuel tank line from vacuum canister. Idle speed adjustments are made as follows:

Engine	Manual Trans. in neutral	Auto. Trans. in drive
250 cu. in.	550 rpm	500 rpm
307, 350, 400 cu. in.	600 rpm *	550 rpm #
350 cu. in. Quadrajet	600 rpm *	550 rpm #
350 cu. in. 4 bbl. Holley	700 rpm +	700 rpm +
402 cu. in. Quadrajet	600 rpm	600 rpm
454 cu. in. 4 bbl. Holley	700 rpm %	700 rpm %

* - Air conditioner off. # - Air conditioner on. + - On Corvette: Then turn one mixture screw in to obtain a 20 rpm drop. Then back off 1/4 turn, repeat for second screw. % - On all except Corvette adjust mixture screws to obtain maximum rpm, then adjust carburetor speed screw to obtain 700 rpm. Turn one mixture screw in to obtain 20 rpm drop, then back off 1/4 turn. Repeat for other mixture screw. Readjust speed screw to obtain 700 rpm.

Adjusting 1970 carburetors: On all models disconnect and plug distributor line. Turn mixture screw in until lightly contacting seat, then back out four turns. For individual models then proceed as follows:

153 C.I.D.: Set mixture screw to obtain maximum idle rpm. Then adjust idle speed screw to obtain 750 rpm with manual transmisssion on and 650 rpm with automatic transmission. Adjust mixture to obtain 20 rpm drop then back out one-quarter turn. Readjust idle to specified rpm.

230, 250 and 350 (250 hp): Adjust solenoid screw to obtain 830 rpm with manual transmission and 630 rpm with automatic transmission. Adjust mixture screw to obtain 750 rpm with manual transmission and 600 rpm with automatic transmission. Disconnect solenoid. Set carburetor idle screw to obtain 400 rpm. Reconnect solenoid.

307 C.I.D. 400 C.I.D. (265 hp): Adjust idle speed to 800 rpm and solenoid screw to 630 rpm. Adjust mixture screws equally to 700 rpm for manual transmission and 600 rpm for automatic transmission. On auto-

matic transmission cars disconnect solenoid electrically. Set carburetor idle speed screw to 450 rpm and reconnect solenoid.

350 C.I.D. (250 hp): Adjust solenoid screw to obtain 830 rpm with manual transmission and 630 rpm with automatic transmission. Adjust mixture screws equally to obtain 750 rpm with manual transmission and 600 rpm with automatic transmission. Disconnect solenoid electrically set carburetor idle to 450 rpm and reconnect solenoid.

350 C.I.D. (300 hp), 400 C.I.D. (330 hp): Adjust carburetor idle speed screws to 775 rpm with manual transmission and 630 rpm with automatic transmission. Adjust mixture screws equally to obtain 700 rpm with manual and 600 rpm with automatic transmission.

396 C.I.D. 400 C.I.D. (375 hp), 454 C.I.D. (450 hp): Set mixture screws, Fig. C-2, to obtain maximum rpm. Set idle speed screws to obtain 750 rpm with manual transmission and 700 rpm with automatic transmission. Turn one mixture screw in to obtain 20 rpm drop. The back out screw one-quarter turn. Readjust idle speed screw to 750 rpm with manual transmission and 700 rpm with automatic transmission.

396 C.I.D. (350 hp) 454 C.I.D. (345 hp), 454 C.I.D. (360 and 390 hp) with automatic transmission: Adjust idle speed screw to obtain 630 rpm. Adjust mixture screws equally to obtain 600 rpm.

FAST IDLE ADJUSTMENT

The fast idle adjustment on Rochester M, 4MV and Holley carburetors is as follows: With the fast idle lever on the high step of cam and choke valve open with the engine warm, set fast idle to give specified engine rpm. Adjust screw on Rochester 4MV and bend fast idle lever on Rochester M and Holley carburetors.

On Carter BV carburetor, the steps on the fast idle cam are correctly proportioned to give correct speed steps so it is only necessary to have correct relationship between fast idle cam position and the choke valve. If necessary, bend choke valve rod to obtain .050 to .070 in. clearance between lower edge of choke valve and bore of carburetor.

To adjust the fast idle on the Carter AFB carburetor, hold the choke valve closed and index mark of fast idle cam should line up with fast idle adjustment screw. If necessary bend fast idle rod.

CHOKE ADJUSTMENT

If the carburetor is provided with a remote type choke, remove the air cleaner and check to see that the choke valve and rods move freely. Disconnect choke rod at choke lever. Check choke adjustment as follows: On all engines except L6 and 390 hp 427 cu. in. engines, hold choke valve closed and push rod downward to contact stop. The top of rod should be even with bottom of hole in choke lever. On L6 and 390 hp 427 cu. in. engines hold choke valve closed and pull rod upward to end of travel. The bottom of rod should be even with top of hole in choke lever. If necessary adjust rod length by bending rod at offset bend. The bend must be such that the rod enters choke lever hole freely and squarely.

Connect rod at choke lever and install air cleaner.

On carburetors with manual chokes proceed as follows: Remove air cleaner. Push hand choke knob to within 1/8 in. of instrument panel. Loosen choke cable clamp at carburetor bracket and adjust cable to the clip until the choke valve is wide open. Tighten cable clamp at carburetor bracket and check operation of choke valve to insure full closed and wide open positions. Replace the air cleaner.

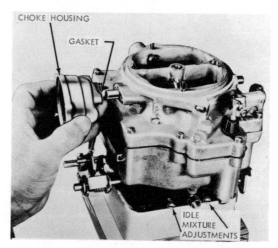

Fig. C-4. Details of Rochester model 4GC carburetor. Note idle mixture adjustment and choke housing.

To adjust a vacuum type choke as used on the Rochester 4GC carburet-or, Fig. C-4, proceed as follows: Remove air cleaner and make sure that choke valve and mechanism move freely. Loosen choke cover, retaining screws, and adjust choke cover to specifications and tighten retainer screws securely. Replace air cleaner.

To adjust choke of Carter WCFB carburetor: Turn the Bakelite housing, Fig. C-5, counterclockwise for leaner setting. Dirt, gum, water and car-bon accumulations are often the cause for poor performance. If necessary, the entire assembly should be thoroughly cleaned.

FLOAT ADJUSTMENT

Most Holley carburetors are provided with a sight plug in the side of the float bowl which permits checking and adjusting the float level without removing the carburetor from the engine, Fig. C-6. On the Holley car-buretors used on 1966-69 models, the procedure is as follows: Remove

Carburetor, Fuel System Service

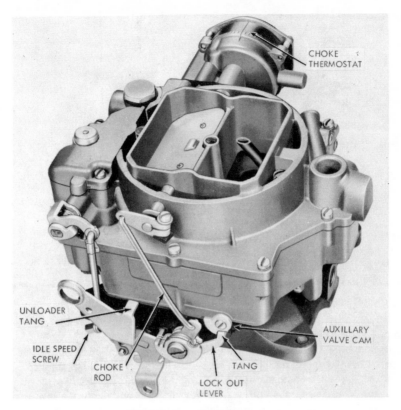

Fig. C-5. Carter WCFB carburetor.

Fig. C-6. Holley carburetor showing fuel level sight plug.

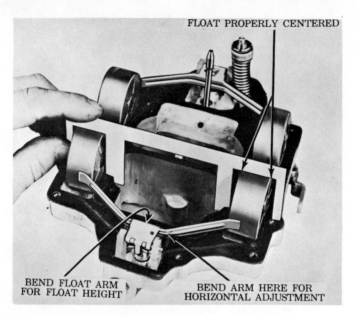

FLOAT PROPERLY CENTERED

BEND FLOAT ARM
FOR FLOAT HEIGHT

BEND ARM HERE FOR
HORIZONTAL ADJUSTMENT

Fig. C-7. Using special gauge to check float level on Rochester 4GC carburetor. Such gauges usually form part of repair kit of parts.

the air cleaner, then remove the fuel level sight plug, Fig. C-6. With the parking brake on and transmission in neutral, start the engine and allow it to idle. With the car on a level surface, the fuel level should be on a level with the threads at the bottom of the sight plug port, plus or minus 1/32 in. If necessary to adjust, either or both bowls, loosen inlet needle lock screw and turn the adjusting nut clockwise to lower or counterclockwise to raise the fuel level, then tighten the lock screw. One-sixth turn of adjusting nut equals approximately 1/16 in. fuel level change. Allow a minute for fuel level to stabilize and recheck the level at sight plug. Readjust if necessary, until the proper level is obtained, and install sight plug and air cleaner. To insure proper secondary float level setting, it is advisable to accelerate primary throttle slightly and hand operate secondary throttle. This assures a stabilized secondary fuel level.

The float level of Carter and Rochester carburetors is adjusted to a specified height and is measured with the aid of a T-scale or special gauge, Fig. C-7. Such gauges are usually provided with each kit of carburetor repair parts.

CARBURETOR FLOAT LEVEL

Carburetor Make and Model	Primary Float	Secondary Float	Measurement
Carter YH	5/8 in.	none	12
Carter YF	1/2 in.	none	1
Carter AVS	1-15/32 in.	none	2
Carter WCFB	7/32 in.	1/4 in.	3

50

Carter AFB	7/32 in.	7/32 in.	4
Holley 4150 (327)	.170 in.	.300 in.	5
Holley 4150 (427)	.350 in.	.450 in.	5
Holley 4160	.170 in.	.300 in.	5
Holley 2100	.350 in.	none	5
Holley 2300	.350 in.	.500 in.	5
Holley 1970-1971 (Use sight plug)			
Rochester BC	5/8 in.	none	6
Rochester 2GC, 1959-1961	1-23/64 in.	none	7
Rochester 4GC	1-33/64 in.	1-37/64 in.	8
Rochester 4GC Low Silhouette	1-1/2 in.	1-5/16 in.	9
Rochester BV	1-9/32 in.	none	10
Rochester HV	1-1/16 in.	none	10
Rochester H	1-1/16 in.	none	10
Rochester 2GV, 1965-1966	3/4 in.	none	11
Rochester 4MV	9/32 in.	none	13
Rochester 4MV (327)	9/32 in.	. . . .	. . . .
Rochester 4MV (396)	3/16 in.	. . . .	. . . .
Rochester M	11/32 in.	. . . .	. . . .
Rochester 2G	3/4 in.	. . . .	. . . .
Rochester M, 1969-1970	1/4 in.	. . . .	. . . .
Rochester MV, 1969-1972	1/4 in.	. . . .	. . . .
Rochester MV Vega, 1971	1/8 in.	. . . .	. . . .
Rochester 2GV 1 1/4, 1969-1970	27/32 in.	. . . .	. . . .
Rochester 2GV 1 1/2, 1967-1969	3/4 in.	. . . .	. . . .
Rochester 2GV 1 1/2, 396-265 hp	5/8 in.	. . . .	. . . .
Rochester 2GV 1 1/2, 1970-1972	23/32 in.	. . . .	. . . .
Rochester 4MV 350 cu. in. 255 hp, 1969	7/32 in.	. . . .	. . . .
Rochester 4MV 350 cu. in. 325 hp, 1969	3/16 in.	. . . .	. . . .
Rochester 4MV 396 cu. in., 1969	1/4 in.	. . . .	. . . .
Rochester 4MV ALL 1970-1972	1/4 in.	. . . .	. . . .

When measuring the float level, the float bowl cover is inverted and measurement is made as follows:

1. Invert float bowl and measure distance between float and float cover at free end of float.
2. With air horn inverted and gasket in place measure from bottom of each float to air horn gasket.
3. With float bowl inverted, measure between top of float and machined surface of casting.
4. With float bowl inverted, measure between top of floats (at outer end) and air horn gasket.
5. Use fuel level sight plug in side of float bowl.
6. With float bowl inverted and gasket in place, measure from gasket surface to bottom of float.

7. With air horn inverted and gasket in place, measure dimension from gasket surface to top of float.
8. With air horn inverted and gasket in place, measure from gasket surface to top of each float next to the seam.
9. With air horn inverted and gasket in place, measure from gasket surface to top of each float next to seam.
10. With air horn inverted and gasket in place, measure distance from gasket surface to bottom of each float.
11. With air horn inverted and gasket in place, measure distance from gasket to lower edge (sharp edge) of float seam at the outer edge of float pontoon.
12. Invert cover and measure from cover gasket to float center.
13. With adjustable T-scale, measure from top of float bowl gasket surface to top of float at toe (locate gauging point 3/16 in. back from toe).

When adjusting the float level the procedure is to bend the float tang, Fig. C-7. On Carter carburetors Model AVS the instructions are to bend the float arm. In the case of Holley carburetors, the float level is provided with a screw adjustment.

CARBURETOR OVERHAUL

Complete instructions covering the overhaul of carburetors are included in the repair parts kits. The procedure is to completely disassemble the carburetor, clean it thoroughly and then install the parts contained in the repair parts kit.

CHEVROLET DUAL WCFB INSTALLATION

Dual Carter WCFB carburetor installations differ from those used on single carburetor equipped engines only in the linkage attachments and metering calibration.

To adjust accelerator linkage, remove the carpet adjacent to area around accelerator pedal to allow for clearance measurements between the toe board and accelerator pedal. Remove air cleaners and throttle pull back springs on both carburetors.

With rear carburetor on wide-open throttle, accelerator pedal should be three-quarter inch from toe board. Adjust accelerator rod by removing spring clip and turning trunnion nut. With rear carburetor on wide-open throttle, adjust front carburetor control shaft until throttle on front carburetor is wide-open and against throttle stop. Tighten lock nut on front control shaft if loosened.

When linkage is properly adjusted, front carburetor will be opened when rear carburetor is at approximately half throttle. Reinstall air cleaners.

Idle speed and mixture: For initial adjustment, set all four mixture adjusting screws three-quarter turn open. With engine at operating tem-

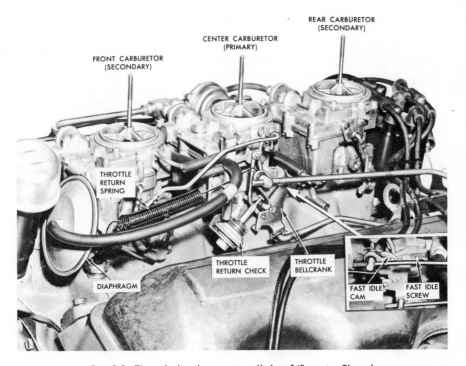

FRONT CARBURETOR
(SECONDARY)

CENTER CARBURETOR
(PRIMARY)

REAR CARBURETOR
(SECONDARY)

THROTTLE
RETURN
SPRING

DIAPHRAGM

THROTTLE
RETURN CHECK

THROTTLE
BELLCRANK

FAST IDLE
CAM

FAST IDLE
SCREW

Fig. C-8. Three dual carburetors installed on 348 cu. in. Chevrolet.

perature, adjust throttle valve setscrew to give an engine speed of about 600 rpm. Adjust all idle mixture screws individually for best engine feel and highest vacuum.

TRIPLE ROCHESTER INSTALLATION

Fig. C-8 illustrates the Rochester installation of three model 2GC carburetors on a 348 cu. in. Chevrolet.

To adjust the pump rod, back off the idle speed adjustment screw until the throttle valves are completely closed. The distance from top of bowl cover to top of pump rod should be 15/16 in. on each of the carburetors. Bend pump rod to make the adjustment tighter. To adjust vacuum valve: First make sure the valve post is fully upward. Then with throttle valve completely closed, the distance from the tang on the pump lever to the actuating post on the vacuum valve should be 1/32 in. A standard 1/32 in. drill can be used as a gauge. To obtain proper clearance, loosen two re- taining screws and move valve assembly up or down.

Front to Rear Carburetor Throttle Rod Adjustment: Be sure throttle valves on front and rear carburetors are completely closed. With front of rod attached to throttle lever on front carburetor, rear of rod must be in the middle of hole in the throttle lever on the rear carburetor. Otherwise bend the rod as required.

Idle Mixture and Speed Adjustment: With a vacuum gauge connected to the engine, bring the engine up to operating temperature until the choke valve is fully open. Start the adjustment by having the idle mixture adjusting screws two turns off their seats. Adjust the idle mixture adjusting screws as required to produce the highest steady engine rpm and vacuum reading.

Fig. C-9. Removing ceramic type fuel filter from carburetor.

FUEL FILTER SERVICE

Fuel filters on recent model Chevrolets are mounted directly in the carburetor. These filters are of two different types. One type known as the bronze, shown in Fig. C-9, and the paper element type shown in Fig. C-10.

To check these fuel filters, first disconnect the fuel line connection at the inlet fuel filter nut. Remove the inlet fuel filter nut from the carburetor with a 1 in. wrench. The filter element, Fig. C-9 and Fig. C-10, can then be removed from the carburetor. Check the bronze element for restriction by blowing on the cone end. Element should allow air to pass freely.

Check paper element by blowing on fuel inlet end. If filter does not allow air to pass freely, replace the element. No attempt should be made to clean filters.

Elements should be replaced if plugged or if flooding of the carburetor occurs. A plugged filter will result in a loss of engine power or rough engine feel, especially at high engine speeds.

Fig. C-10. Paper element type fuel filter as installed on a Rochester carburetor.

Install the spring and the filter element in carburetor. Bronze filters must have small sections of cones facing out. Always install a new gasket or inlet fitting nut and install nut in carburetor and tighten securely.

Filter element should be replaced every twelve months, or 12,000 miles, whichever occurs first.

AIR CLEANER SERVICE

Several different types of air cleaners are used on recent model Chevrolet engines. These include the wire mesh with polyurethane band, oiled paper with polyurethane band, and the oiled paper type. Starting with the 1968 models, most automatic transmission equipped vehicles and emission control systems are provided with a device which thermostatically controls the temperature of the air entering the air cleaner. The thermostatic valve of the device proportions the air from a heat stove on the exhaust manifold with the cooler air from the engine compartment.

The oiled paper filters, Fig. C-11, used in most air cleaner assemblies have both ends of the paper element bonded with Plastisol sealing material. Oil on the paper causes the element to become discolored by a small amount of dirt. This does not necessarily indicate that the element is plugged or reduced in efficiency. It is advisable to rotate the air cleaner element 180 deg. at 12,000 miles and replace it every 24,000 miles. If the vehicle is operated in very dusty conditions the preceding operation should be performed more frequently.

POLYURETHANE ELEMENT

To remove the filter element for cleaning and inspection, remove the cover wing nut, Fig. A-2, which will then permit the filter element to be lifted from its housing. Visibly check the element for tears and rips, and replace if necessary. Clean all accumulated dirt and grime from air cleaner bottom and cover. Discard air horn to air cleaner gaskets. Remove support screen from element and wash element in kerosene or mineral spirits and squeeze out excess solvent, Fig. C-12.

Never use a hot degreaser or any solvent containing acetone or similar solvent to clean the polyurethane element.

After cleaning with kerosene or mineral spirits, dip the element in light engine oil and squeeze out excess oil.

Never shake, swing or wring the element to remove excess oil or solvent, as this may tear the polyurethane material. Instead squeeze the excess from the element.

Install element on screen support. Using new gasket, replace air-cleaner body over carburetor air horns. Replace the element in the air cleaner. Care must be taken that the lower lip of the element is properly placed in the assembly and that the filter material is not folded or creased in any manner that would cause an imperfect seal.

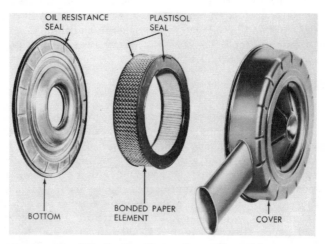

Fig. C-11. Details of paper element type air filter.

OIL WETTED PAPER ELEMENT FILTER

To replace the element of the oil wetted paper type air cleaner, Fig. C-11, first remove the wing nut, washer and cover, Fig. A-2. Remove paper element and discard. Remove bottom section of air cleaner and gasket on air horn of carburetor. Discard air horn gasket. Clean bottom section of air cleaner and cover pieces thoroughly to remove dust and grime. Be sure to check bottom section of air cleaner seal for tears or cracks. Install a new gasket on carburetor air horn and set bottom section of air cleaner on carburetor. Install new paper element on bottom section of air cleaner with either end up. The Plastisol seal is the same material on both ends. Install cover, washer and wing nut to complete the job.

To clean the paper element type filter, tap the element gently against a smooth flat surface to remove any loose dirt. Also if compressed air is available, direct the air gently against the inner side of the element which

Fig. C-12. When cleaning a polyurethane air filter element, it should be squeezed dry, not wrung.

will remove accumulated dirt. Also inspect the element for punctures or splits by looking through the element toward a strong light. If damaged, the element should be replaced.

OIL BATH TYPE AIR CLEANER

Remove the air cleaner assembly. Remove cover and filter element assembly. Empty oil out of cleaner and clean out all oil and accumulated dirt. Wash body with cleaning solvent and wipe dry. Wash filter element by slushing up and down in the cleaning solvent. Dry filter unit with an air hose or let stand until dry. Fill body of cleaner to full mark with SAE 50 engine oil. If expected temperatures are to be consistently below freezing, use SAE 20 engine oil. Assemble filter and cover assembly to body of cleaner. Install cleaner, making sure it fits tight and is set down securely.

THERMOSTATICALLY CONTROLLED AIR CLEANER

This system, Fig. C-13 and Fig. C-14, is designed to improve carburetor operation and engine warm-up characteristics. It achieves this by keeping the air entering the carburetor at a temperature of at least 100 deg. F. or more. The thermostatic air cleaner system includes a temperature sensor, Fig. C-13, a vacuum motor and control damper assembly mounted on the air cleaner, vacuum control hoses, manifold heat stove and connecting pipes. The vacuum motor is controlled by the temperature sensor. The vacuum motor operates the air control damper assembly to regulate the flow of hot air and under-hood air to the carburetor. The hot air is obtained from the heat stove on the exhaust manifold.

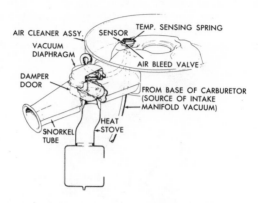

Fig. C-13. Schematic drawing of thermostatically controlled air cleaner.

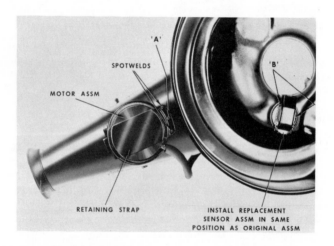

Fig. C-14. Installing replacement sensor assembly.

Visual inspection is made by checking for proper, secure connections at heat pipe and hose connections. Also check for kinked or deteriorated hoses. Repair or replace as required.

Operational inspection is made as follows: Remove air cleaner cover and install thermometer as close as possible to sensor. If engine has been in recent operation allow it to cool to below 85 deg. F. Replace air cleaner cover without the wing nut. Use a mirror if necessary to check the temperature. Start and idle the engine. When control damper assembly begins to open, remove air cleaner cover and observe the temperature reading. Open temperature must be between 85 deg. and 115 deg. F. If damper assembly does not open at the correct temperature, continue with the fol-

Chevrolet's 307 cu. in. V-8 features a carburetor hot air system. In operation, heat from exhaust manifold is ducted to air cleaner and snorkel. Thermostat, control valve and damper blend hot and cold air entering carburetor for better air-fuel vaporization.

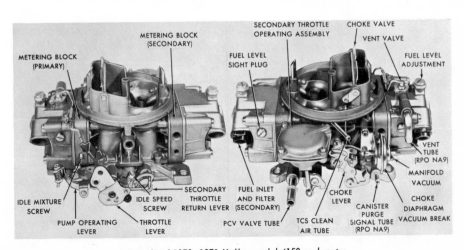

Details of 1970–1971 Holley model 4150 carburetor.

lowing vacuum motor and sensor checks. With the engine off, the position of the control damper assembly should be in the cold air delivery mode. To determine if the vacuum motor is operable, apply at least 9 in. of vacuum (obtained from the intake manifold) to the fitting on the vacuum motor. The control damper should close the cold air passage as long as vacuum is applied (the hot air pipe will be open). If the vacuum motor fails to operate the control damper assembly, with the direct application of vacuum, check to determine if the vacuum motor linkage is properly connected to the door. If the linkage is found satisfactory, then motor replacement is indicated. If the vacuum motor check is found to be satisfactory, then sensor replacement is indicated.

TIPS ON CARBURETOR SERVICE

Most difficulties encountered in the operation of carburetors result from dirt and other foreign material that gets past the fuel filters and forms in the carburetor. It is, therefore, important to make sure that the fuel filters are cleaned at least once each year.

One of the major difficulties arises from moisture that accumulates in the system. This results from condensation. The difficulty is easily overcome by using some of the special preparations that are designed to absorb such moisture. The moisture will then pass through the fine mesh of the filters and the carburetor jets. Such chemicals have various names, but usually imply that freezing of the fuel line will be prevented. Obviously, if this moisture is allowed to accumulate in the fuel system, it will freeze in cold weather with the result that fuel will not reach the carburetor and the engine will not operate. In addition, the fuel pump, filter and carburetor may be damaged by the ice. Moisture that collects in die

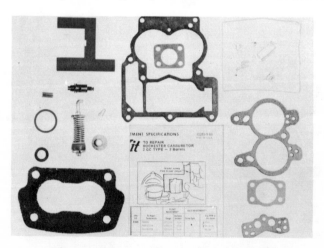

Fig. C-15. Parts contained in a typical kit of parts for overhauling a carburetor. Note illustrated instruction sheet and gauge for setting float level.

cast fuel pumps and carburetors will cause corrosion which will be a cheesy light substance which effectively clogs the system.

When overhauling the carburetor becomes necessary, this will be indicated usually by poor fuel economy, rough running engine, and particularly rough idle. When overhauling becomes necessary, the owner has the option of obtaining a new or rebuilt carburetor, or, purchasing a kit of repair parts and installing them. One of the kits is shown in Fig. C-15. As shown in the illustration, the necessary instructions are included.

Before installing any new parts in a carburetor, it is important that the main body and air horn be carefully cleaned and all the internal passages cleared by blowing out with compressed air. In that connection, a gummy substance frequently forms in the carburetor and it is important that all of it is removed. This is most easily done by special solvents designed for cleaning carburetor parts. Since this gummy substance is formed from the fuel, it is difficult to dissolve it with gasoline or kerosene.

Also before installing new parts in the carburetor, the mating surfaces of the main body and the air horn should be checked to be sure they are true and not warped. This is done with a straightedge, as shown in Fig. C-16. In addition, the two parts should be held together and if one can be rocked on the other, a new unit should be obtained. Unless these two surfaces are true and flat, air leaks will occur and the carburetor will not operate correctly. Be sure to install all new gaskets and other parts contained in the kit.

When disassembling the carburetor, carefully note the position of the various parts, and at the same time study the illustrations contained in the parts kit and the illustrations in this text, so that there will be no confusion when reassembling the unit. Pay particular attention to the location of the ball checks.

Fig. C-16. Checking surface of a carburetor with a straightedge.

SERVICING THE MANIFOLD HEAT CONTROL VALVE

For servicing information on the manifold heat control valve, see the Chapter devoted to the Exhaust System.

QUICK SERVICE ON FUEL PUMPS

Fuel pumps on in-line engines and the V-8 engines are mounted on the right side of the engine. A typical installation on an in-line engine is shown in Fig. A-2. Current type fuel pumps are not serviceable and when difficulty occurs, a new fuel pump must be installed. Fig. C-17 shows a serviceable fuel pump which was used on some installations in 1966 and previous models.

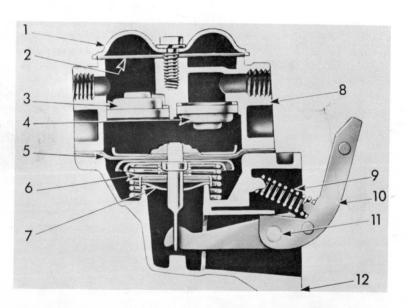

Fig. C-17. Details of a typical fuel pump. 1—Pulsator cover. 2—Pulsator diaphragm. 3—Outlet valve. 4—Inlet valve. 5—Diaphragm assembly. 6—Diaphragm spring. 7—Oil seal. 8—Fuel cover. 9—Rocker arm return spring. 10—Rocker arm and lever assembly. 11—Pivot pin. 12—Pump body.

Fuel pumps are easily removed. All that is necessary is to first disconnect the fuel lines from the pump and then remove the attaching bolts.

A quick test to see if a fuel pump is operating is to disconnect the fuel line at the carburetor and direct the end into a container. Start the engine and note the length of time required to pump one pint of fuel. On four and six cylinder engines, one pint of fuel should be pumped in thirty seconds, and on the larger engines, one pint in twenty seconds. If little or no fuel is pumped, pump may be defective or line to fuel tank may be obstructed.

If a pressure gauge is available, the fuel pump on the V-8 engine should deliver 5 to 8-1/2 lbs. for the 396 and 427 cu. in. engines, and 5-1/4 to 6-1/2 psi for the smaller V-8s. On the six and four cylinder engines, the fuel pump should develop 3 to 4-1/4 psi.

The fuel pump can also be checked by measuring the volume pumped which should be one pint in 30 to 45 seconds.

TROUBLE SHOOTING

See also Ignition, Starting and Engine sections.

ROUGH IDLE

Incorrect idle mixture. Carburetor float needle not seating. Air leaks in carburetor, intake manifold or gasket. Worn valve stem guides. Leaking cylinder head gasket. Incorrect valve lash. Burned or sticking valves.

HARD STARTING

Choke not operating correctly. Throttle not set correctly. Carburetor dirty and passages restricted. Clogged fuel filter. Clogged air filter.

POPPING AND SPITTING

Manifold heat control valve not properly installed. Manifold heat control valve sticking. Lean mixture. Dirt in carburetor. Clogged fuel filter. Leaky carburetor or intake manifold gaskets.

LACK OF POWER

Air cleaner dirty. Wrong jets for altitude in which car is being operated. Carburetor choke partly closed.

MISSES ON ACCELERATION

Accelerating pump incorrectly adjusted. Vapor vent ball in pump plunger not working. Lean mixture.

EXCESSIVE FUEL CONSUMPTION

Check complete system for fuel leaks. Worn or incorrect jets in carburetor. High fuel level in float bowl. Low engine compression. Worn, burned or sticking engine valves. Incorrect valve lash. Air leaks in carburetor, manifold gasket or intake valve stems. Incorrect spark advance. Fast driving. Excessive friction from dragging brakes, misaligned wheels, etc. Excessive engine idling.

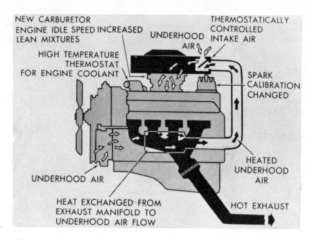

NEW CARBURETOR
ENGINE IDLE SPEED INCREASED
LEAN MIXTURES

HIGH TEMPERATURE
THERMOSTAT
FOR ENGINE COOLANT

UNDERHOOD
AIR

THERMOSTATICALLY
CONTROLLED
INTAKE AIR

SPARK
CALIBRATION
CHANGED

UNDERHOOD AIR

HEAT EXCHANGED FROM
EXHAUST MANIFOLD TO
UNDERHOOD AIR FLOW

HEATED
UNDERHOOD
AIR

HOT EXHAUST

Fig. C-18. Schematic diagram of Controlled Combustion System (C.C.S.)

FUEL PUMP NOISE

Fuel pump loose at mounting. Worn rocker arm. Broken or weak spring.

INSUFFICIENT FUEL DELIVERY

Loose fuel line fittings. Damaged diaphragm. Cracked fuel line.

EXCESSIVE PINGING

Low octane fuel being used. Spark advanced too far. Excessive carbon in combustion chamber.

CRANKCASE AND EXHAUST EMISSION SYSTEMS

In order to combat air pollution resulting from blow-by gases in the crankcase and the engine exhaust, Chevrolet cars are now provided with positive crankcase ventilating systems to take care of the blow-by gases, and either the control combustion system, Fig. C-18, or the air injection reaction system, Fig. C-19, to take care of the exhaust emission gases.

In the positive crankcase ventilating system, fresh air from the air filter is circulated through the crankcase where it mixes with the blow-by gases. This mixture is then carried through the PCV valve into the intake manifold, and then into the combustion chamber where it is reburned. The entire system must be clean and free from sludge.

The PCV valve, Fig. C-20, should be replaced every twelve months or 12,000 miles and the breather filter every 24,000 miles. To check the condition of the PCV valve, disconnect the ventilation hose at the valve and block opening of the valve and note the change in the engine speed. A change of less than 50 rpm indicates a plugged ventilation valve, and the valve should then be replaced.

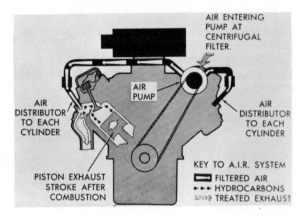

AIR ENTERING
PUMP AT
CENTRIFUGAL
FILTER.

AIR
PUMP

AIR
DISTRIBUTOR
TO EACH
CYLINDER

AIR
DISTRIBUTOR
TO EACH
CYLINDER

PISTON EXHAUST
STROKE AFTER
COMBUSTION

KEY TO A.I.R. SYSTEM
▭ FILTERED AIR
•••• HYDROCARBONS
⇢ TREATED EXHAUST

Fig. C-19. Schematic drawing of Air Injection Reactor system (A.I.R.)

The control combustion system (C.C.S.), Fig. C-18, includes a special air cleaner, Fig. C-14, which is designed to supply heated air to the carburetor, thereby improving combustion. Both carburetor and distributor are especially calibrated so that an efficient mixture is properly ignited, thereby reducing the generation of the excessive hydrocarbons and carbon monoxide. The system should be checked every 12,000 miles or twelve months, whichever occurs first. Special care must be observed when doing a tune-up job, particularly in regard to idle speed and mixture adjustment and ignition timing.

The air injection reactor system (A.I.R.), Figs. C-19 and C-21, is another method used to reduce the production of noxious gases and is used on some Chevrolet engines. It does this by reburning the exhaust gases.

FLOW

Fig. C-20. Details of Positive Crankcase Ventilating valve (PCV)

This system, Fig. C-19, is composed of the air injector pump, Fig. C-22, air injector tubes (one for each cylinder), air diverter valve, check valves (one for in-line engines and two for V-8 engines), and air manifold assemblies, tubes and hoses necessary to connect the various components.

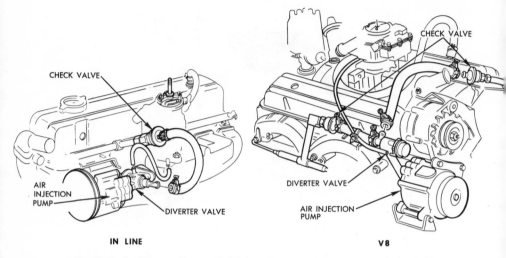

Fig. C-21. *Air Injection Reactor (A.I.R.) system as installed on in-line and V-8 engines.*

Carburetors and distributors for engines with the A.I.R. system are designed particularly for these engines, and therefore they should not be interchanged with or replaced by a carburetor or distributor designed for engines without this system.

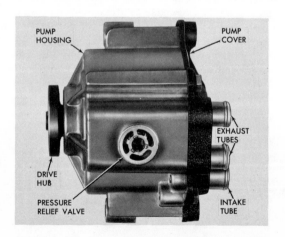

Fig. C-22. *Note pressure relief valve on air injection pump.*

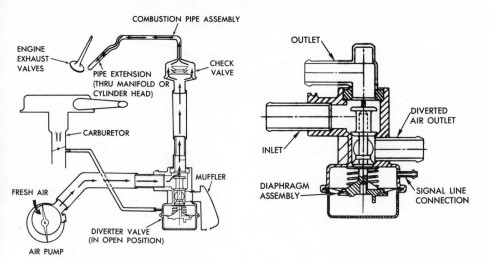

Fig. C-23. Left. Air Injection Reactor system as installed on 1969 models.
Fig. C-24. Right. Typical diverter valve. Open position.

The air injector pump, Fig. C-22, with an integral filter, compresses the air and injects it through the air manifold, hoses and injection tubes into the exhaust system into the area of the exhaust valves, Fig. C-23. The fresh air ignites and burns the unburned portion of the exhaust gases in the exhaust system, thus minimizing exhaust contamination.

The diverter valve, Fig. C-24, when triggered by a sharp increase in manifold vacuum, shuts off the injected air to the exhaust port areas, and prevents backfiring during this richer period.

On engine over-run the total air supply is dumped through the muffler on the diverter valve. At high engine speeds the excess air is dumped through the pressure relief valve when the pressure relief valve is part of the air pump and to the diverter valve when the pressure relief valve is part of the diverter valve.

The check valves prevent exhaust gases from entering and damaging air injector pump, as back flow can occur even under normal conditions.

Because of the relationship between engine tune-up and unburned exhaust gases, the condition of the engine tune-up should be checked whenever the A.I.R. system seems to be malfunctioning. Pay particular attention to the crankcase ventilating system, carburetor, carburetor air cleaner, and ignition system.

Always make sure that the air injection pump drive belt is properly adjusted. When necessary the pump filter should be replaced, and to do so it is first necessary to remove the drive belt and pump pulley. When installing a new filter, be sure to draw it on with the pulley and pulley bolts. Do not attempt to install a filter by hammering or pressing it on. Draw the filter down evenly by alternately torquing the bolts.

Be sure to inspect the air manifold, hoses and tubes for any signs of deterioration and replace as necessary.

The check valve should be inspected whenever the hose is disconnected,

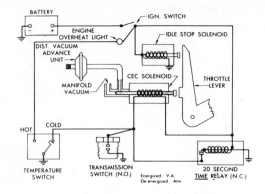

Fig. C-25. Schematic drawing of transmission control spark system as installed on 1972 L-6 engines. (Engine off.)

and a simple check of the check valve can be made by blowing through the check valve (toward the air manifold) and then attempt to suck back through the check valve. Air flow should be only toward the air manifold.

1970-1972 EMISSION CONTROL SYSTEMS

Some improvements and additions have been made to the preceeding systems in order to still further control the emission of noxious gases. The systems now include: Positive Crankcase Ventilating System, Controlled Combustion System, Evaporative Emission Control, Transmission Controlled Spark, and the Air Injector Reactor System.

The Evaporative Emission Control System and the Transmission Controlled Spark are new. The former system is designed to reduce fuel vapor emission that normally vents to the atmosphere from the fuel tank and carburetor fuel bowl. When the engine is running, vapors are piped from the fuel tank (which has a non-vented cap) into the intake snorkel of the air cleaner. When the engine is stopped, the vapors are stored in a carbon canister. An air cleaner at the bottom of the canister requires removal and oiling every 12,000 miles.

In the transmission controlled spark system, the distributor vacuum advance has been eliminated in the low forward speeds in both manual and automatic transmission cars. The control of the vacuum advance is accomplished by means of a solenoid switch energized by the low transmission gears by a grounding switch at the transmission, Fig. C-25. When the solenoid is energized, the vacuum source to the distributor is cut off and the vacuum advance is vented to the atmosphere by a connection to the carburetor air hose. The transmission controlled spark system also includes a temperature override system which provides full spark advance when the engine is cold.

In addition to the foregoing controls, all engines offered to California in 1972 will be equipped with new camshafts, except the high performance 255 hp Turbo-fire 350 engines and all those assemblies not requiring Air Injection Reactor Systems will be so equipped.

Shortcuts on
ENGINE DISASSEMBLY

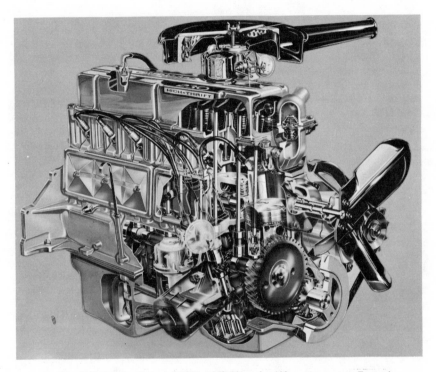

Fig. D-1. Sectional view of 1963–1970 Chevrolet 230 cu. in. engine. Typical.

This Chapter deals with short cut methods of removing different engine parts and their reinstallation. Details of servicing procedures for repairing these individual parts, together with further information of disassembling after these parts are removed are given in the Chapter on Simplified Engine Repairs.

HOW TO REMOVE THE CYLINDER HEAD

In-line Engines: The procedure for removing the cylinder head on in-line engines, which include the 153, 194, 230,235 and 250 cu. in. engines, Figs. B-22 and D-1, is basically the same and is as follows:

Drain the cooling system and disconnect the radiator upper hose. Remove the air cleaner. Disconnect the accelerator and choke linkage from the carburetor. Disconnect fuel and vacuum lines at the carburetor. Disconnect wire harness from the engine temperature sending unit. Disconnect wires and remove spark plugs. Remove ignition coil on L6 engines only. On the 135, 194, 230 and 250 cu. in. engines, disconnect exhaust pipe at manifold flange, then remove manifold bolts and clamps and remove the manifold and carburetor as an assembly.

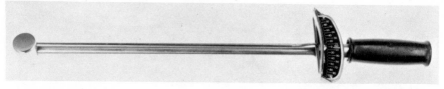

Fig. D-2. Always use a torque wrench to tighten cylinder head bolts to the specified torque.

On the 235 cu. in Six, remove bolts and clamps that attach manifold assembly to cylinder head and pull manifold assembly off the manifold studs. Also remove intake pilot sleeves.

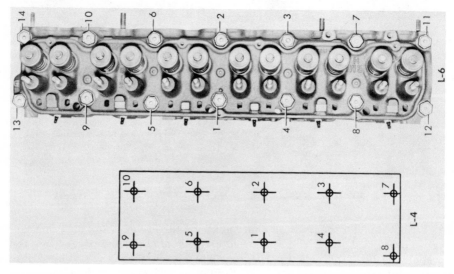

Fig. D-3. Correct sequence for tightening cylinder head bolts on 194, 230, 250 cu. in. six cylinder engines (upper) and 153 cu. in. four cylinder engine (lower). Torque for all these engines is 90 to 95 ft. lb.

On all engines remove battery ground strap. On engines with positive crankcase ventilation, remove air cleaner attachment to rocker arm cover. Remove rocker arm cover.

On the 235 cu. in. Six, 1950 to 1962, remove rocker arm assembly. On other in-line engines, back off rocker arm nuts, then pivot rocker arm to clear push rods.

Engine Disassembly

On all engines remove push rods, taking care to identify each rod so that it can be replaced in its original position. Remove cylinder head bolts and lift off cylinder head. Clean all gasket surfaces.

When replacing the cylinder head, torque the bolts to the specified torque, and in the sequence shown in Figs. D-2, D-3, and D-4.

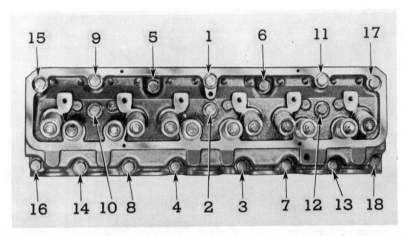

Fig. D-4. Tightening sequence of cylinder head bolts on 1953 to 1962 Chevrolet Six 235 cu. in. Correct torque is 90 to 95 ft. lb.

Also, when installing the rocker arms and shaft on the 235 cu. in. Six, 1954 to 1962, be sure that rocker arms are installed as shown in Fig. D-5.

V-8 Engine Cylinder Head Removal: Drain cooling system and remove air cleaner. Disconnect radiator upper hose and heater hoses. Disconnect

Fig. D-5. Angles of rocker arms on 1953 to 1962 Chevrolet Six. When replacing rocker arms they must be replaced as shown.

throttle rods from carburetor. On Power Glide and Turbo-Glide models; disconnect transmission throttle rod. Disconnect fuel and vacuum lines at carburetor. On overdrive models, disconnect kick-down switch wire from switch. Disconnect and remove ignition coil and distributor. Disconnect battery. Disconnect and remove spark plugs. Disconnect power brake hose

Fig. D-6. Details of 283 cu. in. V-8 engine.

at carburetor when installed. Disconnect crank case ventilating hoses as required. Disconnect air injector reaction hoses when installed. Disconnect spark advance hose at distributor. Remove temperature indicator unit at intake manifold. Remove fan belts. On 283 cu. in. V-8, Fig. D-6, remove exhaust manifold to exhaust crossover pipe stud nuts and allow crossover pipe to drop. Disconnect wires from generator.

Remove exhaust manifold. On 283 cu. in. engines, remove choke heat tubes. On all models, remove rocker arm covers, Fig. D-7. Back off rocker arm nuts and pivot rocker arms to clear push rods. Remove push rods, taking care to identify each rod so it can be replaced in its original position. Be sure that push rod seats on solid lifters do not come off of

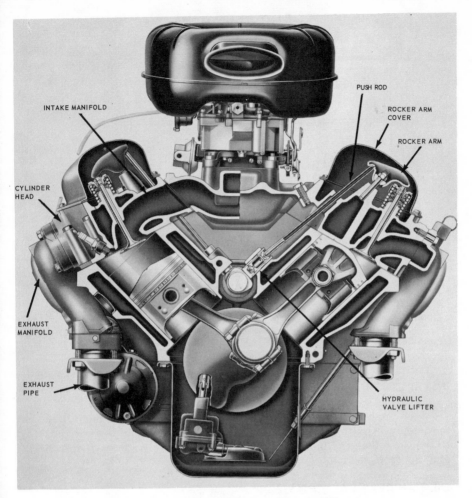

Fig. D-7. Sectional view of 348 cu. in. Chevrolet V-8 engine.

lifters. Snap push rod lower end to one side before lifting to break push rods loose from seats. Note on the 348 cu. in. engine, Fig. D-7, the exhaust push rods are longer than the intake push rods.

Remove cylinder head bolts and lift off cylinder heads. On 348 cu. in. models, before removing left cylinder heads, remove generator. Also on 348 cu. in. and 409 cu. in. engines.equipped with air conditioning units, remove air compressor before removing right cylinder head. Note: Special equipment is needed to evacuate the air conditioning system before disconnecting the compressor.

When removing bolts from the cylinder head, always note carefully the length of each bolt and the position from which it was removed so that it can be replaced in its original position. The cylinder bolt tightening sequences for V-8 engines are shown in Figs. D-8 and D-9. Use no sealers with composition steel gaskets.

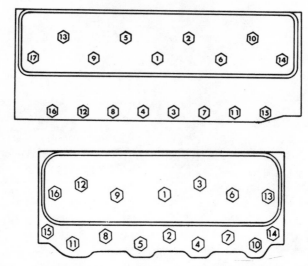

Fig. D-8. Upper: Correct cylinder head bolt tightening sequence for the 265, 283, 302, 307, 327, 350 cu. in. engines. Correct torque is 65 ft. lbs. Lower: Tightening sequence for the 396, 402, 427 and 454 cu. in. V-8 engines. Torque is 80 ft. lbs. except aluminum head short bolts 65 ft. lbs. and long bolts 75 ft. lbs.

INSTALLING INTAKE MANIFOLD

When installing the intake manifold on V-8 engines, care must be taken to tighten the bolts in their proper sequence. An example is shown in Fig. D-10. Note that the bolts are tightened alternately across the manifold starting from the center. Final torque should be 25 to 35 ft. lb.

OIL PAN REMOVAL KINKS

To remove an oil pan where gasket adhesion has caused the pan to stick, do not attempt to pry the pan loose. Instead use a wide bladed putty knife to loosen the gasket. Once the putty knife has been used at all accessible locations, knock the oil pan loose by using a wide-faced rubber hammer.

1959-1961 348 cu. in. To remove the oil pan from the 348 cu. in. V-8 with either three-speed, four-speed or automatic transmission: Raise front of vehicle and place on jack stands. Drain engine oil. Drain radiator and disconnect radiator hoses at radiator. Disconnect battery ground strap at engine. Disconnect clutch pedal push rod at clutch pedal control, intermediate lever and shaft assembly. Remove clutch pedal control, intermediate lever and shaft assembly at mounting bracket leaving shaft assembly attached to engine. Disconnect fuel feed pipe at fuel pump and remove fuel pump. Remove accelerator control rod from accelerator control rod lever. Remove oil level gauge tube. If power brake equipped, remove power brake vacuum hose at valve on engine manifold. Disconnect generator brace and rotate away from engine. Remove transmission lower control rods at transmission shift levers. Remove exhaust pipe flange to exhaust manifold. Lower exhaust pipe and muffler assembly. Remove oil filter. Loosen transmission mounting bolts. Remove long bolt from each front engine mounting bolt. Turn crankshaft so harmonic balancer key-way is at bottom of engine. This will permit oil pan to clear counterweights on crankshaft. Engine may be raised from below at har-

Fig. D-9. Correct torque for tightening cylinder head bolts on 348 and 409 cu. in. V-8 engines is 60 to 70 ft. lb. Correct sequence is indicated.

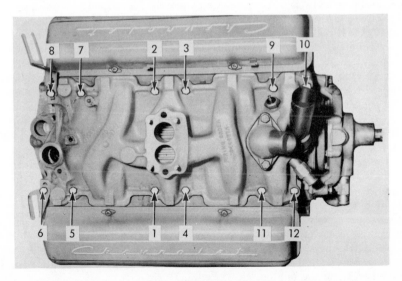

Fig. D-10. Typical tightening sequence of intake manifold bolts on V-8 engines. Correct torque is 25–35 ft. lb. A pilot tool made of wood and inserted in hole for distributor shaft will help guide the manifold in place and reduce the possibility of the manifold end seals slipping out of place.

monic balancer. Engine will have to be raised 2 3/4 in.

Raise engine until transmission housing comes in contact with underbody toe pan. Note clearance at fan blade and shroud when lifting engine and adjust for clearance as required. Remove oil pan bolts, using a universal socket and long extension handle. Tilt pan while removing. In the case of a Turboglide equipped car, it is also necessary to remove the transmission control lever corss-shaft at the transmission shifter lever and shaft assembly.

1959 to 1962 Six: Remove oil pan drain plug and drain crankcase oil. Raise front of vehicle and place on jack stand. Drain water and disconnect radiator hoses at radiator. Disconnect battery ground strap at engine. Disconnect gas tank to fuel pump feed line at fuel pump. Disconnect accelerator control rod at the accelerator control rod lever. Remove overdrive solenoid, if so equipped. Disconnect power brake hose at check valve. Remove oil filter and support bracket assembly to clear power brake master cylinder. Remove exhaust pipe flange to exhaust manifold nuts and gasket. Disconnect transmission lower control rods at the transmission shifter lever. Disconnect clutch fork push rod at the clutch fork. Disconnect clutch pedal control, intermediate lever, and shaft assembly from the engine. Loosen transmission mounting bolts and remove front engine mounting bolts. Remove hood and lift engine with a hoist approximately three inches, or until valve rocker cover comes in contact with the dash upper panel. Remove oil pan retaining bolts. If synchromesh transmission equipped, remove flywheel underpan extension and remove oil pan.

When replacing the oil pan, install the pan side gaskets on the cylinder block using grease as a retainer or adhesive. Install oil pan end gaskets and grooves in front and rear main bearing caps.

1963-1964, 230 cu. in. Six: To remove oil pan, drain radiator and oil pan. Disconnect fuel line at pump and radiator connections at radiator. Disconnect battery. Remove clutch housing-to-engine block bolt above dowel at right side. Raise engine on jack stands. Rotate engine to align distributor rotor between No. 3 and No. 5 plug wires to get No. 6 crank throw out of the way. Remove starter assembly and flywheel front cover plate. Remove front mount bolts. Do not loosen rear mounts. Jack engine as high as it will go with left side of clutch housing flange riding in body tunnel and right side just clearing tunnel, and riding against fire wall, Fig. D-11. The preferred method to jack up engine is to install an extension on crankshaft and operate the jacks against the extension. With the engine jacked up, remove engine front mount frame bracket on right side and remove oil filter. Remove oil pan screws and lower oil pan to frame, Fig. D-11. Remove oil pump to gain pan clearance, then remove oil pan by sliding and rotating front of pan to right of engine, then rearward, down and out at an angle to left rear corner of engine. The oil pan gasket surfaces can be cleaned and new gaskets installed without completely removing the pan from the engine.

1962-1964 409 cu. in.: To perform any operation on the 409 engine requiring oil pan removal, the engine must be removed from the vehicle.

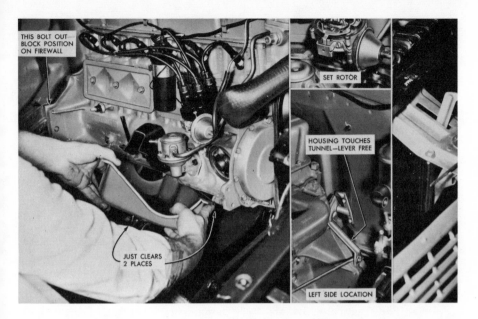

Inside the image: THIS BOLT OUT—BLOCK POSITION ON FIREWALL · SET ROTOR · HOUSING TOUCHES TUNNEL—LEVER FREE · JUST CLEARS 2 PLACES · LEFT SIDE LOCATION

Fig. D-11. Steps to follow when removing oil pan on 1963–1964 Chevrolet Six.

1959-1964 283, 327 V-8: Raise front of vehicle. Place on jacks. Drain the engine oil. Drain water and disconnect radiator hose at radiator. Disconnect battery ground strap at engine. Disconnect the clutch pedal push rod at clutch pedal control intermediate lever and shaft. Remove clutch pedal control, intermediate lever and shaft assembly at frame mounting bracket, leaving shaft assembly attached to engine. Remove carburetor fuel feed pipe at fuel pump. Remove fuel pump from engine. Remove accelerator control rod from accelerator control rod lever. If power brake equipped, remove power brake vacuum hose at check valve on the engine manifold. If power steering equipped, move power steering pump to clear. Remove transmission lower control rod at transmission shift levers. Remove exhaust pipe flange to exhaust manifold nuts and gasket. Lower exhaust pipe and muffler assembly. Remove oil filter. Loosen transmission mounting bolts. Remove nut, washer and long bolt from each front mounting. Turn crankshaft so that harmonic balancer key-way slot is at bottom of engine. Engine may now be raised from below at harmonic balancer. Remove oil pan bolts using a universal socket and long extension handle. Tilt oil pan while removing. On 1963, 283 and 327 cu. in. models the flange mounted starter must be removed to provide clearance. When replacing the oil pan, use grease as an adhesive to hold the gaskets in place. Install rear oil pan seal in groove and rear main bearing cap. Tuck ends into groove opening in cylinder block. Install oil pan front seal in groove in front end cover with end cutting side gasket.

1964-1968 Chevelle: To remove the oil pan it is first necessary to remove engine from the chassis.

1964 283 cu. in. Chevy II: Disconnect battery ground strap at battery.

Drain oil. Disconnect battery cable and small wires at solenoid then remove starter. Disconnect dip stick tube bracket at manifold, then disconnect steering idler arm bracket at right hand frame rail and swing steering linkage down for pan clearance. Disconnect exhaust crossover at manifolds and allow crossover to hang free. Remove oil pan bolts, oil pan gaskets and end seals.

1964-1967 Chevy II: Disconnect battery ground strap at battery and drain oil from crankcase. Remove starting motor. Disconnect steering idler arm bracket at right hand frame rail and swing steering linkage down for clearance. On six cylinder models only, remove front cross member. On station wagon, let stabilizer bar hang while removing cross member. Then remove oil pan bolts and lower oil pan to ground. When replacing the oil pan, be sure all gasket surfaces are clean and install rear seal in rear main bearing cap. Also install front seal on timing gear cover, pressing tips into holes provided. Use grease as an adhesive to secure the side gaskets to the oil pan. Screws into timing gear cover should be installed last and after the rest of pan bolts have been tightened.

1965-1968 Chevrolet Six and V-8, Camaro and 1968 Chevy II: To remove the oil pan on these models, disconnect battery. Remove distributor cap and fuel pump. Remove through bolts from engine front mounts. Drain radiator and then disconnect upper and lower radiator hoses at radiator. Remove fan blade. Raise vehicle and then drain engine oil. Disconnect and remove starter. On vehicles equipped with automatic transmissions, disconnect transmission cooler lines at transmission and remove converter housing under pan. Disconnect steering rod at idler lever, then swing steering linkage for oil pan clearance. Rotate crankshaft until timing mark on torsional damper is at six o'clock position. Using a suitable jack and a block of wood to prevent damaging the oil pan, raise engine enough to insert 2 x 4 in. wood blocks under the engine mounts, Fig. D-10A. Then lower engine onto blocks. On Chevrolet models remove oil pan and discard gaskets and seals. On Camaro and Chevy II, remove oil pan retaining screws and lower pan. Remove the two bolts securing the oil pump assembly and the one bolt securing the intake pipe and screen to the block. Remove oil pump and pan and discard gaskets and seals.

1969 In-Line Engine, Chevelle With Automatic Transmission: Disconnect battery. Remove radiator upper mounting panel and place a piece of heavy cardboard between fan and radiator. Disconnect starter brace at starter and disconnect and plug fuel line at fuel pump. Raise vehicle on hoist and drain engine oil. Remove converter under pan and splash shield. Remove inboard starter bolt and loosen outboard starter bolt. Swing starter outboard to gain adequate clearance for pan removal. Rotate crankshaft until timing mark on damper is at 6 o'clock position. Remove both engine mount through bolts. Raise front of engine until mounts separate from frame brackets. Remove the right motor mount from engine and install two bolts in mount holes. Continue to raise engine until a 4 1/2 in. block of wood can be inserted on right side between the bolts and the frame bracket and a 4 in. block on the left side, Fig. D-12. Remove retaining

Engine Disassembly

bolts and lower pan. Remove front main bearing cap then remove pan.

1969 In-Line Engine, Chevelle with Manual Transmission: To remove oil pan on this model it is first necessary to remove engine from chassis.

*Fig. D-12. Note blocks of wood used to keep engine
in raised position while oil pan is being removed.*

1969 - All Chevelle 396 cu. in. engines and 307 and 350 cu. in. engines equipped with manual transmissions: Disconnect battery positive cable. Remove air cleaner, dip stick and distributor cap. Remove radiator shroud and upper mounting panel to provide clearance. On 396 cu. in. engines, place a heavy piece of cardboard between radiator and shroud as protection. Disconnect engine ground straps at engine. On 307 and 350 cu. in. engines remove fuel pump and plug line from supply tank. Disconnect accelerator control cable from engine. Place a hook fabricated from steel strap stock and formed as shown in Fig. D-12a and suitable chain (approximately 4 ft. long) over cowl. Install a bolt through the holes in the hook and center link of chain. Raise vehicle on hoist, drain oil and remove oil filter on 307 and 350 cu. in. engines. Disconnect starter brace at starter. Remove inboard starter bolt and loosen outboard starter bolt and swing starter outboard to provide clearance. Remove propeller shaft and plug rear of transmission. On all floor shift manual transmissions, remove two bolts securing shift lever to linkage. On all other models disconnect transmission linkage at transmission. Disconnect speedometer cable and back-up lamp switch connector. On manual transmission vehicles disconnect clutch cordon shaft at frame. On automatic transmission vehicles disconnect cooler lines, detent cable, rod or switch wire and modulator pipe. Remove crossmember bolts and place jack under engine. Raise engine and move crossmember toward rear of engine. On engines with single exhaust, remove crossover pipe. On engines with dual exhaust, disconnect exhaust pipes. Remove flywheel housing cover. Remove transmission attaching bolts and remove transmission. On manual transmission models remove flywheel housing and throwout bearing. Remove engine mount through bolts. Raise rear of engine approximately

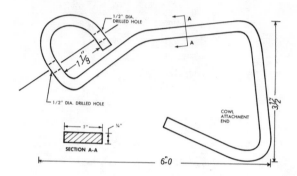

Fig. D-12a. Drawing of fabricated hook.

4 in. Attach each end of chain from fabricated hook using bell housing bolts (manual transmission) or transmission mounting bolts (automatic transmission). Lower jack and move to front of engine. Raise front of engine and insert 2 in. blocks of wood under front engine mounts. Rotate crankshaft until timing mark on torsional damper is at 6 o'clock position. Remove oil pan bolts and remove oil pan.

1969 In-Line Engines, Chevrolet, Camaro, Nova: Disconnect battery. Remove upper radiator mounting panel or side mount bolts. Place a piece of heavy cardboard between radiator and fan. Drain engine oil. Remove starter. On automatic transmission cars remove converter housing under-pan. Disconnect steering rod at idler lever and swing linkage for oil pan clearance. Rotate crankshaft until timing mark is at six o'clock position. On Chevrolet and Camaro, raise engine enough to insert 2 x 4 in. wood blocks under engine mounts, Fig. D-12. On Chevrolet, remove oil pan and discard gaskets. On Camaro remove oil pan retaining screws and lower pan. Remove two bolts securing oil pump assembly and one nut securing intake pipe and screen to block. Remove oil pan and pump. Discard gasket and seals. On Nova, remove hood hinge front bolts. Loosen rear bolts and prop up hood. With chain hoist, raise engine approximately 2 in. Then remove left engine mount and frame bracket. Remove oil pan by lowering it slightly and then rolling it into opening created by removal of left engine mount until oil pan is cleared. Tilt front of pan upward and remove by pulling pan down and to rear of vehicle.

1969 V-8 Chevrolet, Camaro, Monte Carlo, Nova and Chevelle: To remove oil pan on these cars with V-8 engines (except those with 396 cu. in.

engine or manual transmission) disconnect battery. Remove distributor cap. Remove radiator upper mounting panel (except Chevrolet). On Chevrolet remove six radiator support bolts. Remove fan shroud. Place piece of heavy cardboard between radiator and fan. Raise car and drain oil. Disconnect exhaust or crossover pipes. Remove automatic transmission converter housing under pan and splash shield if so equipped. Disconnect steering idler lever at frame and swing steering linkage down for oil pan clearance. Rotate crankshaft until timing mark on damper is at 6 o'clock position. Disconnect starter brace at starter. Remove inboard starter bolt and loosen outboard starter bolt. Swing starter outboard to obtain clearance for pan removal. Remove fuel pump and plug fuel line from gas tank. Remove through bolts from engine front mount. Raise front of engine. On Nova and Camaro 302, 307, 327, and 350 engines a special screw type jack is used to raise engine at fan pulley. Engine should be raised until wood blocks of 4 in. on Chevrolet, 2 in. on Nova and Camaro and 3 in. on Chevelle can be inserted under engine mounts. Remove pan. On 1971 Chevelle with Mark IV engine also remove transmission, disconnect exhaust pipe, remove engine mounts, raise engine.

1970-1972: Oil pan removal on these cars is basically similar to that listed for the 1969 models.

HOW TO REMOVE CONNECTING RODS

To remove connecting rods it is first necessary to remove the cylinder head and oil pan. Carefully note the identification numbers on each of the connecting rods and caps. If numbers are not visible center punch rods and caps with appropriate number of punch marks for identification.

If a ridge has been worn at the top of the cylinder bore, which is usually the case, this must be removed by special cutter before the rods are removed. If this is not done, the pistons will be damaged as the assemblies are removed. Before removing ridge, crank engine until piston is at bottom of its stroke and place an oiled rag on the top of the piston. As the ridge is removed with the cutter, the metal chips will be caught on the rag. At the completion of the ridge removal, the engine is cranked until piston is at the top and the rag with the chips is then removed. Then remove a connecting rod cap and push the rod and piston up and out of the top of the cylinder. Replace the cap on the connecting rod and proceed to remove the remaining rods in a similar manner.

It is important that the connecting rod caps be always replaced on their original rods and also that the bearing inserts are not mixed.

REMOVING THE TIMING CASE COVER

Removal of the timing case cover is basically the same on all Chevrolet built engines, four, six and eight models.

Remove the radiator and fan belt. On most late model V-8 engines, remove fan shroud and water pump. On all models except the Chevy

II four cylinder, remove harmonic balancer. On Chevy II four cylinder, remove fan pulley. On all models remove oil pan. On 235 cu. in. Six remove two bolts installed from back through front main bearing. Then after removing the timing case cover bolts, the cover can be removed.

On all models, except the 235 cu. in. Six engine, the front cover seal can be replaced without removing the cover. Remove vibration damper. Pry out old seal. Install new seal so that open end of seal is toward inside of cover. Fig. D-13 shows a new oil seal being driven into position with the cover removed.

Fig. D-13. Installing an oil seal in timing case cover.

REMOVING THE ENGINE

Removal and installation of an engine becomes necessary when a rebuilt engine is installed. As an engine assembly weighs six to seven hundred pounds, an overhead beam capable of supporting such a weight, together with a chain hoist is necessary.

The basic procedure applicable in general to all engines is as follows: Drain the cooling system, crankcase and transmission. Scribe alignment marks on the hood around the hinges, and remove the hood from the hinges. Remove the radiator hoses and heater hoses on models so equipped. Remove battery and battery cables. Remove fan shroud on cars so equipped. On Power Glide and Turbo-Glide models, remove and plug oil cooler lines. Remove radiator core.

Engine Disassembly

Disconnect starter and generator wires, engine to body ground strap, oil pressure indicator wire at sending unit on block, and ignition coil wires.

Remove temperature indicator element wire. Remove oil filter assembly. Remove air cleaner. Remove air conditioning on cars so equipped. Note that special equipment is needed to evacuate the air conditioning system before it can be removed. Disconnect fuel and vacuum lines. On eight cylinder models it is necessary to remove the distributor cap. If the car has power steering, this unit should be removed. Disconnect carburetor control rod from belt crank and throttle valve lever on transmission, if the car has an automatic transmission.

Remove exhaust pipe flange nuts and lower exhaust pipes and muffler. Remove road draft tube, if so equipped.

Remove exhaust crossover pipe and manifold heat valve from right hand exhaust manifold on eight cylinder models. Remove transmission control rods. On overdrive models, disconnect wires and cables. Remove clutch control belt crank and control rods on conventional transmission

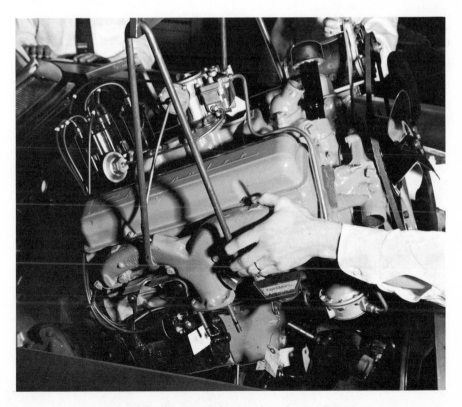

Fig. D-14. Removing V-8 engine from chassis. Typical.

models. On automatic transmission models, remove oil filter tube and plug the opening. Disconnect speedometer cable at the transmission. Remove the propeller shaft. Raise engine to take weight off front mounts and remove front mount through bolts. Remove rear mount to cross member bolts. Raise engine to take weight off rear mounts, then remove cross member.

If eye bolts fitting the cylinder head bolts are available, these should be screwed into the cylinder head for attaching the lifting hooks from the hoist. If not, use a chain sling around the engine. The engine and transmission, Fig. D-14, can then be lifted from the engine as a unit.

Simplified
ENGINE REPAIRS

General repair work on the Chevrolet, Chevelle, Chevy II, Nova, Camaro and Corvette engines is not difficult. In this chapter of Fix Your Chevrolet instructions covering the repair of different parts of the engine, applicable to all Chevrolet built engines, will be discussed.

In order to recondition or replace an engine part, it is, of course, necessary to first disassemble the engine, either partly or completely. Removal procedure was discussed in the preceding chapter. This chapter will be devoted to servicing and disassembly of the different parts after they have been removed from the engine.

WHEN SHOULD VALVES BE RECONDITIONED?

Due to incorrect valve tappet clearance, gummy valve stems, defective hydraulic valve lifters, the use of low octane fuel, unequal tightening of the cylinder head bolts, etc., valve life is often materially shortened. As a result, the face and seat of the valve become burned and pitted, as shown

Fig. E-1. Example of badly burned and carboned valve. Carbon under valve head usually indicates worn valve guide or defective seal.

in Fig. E-1. As a further result, compression of the combustible gases will not reach its maximum value. In extreme cases it will be necessary to replace the valve and also the valve seat. In cases not so extreme, the valve and seat can be reconditioned to give many more thousands of miles of useful service.

It is necessary to recondition the valves of Chevrolet built engines when compression tests indicate the valves are leaking. Leaking valves will also be indicated by loss of power and reduced fuel economy.

HOW TO REMOVE ENGINE VALVES

Before removing the valves, it is necessary to remove the cylinder head from the engine. After removing the cylinder head, as explained in the preceding chapter, procedure for removing the valves from the 153, 194, 230 and 250 cu. in. in-line engines, and all the V-8 engines is as follows:

Swing the rocker arm on the rocker arm stud so it does not cover the end of the valve stem, Fig. E-2, or remove the rocker arm nuts, rocker arm bolts and rocker arms.

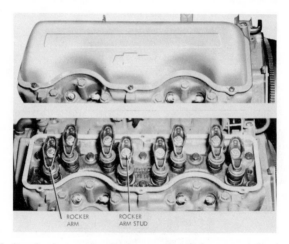

Fig. E-2. Details of types of rocker arms used on V-8 engines and in-line Sixes, except the 235 cu. in. Six.

On the 1950 to 1962 L-head Six, Fig. E-3, remove the bolts which retain the rocker arm assembly to the cylinder head, and remove the assembly. After the rocker arm shaft has been removed, or the rocker arm swung to one side, the valves can be removed.

To remove the valves from the cylinder head, a C-type valve spring compressor is used, Fig. E-4. While it is possible to compress the valve springs by pressing down on the valve spring retainers with two screw drivers, this is a difficult and tedious method. With the valve springs compressed, the valve locks, cap and seal are removed, Figs. E-3 and E-4.

Any valve with a bent stem, or a stem that is worn more than .002 in. should be replaced.

Fig. E-3. Rocker arm and shaft construction on 235 cu. in. 1962 and earlier in-line Six.

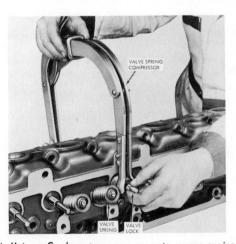

Fig. E-4. Using a C—clamp type compressor to remove engine valves.

Micrometers are used to measure the wear on valve stems. First measure the diameter on the valve stem of a new valve, or the unworn portion of an old valve. This is then compared to the diameter of the worn portion of the old valve.

Wear in excess of .002 in. will result in poor seating of the valve. In addition, air and oil will be drawn past the valve stem. The air will dilute the fuel mixture and the oil will cause increased oil consumption.

If the valve is not bent, or the stem worn, the valve can be refaced.

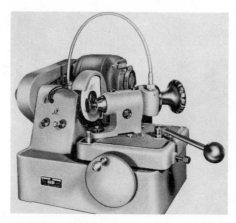

Fig. E-5. One type of valve refacing machine.

This is done on a valve refacing machine, Fig. E-5. Any automotive machine shop will perform this operation at a low cost. After a valve is refaced, the head should be checked to make sure it is not too thin. If the edge of the valve head is less than 1/32 in. thick, Fig. E-6, the valve should be replaced.

In addition to refacing the valve, the valve seat should also be reconditioned. Special valve seat reconditioning equipment is available for doing such work. By using 30, 45, and 60 deg. seat cutters, the proper seat width of 1/16 in. can be obtained.

The angle of the valve seats and valves of the different Chevrolet built engines is as follows:

	Intake		Exhaust	
	Seat	Face	Seat	Face
Engine	Angle	Angle	Angle	Angle
235 Six	31	30	46	45
Corvair (1960-1968)	45	44	45	44
Others	46*	45	46*	45

* Aluminum heads 45 deg.

RECONDITIONING VALVES WITHOUT SPECIAL EQUIPMENT

It is possible to recondition valves and valve seats without the use of special equipment, but the final job is not as satisfactory as is the case when special equipment is used. However, it is often resorted to when an auto machine shop is not immediately available, or when the costs are of major importance.

The procedure is to use fine carborundum powder, or special valve grinding compound, and grind or lap the valve to the seat. A very light coating of a valve grinding compound is placed on the face of the valve, and the valve is placed in position in the cylinder head. Then with a valve lapping tool, the valve is rotated back and forth on its seat. The valve lapping tool is basically a vacuum cup attached to the end of a short handle. The valve grinding compound grinds away the metal of both the seat and the valve until both are smooth and free from pits or other defects.

To keep the valve grinding compound evenly distributed, the valve should be raised occasionally from its seat and given a half-turn before the lapping process is renewed. Only light pressure should be placed on the valve during the grinding process.

The lapping is continued until all of the pit marks are ground away from both the valve and its seat. If the valves are badly pitted, it will be found that a groove will be ground in the face of the valve during the lapping process. Such a condition is not desirable, as the valve will then quickly pit again. The groove affords a place for carbon and other combustion products to lodge. That is why refacing the valve head and seat is the preferred method.

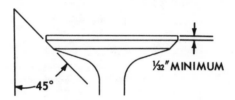

Fig. E-6. If edge of valve is less than 1/32 in. thick, valve should be replaced.

When the lapping process is completed, great care must be exercised to remove all traces of the grinding compound. Should any of the compounds remain in the intake valve seat, it will be drawn into the engine and cause rapid wear of all parts. On the exhaust valve it will cause the stem to be worn and in turn the valve will seat poorly, resulting in compression loss followed by burning of the valve and seat.

The width of the intake valve seat should range from .060 in. to .080 in., while the limits of exhaust valve seat width should range from .070 in. to .090 in. This is important because if the seats are too narrow, the valves will operate at too high a temperature and will soon become burned. If the seat width is too wide, there is a tendency for carbon to lodge on the seat and the valve will soon become pitted and not hold compression.

The finished valve seat should contact the approximate center of the valve face. This can be determined by placing a slight amount of Prussian Blue on the valve seat. Set the valve in position and rotate the valve with light pressure. The Blue will be transferred to the face of the valve and show clearly whether it is centered or not.

Another point to check on an engine valve is the condition of the end of the valve stem. If the end of the valve stem is rough, it will be difficult to accurately adjust the valve tappet clearance. When necessary, the end of the valve stem can be ground on the same machine that refaces the valve face.

As pointed out previously, it is possible to recondition valves by hand grinding but a better job can be done by using specialized equipment. Consequently many car owners and operators of small garages, not having their own equipment, take advantage of the facilities of the automotive machine shop. This is particularly true in the case of overhead type en-

Fig. E-7. One method of checking strength of valve spring.

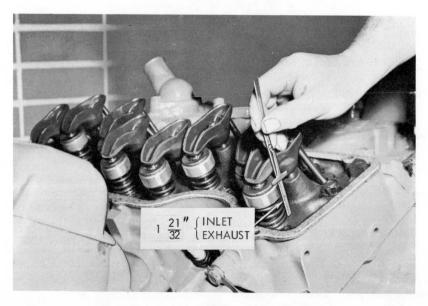

Fig. E-8. Measuring installed height of valve spring.
Indicated dimension does not apply to all engines.

gines, such as Chevrolet. In such cases all that is necessary is to remove the cylinder heads from the engine and take them to the machine shop where the head will be completely disassembled, cleaned and reconditioned.

QUICK CHECKS ON SPRINGS

It is important to check the condition of the valve springs, for if any of them are weak, full power will not be developed, particularly at higher engine speeds. Special testers are available for testing the compression strength of the valve springs, Fig. E-7. However, a fairly accurate check can be made by comparing the length of a used spring with that of a new spring. The end of the spring should be flat, and neither flatness nor length should vary more than 1/16 in.

After the valve and seat have been reconditioned, the valve springs will not exert as much pressure as they did originally because of the assembled height of the spring, which will be greater. In other words, it will not be compressed as much as it was originally.

It is, therefore, necessary to measure the length of the valve spring after it is reassembled in the engine, Fig. E-8. If it exceeds the specified amount, it is necessary to install spacers, between the cylinder heads and valve springs, in order to restore the spring to its normal compression. The assembled valve spring height for the various Chevrolet engines is as follows:

Assembled Valve Spring Height

Engine	Height	Engine	Height
153 cu. in.	1-21/32 in.	327 cu. in. 1967-68	1-5/32 in.
194 cu. in.	1-21/32 in.	348 cu. in.	1-21/32-1-23/32
230 cu. in.	1-21/32-1-23/32	350 cu. in. 1967-69	1-5/32 in.
235 cu. in.	1-51/64-1-7/8 in.	350 cu. in. 1970-71	1-23/32 in.
250 cu. in.	1-21/32 in.	396 cu. in.	1-7/8 in.
265 cu. in.	1-9/16-1-5/8 in.	400 cu. in. 1970	1-7/8 in.
283 cu. in. to 1966	1-21/32 in.	400 cu. in. 1971	1-23/32 in.
283 cu. in. 1967	1-5/32 in.	402 cu. in. 1971	1-23/32 in.
302 cu. in.	1-5/32 in.	409 cu. in.	1-5/8-1-11/16 in.
307 cu. in. 1969	1-5/32 in.	427 cu. in.	1-7/8 in.
327 cu. in.	1-21/32 in.	454 cu. in.	1-7/8 in.

REPLACING VALVE STEM SEAL OR VALVE SPRING

Occasionally it is necessary to replace a valve seal, or a valve spring, without doing any work on the valve itself, and this can be done as follows: Remove rocker arm cover, and the spark plug, rocker arm and push rod on the cylinders to be serviced. Apply compressed air to the spark plug hole to hold the valves in place.

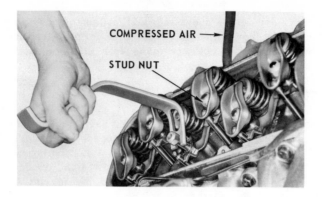

Fig. E-9. Illustrating method of compressing valve spring in order to replace oil seals or springs without removing head from engine. Note compressed air hose which supplies air pressure at spark plug hole.

A tool to apply the compressed air to the cylinder can be made from an old spark plug by removing the porcelain insulator from the plug. Then using a 3/8 in. pipe tap, cut threads in the remaining portion of the spark plug. A compressed air hose adaptor can then be screwed into the spark plug and the spark plug in turn into the cylinder head.

Compress the valve spring as shown in Fig. E-9. Then with the spring compressed, remove the valve locks, valve tap, valve shield, and the valve spring and damper. Also remove the valve stem oil seal. A new seal and spring can then be installed. A light coat of oil on the seal will help prevent twisting.

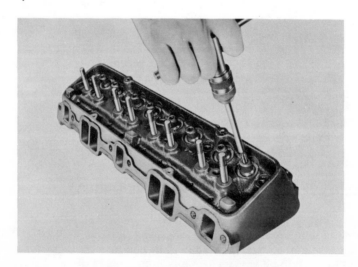

Fig. E-10. Reaming a valve guide.

Engine Repairs

WHAT TO DO ABOUT VALVE GUIDES

Only the 235 cu. in. Chevrolet Six, built in 1962 and earlier, is provided with the removable type valve guide. On other engines, valve guide holes are accurately reamed directly in the cylinder head. This has the advantage of cooler operating valves. However, when the valve guide holes in the cylinder head become worn more than .0045 in., it is necessary to recondition the holes by reaming, or by knurling, and then installing new valves with oversized valve stems. As this is a precision operation, it is generally necessary to have such work done by an automotive machine shop. Fig. E-10 shows a guide being reamed. Valves with oversized stems are available for intake and exhaust valves in the following oversizes, .003 in., .015 in., .030 in.

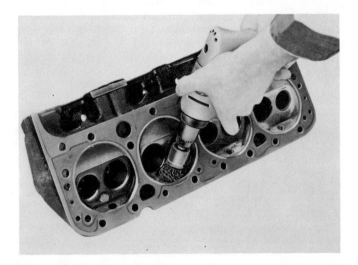

Fig. E-11. Cleaning carbon from cylinder head with a wire brush driven by an electric drill.

CLEANING THE CYLINDER HEAD

Before assembling the valves to the cylinder head, the head should be thoroughly cleaned. Carbon and combustion deposits should be removed from the combustion chambers. This can be done by scraping with a putty knife, or by means of an electric drill equipped with a wire brush, Fig. E-11. Be sure all carbon accumulations are removed, as any particles remaining may result in preignition. Also all grease should be removed from the outer side of the cylinder head and the water jacket thoroughly flushed to remove all traces of rust accumulation. All carbon accumulations must also be removed from the top of the piston.

It is also essential to check the surface of the cylinder head that mates with the cylinder block. This can be done with a straightedge and a feeler or thickness gauge. The straightedge should be held diagonally and then across the center of the cylinder head while checking the clearance between the straightedge and the cylinder head by means of a feeler gauge. Warpage should not exceed .003 in. in any six inches, or .006 in. overall.

In addition, the cylinder head should be carefully examined for any cracks, particularly around the valve seats and around the water jacket. Special spray-on type chemicals are available which will help greatly in revealing any cracks that may be present. While the head is off, it is also an excellent time to check and make sure the core plugs are tight and have not rusted. If there is any indication of rust around any of the core plugs, they should be replaced as explained in the Chapter on Cooling Systems.

It also pays to clean the interior of the water jacket so as to be sure that all rust accumulations are removed and in that way reduce the possibilities of overheating. This can be done by filling the cylinder head with radiator cleaning solution, which is allowed to remain in the head for approximately twenty-four hours.

HOW TO INSTALL PISTON RINGS

After the connecting rod and piston assemblies are removed from the engine, they should be thoroughly cleaned in a solvent designed for cleaning engine parts. If such special solvent is not available, kerosene can be used, but that is not nearly as effective as commercial cleaning solvent. After the assemblies have been cleaned, the rings can be removed as they will not be used again. The usual practice is to grab the end of the ring with a pair of pliers and pull out. In the case of cast iron rings, this will break the ring so that both parts are easily removed from the groove. Steel rings are removed in the same manner, but instead of breaking, the ring can be easily worked out of the groove and once one end is free, the

Fig. E-12. Cleaning piston ring groove with a special tool.

rest will easily spiral out of the groove. Always be sure to remove the steel expander ring from the bottom of each groove where such rings are used. Then with the rings removed from each piston, the groove can be thoroughly cleaned. The preferred method of cleaning is to use a special ring groove cleaning tool, such as is illustrated in Fig. E-12. Such tools quickly cut the carbon from the groove without danger of scratching or otherwise damaging the sides of the ring groove.

If such a tool is not available, a substitute method is to use a broken segment of a cast iron piston ring. This is used as a scraper. This method is long and tedious and there is also a possiblility of marring the surface of the sides of the ring grooves. This could result in loss of compression. It also tends to increase oil consumption.

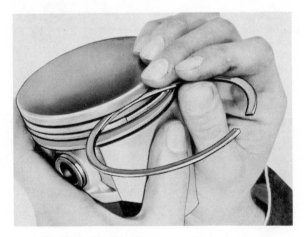

Fig. E-13. Checking fit of piston ring in ring groove.

It should be pointed out that if new piston pins are fitted, that most shops will not bother to clean the piston and rod assemblies. Instead they send them to an automotive machine shop to clean the assemblies, and install the new pins and rings. Or, if desired, the ring installation can be left to the mechanic doing the actual overhaul job. In general, when new rings are found to be necessary, it is always advisable to install new piston pins at the same time. The reason being that the pins generally wear out about the same time as the rings do.

Before installing new rings on the pistons, or fitting new piston pins, the pistons should be carefully checked to make sure they are in good condition and are still serviceable. In addition, the difference in diameter between the piston and the cylinder wall should be checked. This is known as piston clearance and is discussed in later paragraphs.

When examining the piston, make sure the ring grooves are in good condition, that the sides of the grooves are smooth, and without any groove worn by the rings. The sides of the grooves must be at right angles with the center line of the piston. A good method of checking the grooves is to roll a new piston ring around the groove, Fig. E-13. It should roll freely, without binding, but also without any side play. If the clearance between the side of the ring and the piston groove exceeds .005 in., Fig. E-14, the piston should be discarded. However, if desired, the pistons can be placed in a lathe and the grooves trued. A spacing ring is then inserted to compensate for the amount of metal removed from the side of the groove. When checking pistons, make sure there are no burned areas around the ring lands. In addition, make sure there are no cracks. If the piston of the steel strut type, make sure the strut has not become loose.

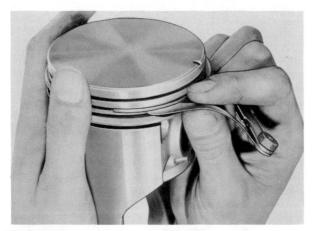

Fig. E-14. Checking clearance of ring in groove with a feeler gauge.

Spongy, eroded areas near the top of the pistons are usually caused by detonation or preignition. A shiny surface on the thrust surface of the piston, offset from the center line between the piston pin holes, can be caused by a bent connecting rod. Replace pistons that show signs of excessive wear, wavy ring lands, fractures and/or damage from detonation or preignition.

FITTING PISTON RINGS

Replacement type piston rings are designed to compensate for a certain amount of wear in the cylinders. The claims made by some manufacturers are extreme, but in general, replacement type rings should not be installed in the cylinders that have more than .010 in. taper, or .005 in. out-of-round. For details on measuring cylinder wear, see paragraph entitled "Should Cylinders be Reconditioned."

When selecting a piston ring set for an engine, it is necessary to select the proper size. To do this, position the ring in the cylinder bore in which it is going to be used. Push the ring down into the bore area where normal ring wear is encountered. Use the head of a piston to position the ring in the bore so the ring is square within the cylinder wall. Be careful to avoid damage to the ring or cylinder bore.

Measure the gap between the ends of the ring with a feeler gauge, as shown in Fig. E-15. The size of this gap is dependent on the make of the piston ring, and also on the diameter of the cylinder bore. In general this gap should be .003 in. for each inch of diameter. In other words, the correct ring gap for a 3 in. bore cylinder should be three times .003 in. or .009 in.

Fig. E-15. Measuring end gap of piston ring with a feeler gauge.

The side clearance of the piston ring in the groove should not be less than .001 in. for both oil and compression rings.

Piston rings are easily installed on the pistons. Some mechanics use special ring spreader tools, which, of course, make the installation quite simple, and without any danger of breaking the ring. Other mechanics will not use a special tool, but will spread the rings by hand. On the cast iron type rings, the procedure is to place a thumb over each end of a ring and spread the end of the ring apart. This will enlarge the diameter sufficiently so that it can be slid down over the piston to its proper groove. Be careful to follow the manufacturer's instructions so each ring is placed in the correct groove. In some designs it is necessary that one side of the ring be toward the top of the piston. If rings are not placed in the proper groove and with the right side up, excessive oil consumption will result.

Instructions for installing the pistons with its connecting rod in the cylinder bores are given in the paragraph entitled "Installing Connecting Rod Assemblies."

Fig. E-16. Checking piston clearance with a feeler gauge and spring balance to measure the pull.

ARE NEW PISTONS NECESSARY?

When new piston rings are installed without reconditioning the cylinders, it is seldom necessary to install new pistons. Naturally, if the ring lands are badly worn, or if the pistons have been badly damaged as a result of preignition, and excessive blow-by, new pistons will be required. When the original pistons are in good condition, as is usually the case, they can be used again. However, it is usually necessary to expand the pistons to obtain the desired clearance between the piston and the cylinder.

The normal piston clearance at the skirt is listed below. However, on the high performance models, skirt clearance is increased materially.

Engine	Skirt	Engine	Skirt
153 cu. in.	.0006-.0010 in.	350 cu. in.	.0005-.0011 in.
194 cu. in.	.0006-.0010 in.	350 cu. in. (1971)	.0007-.0013 in.
230 cu. in.	.0005-.0011 in.	350 cu. in. (330 hp)	.0061 in.
235 cu. in.	.0005-.0011 in.	396 cu. in.	.0018-.0026 in.
250 cu. in.	.0005-.0011 in.	400 cu. in.	.0014-.0020 in.
265 cu. in.	.0005-.0011 in.	402 cu. in. (1971)	.0018-.0026 in.
283 cu. in.	.0006-.0010 in.	409 cu. in.	.0031-.0035 in.
302 cu. in.	.0024-.0030 in.	427 cu. in.	.0009-.0015 in.
307 cu. in.	.0005-.0011 in.	454 cu. in.	.0024-.0034 in.
327 cu. in.	.0005-.0011 in.	454 cu. in. (365 hp)	.0024-.0034 in.
348 cu. in.	.0006-.0010 in.	454 cu. in. (425 hp)	.0040-.0050 in.

MEASURING PISTON CLEARANCE

One method of measuring piston clearance is to use one-half in. wide feeler gauge stock. Such a feeler gauge of the desired width and thickness can be secured in lengths of approximately 12 in. long. The procedure is to place the feeler gauge along the side of the piston, 90 deg. around the piston from the piston pin. The piston and feeler gauge are then inserted into the cylinder bore, Fig. E-16. If the clearance is correct, the piston should push the cylinder with light pressure, but it should lock if a feeler gauge of .001 in. more than standard clearance is used. Another method is to measure the pull required to pull the feeler gauge from between the piston and the cylinder wall. The feeler gauge should be pulled straight up and out by means of a scale, Fig. E-16, and the reading should be between 7 and 18 lb. If less than that amount, the clearance is excessive and if more than that amount the clearance is insufficient.

Still another method of measuring the piston clearance is to use micrometers, Fig. E-17. In this case the diameter of the cylinder bore is measured with inside micrometers, and the diameter of the piston is measured with outside micrometers. When measuring the cylinder bore, it is measured across the width of the engine, and the diameter of the piston is measured across its thrust faces. The difference between the two diameters will then be the piston clearance.

If the clearance is in excess of the amount specified, the pistons should be expanded sufficiently to obtain the desired clearance. Automotive machine shops have the necessary equipment for expanding the pistons.

Fig. E-17. Measuring piston diameter with outside micrometers.

CHECKING PISTON PINS

It is often difficult to determine whether a piston pin requires replacement. In general, a piston pin knock will sound very much like a loose valve tappet, and in many cases is worse when the engine is cold, than after it has reached operating temperature. However, when a car has traveled a distance sufficient to require replacement of piston rings and bearings, it will be poor economy not to replace the piston pins also. Furthermore, when new piston rings have been installed, and particularly when pistons have been expanded, piston pins with only a slight amount of excess clearance will cause a knock. This knock will in some cases disappear after the piston rings have been run in.

When examining the condition of the piston pins, any appreciable looseness or wear is sufficient cause for rejection. An inexperienced mechanic will sometimes confuse side play of the pins and the piston boss with pin wear.

The method of judging the fit of new pins will depend largely on the method used in fitting the pins. When a hone is used to fit the pins, they will seem to be relatively loose. If a reamer is used for fitting the pins, they will appear to be tighter than if they have been fitted by the hone method.

When the hone method is used, the end of the rod will drop quickly of its own weight when the assembly is held by the piston. If the reamer method is used to fit the pin, the rod will not drop of its own weight when the assembly is held by the piston.

BE SURE TO CHECK ROD ALIGNMENT

Along with the job of fitting the piston pin, is the job of checking the connecting rods for alignment. Obviously, if the rod is bent, or twisted, the piston will not move in a straight line at right angles to the center line of the crankshaft. The equipment for aligning connecting rods forms part of every well equipped shop.

If the equipment is not available, an approximation of the trueness of the connecting rod can be obtained by viewing the movement of the upper end of the connecting rod, as the engine is cranked. To do this, the oil pan is removed and the rod and piston assemblies are in position on the crankshaft. While the engine is cranked by the starter, the mechanic underneath the engine views the movement of the upper end of the connecting rod. This should remain centrally located on the piston pin, with equal clearance on each side of the piston pin bosses, and the end of the connecting rod. If the end of the connecting rod moves back and forth between the piston bosses, or if it remains pressed firmly against one of the bosses, the rod is bent.

TIPS ON REPLACING ENGINE BEARINGS

After the connecting rods have been removed from the engine, it is important to check the connecting rod bearings to determine whether they can be used again. It is often difficult to determine the condition of a bearing, and many bearings are discarded when actually they still retain many miles of useful life. First of all, the color of bearing surface is no gauge of the condition of the bearing.

In many cases the bearing surface will be stained a dark gray, or black. Such bearings are usually still serviceable. If any of the bearing metal has dropped from the backing, the bearing should be discarded. Also if the bearing surface is deeply grooved, scratched or pitted, replacement is indicated. If the back of a bearing which contacts the connecting rod or cap shows areas that are black, it indicates that there was dirt between the shell and the rod and the bearing should be replaced. If there are

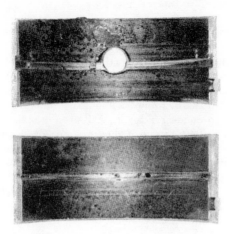

Fig. E-18. Example of worn engine bearings. In case illustrated, the bearings have been worn and gouged as the result of dirt.

groove marks on the back of the bearing shell, the shell has been slipping in the rod, and such bearing should also be replaced. An illustration of a bearing that has failed is shown in Fig. E-18.

Another test for a bearing is to measure the thickness of the shell. Such measurements are made with special micrometers, with a button on

Fig. E-19. Note grooves worn in these engine bearing journals as the result of dirt in the oil.

the rounded end of the anvil. Manufacturers of bearings provide specifications giving the thicknesses of different bearings. One of the best methods of determining the condition of a bearing is to make an oil leak test. This test is described later in this chapter.

CHECKING THE CRANKSHAFT

Before replacing any connecting rod bearings, the connecting rod bearing journal should be carefully measured for wear and roughness. Ordinary three inch outside micrometers are used for measuring connecting rod journals. The throws or journals should be measured at several points along their length to check for taper, and also measured at two points at right angles to each other to see if they are out-of-round.

Generally accepted limits for taper and out-of-round are .001 in. and .0015 in., respectively. If the wear exceeds these values, the crankshaft should be reground. If there is any roughness as shown in Fig. E-19, the journal should be reground. When journals are tapered, out-of-round or scored it will be impossible to fit the bearing correctly with the result that the bearing will knock, lose an excessive amount of oil, and will soon fail completely.

Equipment is available for reconditioning connecting rod journals without removing the crankshaft from the engine.

RODS MUST FIT BEARINGS

When overhauling an old engine, it is often found that a previous mechanic has filed down the bearing caps in an effort to make a worn-out bearing last a little longer. The result of this is that the bearing bore of the connecting rod is no longer round, and it will be impossible to install a new bearing shell. When such a condition is found, it will be necessary to rebore the big end of the connecting rod in order to return true circularity.

It is important that a bearing shall be a snug fit in the connecting rod. To insure such a fit in the conventional connecting rod, bearing manufac-

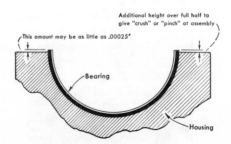

Fig. E-20. Bearing shells should extend approximately .00025 in. above surface of bearing cap, prior to being bolted in position.

turers make the bearing half slightly bigger than an exact half. As a result, the bearing half will extend slightly beyond the edge of the bearing cap. This is known as bearing crush, and is illustrated in Fig. E-20.

Conventional type bearings are keyed to the connecting rods, and are often adjusted by the feel or drag as the rod is swung back and forth on the connecting rod journal.

Some mechanics use "Plastigage" for checking the fit of these bearings. Plastigage consists essentially of slender rods of plastic. A short length of Plastigage is placed between the bearing journal and the bearing, and the connecting rod caps are tightened to approximately 65 ft. lb. tension. The connecting rod is then removed and the width of the crushed Plastigage is compared with a gauge provided by the manufacturer, Fig. E-21. The gauge reading gives the clearance of the bearing directly in thousandths of an inch.

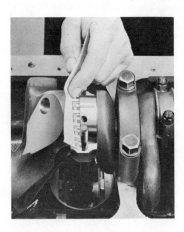

Fig. E-21. Checking engine bearing clearance by means of Plastigage.

HOW TO FIT ROD BEARING

Another method of fitting connecting rod bearings is to place a piece of .002 in. metal feeler stock that is one-half inch wide and 7/8 in. long between the bearing and the crank pin as shown in Fig. E-22. Bolt the connecting rod on the crank pin but with the piston end down, instead of in the conventional manner. Then with the rod bolts tight, the piston end of the rod is swung back and forth, presenting some resistance. If no resistance is felt, the clearance is excessive. If the rod cannot be swung back and forth on the crank pin, the clearance is too little. The correct clearance is obtained when the piston is swung to approximately a horizontal position and then will gradually sink to a vertical position. Be sure to remove the piece of shim stock from between the bearing and bearing journal before the final assembly of the rod to the crankshaft.

USE TORQUE WRENCH ON ROD NUTS

After all of the connecting rod bearings have been adjusted, the bearing cap nuts should be tightened to the correct torque, as specified in the table at the back of this book.

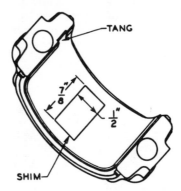

Fig. E-22. Using a piece of .002 in. thick feeler stock to check clearance of engine bearing.

CHECKING AND REPLACING MAIN BEARINGS

The usual procedure when replacing main bearings, is to replace one bearing at a time, leaving the other bearings to support the shaft. After removing the bearing cap, the upper half of the bearing shell must be removed from the cylinder block. There are several ways in which this can be accomplished without removing the crankshaft. A putty knife or some similar tool with a bent blade can be used to rotate the bearing shell around the shaft until it can be removed. Another method is to bend a cotter pin, as shown in Fig. E-23. Insert the eye end of the cotter pin in the oil hole in the bearing journal. Rotate the crankshaft, and the bent end of the cotter pin will force out the bearing shell.

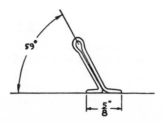

Fig. E-23. Method of bending a cotter pin so it can be used to remove upper half of main bearing shell.

1972 Chevelle Malibu.

Fig. E-24. Using special micrometers to measure diameter of crankshaft without removing shaft from the engine block.

After both halves of the bearing shell have been removed, the crankshaft journal should be checked for wear. Special micrometers are required to check these journals, Fig. E-24. Conventional micrometers cannot be used, as they will not reach up and measure the full diameter. If the journal has more than .001 in. taper, or is more than .0015 in. out-of-round, the crankshaft should be reground. To do this, it will have to be removed from the engine. The correct torque for the main bearing bolts is given in the specification tables at the back of this book.

When the proper size main bearing shells are obtained, the upper one is slid into place in the upper half of the bearing journal. Then the lower half is placed in the cap and the cap installed.

To check main bearing clearance, the Plastigage method can be used or a piece of shim stock, as described in the section devoted to fitting rod bearings.

WHEN SHOULD MAIN BEARINGS BE REPLACED

Main bearings should be replaced when they are worn to such an extent that the engine will knock, or when there is excessive oil leakage, as indicated by an oil leak test. Main bearing knocks will become most evident when the engine is under a heavy load, such as when pulling a steep grade.

HOW TO MAKE AN OIL LEAK TEST

One of the best methods of checking engine bearings for proper fit and wear, and also to determine when they need replacing, is to make an oil pressure, or oil leak test, as shown in Fig. E-25. Such a test will also show whether the entire engine lubricating system is clear and unobstructed so as to permit a full flow of oil to all the engine bearings.

The equipment for making such a test as illustrated, is designed to supply oil under pressure to the engine lubricating system.

Engine Repairs

Basically the equipment consists of a small tank of about five gal. capacity. This is partly filled with oil of SAE 30 grade. Compressed air is then applied to the tank until the pressure reaches approximately 25 lb., or the normal operating oil pressure of the engine. By means of suitable tubing, the tank is connected to the engine oil system. The engine is then cranked slowly and at the same time the engine bearings and the entire oiling system are carefully observed. Under these conditions, copper alloy bearings in good condition will leak at a rate of approximately 50 drops per minute. Engine bearings leaking oil at a faster rate, particularly those leaking in a steady stream, have too much clearance. Bearings showing a slower leakage than 30 drops per minute may have insufficient clearance, or the oil line to the bearing may be clogged. Babbitt type bearings should leak at a rate of 20 to 150 drops per minute.

In addition to the main and rod bearings, it is important to observe other bearings which may receive pressure lubrication, such as camshaft bearings and piston pin bearings. It is also important to check the plug at the rear of the camshaft rear bearing. This plug will occasionally get loose and excessive oil leakage will occur. As this oil will drop down past the rear main bearing, it is often mistaken for a leaking rear main bearing.

Fig. E-25. Making an oil pressure test on an engine to determine condition of engine bearings.

Instead of a pressure tank for making this test, some mechanics will use an oil pump. The intake of the pump is immersed in a pan of oil, and the outlet is connected to the engine oiling system. An electric drill is then used to drive the pump.

Regardless of the type of equipment used in making this test, it is important that the oil used is not heavier than SAE 30. In addition it is important that the oil is not cold, but should be at least 75 deg. F.

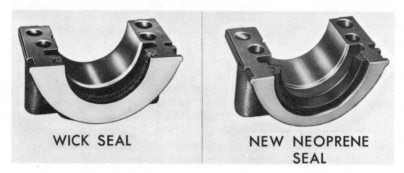

WICK SEAL   NEW NEOPRENE
                         SEAL

Fig. E-26. Illustrating two types of rear main bearing oil seals.

REPLACING REAR MAIN OIL SEALS

To prevent leakage of oil from the rear main bearing, special seals are provided. Typical seals are illustrated in Figs. E-26 and E-27. The wick type seal, Fig. E-26 was used as original equipment on the 235 cu. in. six cylinder engine, and also on the V-8 prior to 1959. A lip type rubber molded seal over a steel core is now available for replacement of the wick type seal used originally. This seal must be installed in sets of two per engine, and is so supplied. To replace the wick type seal, first remove the

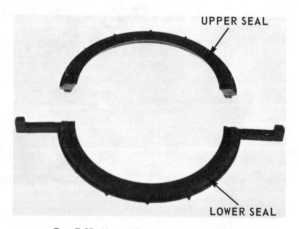

UPPER SEAL

LOWER SEAL

Fig. E-27. Note side extension on this oil seal.

bearing cap and pry the old seal from the bearing cap, using a small screwdriver. Loosen the remaining bearing caps to allow the crankshaft to drop slightly. In some cases it will be necessary to use a lever, placed between the crankshaft and the cylinder block to force the crankshaft down. Using a screwdriver or a blunt punch, push the seal out of the upper bearing sufficiently to pull it out completely with the end of a pair of pliers. Rotating the crankshaft in the same direction will often help pull the seal out.

To replace the wick type seal with a lip type rubber molded seal, after removing the wick type seal, first make sure that the upper and lower grooves are clean. Inspect the crankshaft seal contact area, and remove any imperfections with a fine oilstone. Dip the new seal in engine oil. Handle seals carefully to avoid marring the lip surfaces. Insert the upper seal in groove in engine block with lip of seal toward the front of the engine. Rotate the seal into the groove. Install the lower seal in the bearing cap with the lip toward the front of the engine.

To replace the neoprene type seal used on V-8 engines and illustrated in Fig. E-26, first remove the rear main bearing cap. Remove oil seal from groove, prying from bottom, using a small screwdriver. Always clean crankshaft surface before installing a new seal. New seals should be well lubricated with engine oil on lip only. Be careful not to get oil on

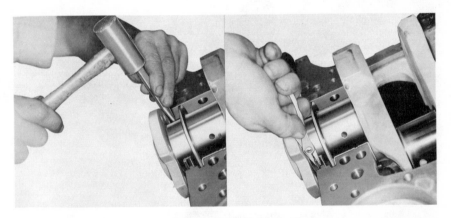

Fig. E-28. Using a pin punch to drive the oil seal (left) and then pliers to pull it through the remainder of the way.

parting line surface as this is treated with adhesive. The lip should face toward the front of the engine. With finger and thumb, roll seal into place being careful not to cut bead on back of seal with seal tangs at parting line.

Always replace upper and lower seal as a unit.

To replace the upper half of the seal, use a small hammer and tap a brass pin punch on one end of the seal until it protrudes far enough to be removed with pliers, Fig. E-28.

Always wipe crankshaft surface clean before installing a new seal.

Lubricate the lip of a new seal with engine oil, taking care to keep oil off the parting line surface. Gradually push with a hammer handle, while turning the crankshaft, until seal is rolled into place. Be careful the seal tangs at parting line do not cut bead on back of seal. Use sealer at parting

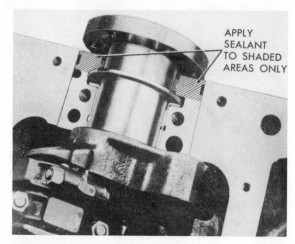

APPLY
SEALANT
TO SHADED
AREAS ONLY

Fig. E-29. Sealer should be applied to the area indicated and also to the bearing cap in order to prevent leakage of oil.

Fig. E-30. Using a dial gauge to check a cylinder for taper and out-of-round.

Fig. E-31. Piston, ring and rod assembly being installed in a cylinder. Note ring compressor used to compress rings into their grooves.

line on cap half of seal. Install the rear main bearing cap with new seal and torque to specifications.

Be sure to use sealer at parting line of cap half of seal and seal area of cylinder block as shown in Fig. E-29.

SHOULD CYLINDERS BE RECONDITIONED?

In most cases cylinders will require reconditioning only after 100,000 miles of operation or when the cylinder is more than .003 in. out-of-round, or when the taper exceeds .006 in.

It should be pointed out that when the car is used mostly in city driving, which consists of short trips of less than five miles, engine wear increases more rapidly than it does on long trips of many miles duration.

The most satisfactory method of determining the wear in a cylinder is to use a dial gauge as shown in Fig. E-30. The measurement is taken across the cylinder and the reading of the gauge is noted as it is moved up and down for the entire length of piston travel. This will measure the taper which should not exceed .010 in. Then measure the fore-and-aft diameter and the difference between that and the taper will give the amount of out-of-round which should not exceed .005 in.

Cylinders can be reconditoned either by means of a boring bar or by means of a cylinder hone. Boring bars are generally used when considerable metal must be removed. Final finish is usually made with a hone.

Automotive machine shops with necessary equipment will do the reconditioning. However, even when cylinder wear is not excessive, the glaze should be removed from the cylinders before installing new piston rings. If the glaze is not removed from the cylinders, the engine will continue to use considerable oil. Removing the glaze is accomplished by means of deglazing hone. The hone is driven by an electric drill, and all that is necessary is to move the rotating hone several times up and down the cylinder until the glaze is removed.

If a deglazing hone is not available, it is advisable to use a relatively fine abrasive paper and rub the surface of the cylinder to remove the glaze. The abrasive paper should be moved spirally around the cylinder bore when deglazing by hand.

Before deglazing the cylinders, cloth should be placed over each of the crankshaft throws so that abrasive particles from the hone will be caught in the cloth.

INSTALLING CONNECTING ROD ASSEMBLIES

After the main bearings have been replaced, new rod bearings selected, pins fitted, pistons expanded, and rings installed on the pistons, the connecting rod and piston assemblies are ready to be installed in their original cylinders. To do this, it is necessary to use a ring compressor as shown in Fig. E-31. This is essentially a sleeve, which compresses the piston rings in their grooves, so the pistons can be replaced in the cylinders. Before compressing the rings, however, the piston and rings should be given a liberal coating of engine oil. Similarly, the cylinders should be covered with oil. With the rings compressed, insert the connecting rod and piston assembly in the top of the cylinder. The assembly will be prevented from dropping through the cylinder by the pressure of the expanded piston against the cylinder walls and by the ring compressor. The assembly is driven the rest of the distance into the cylinder by tapping the top of the piston with the handle of a heavy hammer, Fig. E-31.

On all engines except the 348 cu. in. V-8, be sure the indentation mark or arrow on top of the piston is toward the front of the engine. On the 348 cu. in. V-8 engine, the indentation mark on the top of the piston should be toward the front of the engine on the left bank of cylinders, and to the rear on the right bank of cylinders.

It is important that the gaps of the piston ring should be correctly located around the piston, as indicated in Fig. E-32.

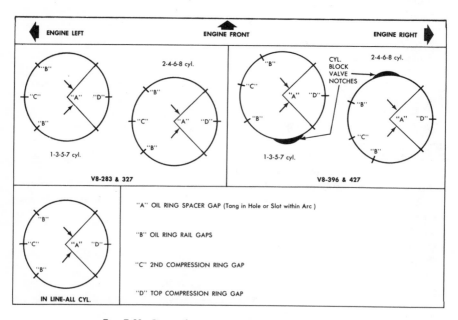

Fig. E-32. Correct location of piston ring gaps is important.

When installing rod and piston assemblies, one mechanic should be underneath the engine to guide the lower end of the connecting rod so it does not strike and mar the connecting rod throw on the crankshaft.

If it proves difficult to force the piston fully into the cylinder, the trouble is probably caused by the piston rings not having been compressed into their respective grooves, with the result that the rings are extending over the edge of the cylinder. In such cases, remove the ring compressor and then making sure that none of the rings have been damaged, again compress the rings carefully and install the piston assembly in the cylinder.

Always check and double check to be sure that the rod and piston assemblies have been correctly assembled and placed in their respective bores from which they were originally removed. On V-8 engines install with connecting rod bearing tang slots on side opposite cam shaft. In-line engines must have pistons with the piston notch facing front of engine. Unless assembly and installation is made correctly, there will be danger of the valves striking the top of the piston and doing considerable damage.

TIGHTENING CONNECTING ROD CAPS

When installing and tightening connecting rod bolts, it is important to place the caps on the rods from which they were originally removed, and also in their original relative position. Be sure to apply a liberal coating of oil to the crankshaft throw before attaching the connecting rod and cap. The socket used to tighten the nuts must be of the thin wall type, as there is very little clearance. Some mechanics will tighten these nuts as much as possible. This is poor practice as it distorts the bearings and connecting rod caps with the result that they are no longer round. Under such conditions, oil leaks from the bearings, bearing life will be materially shortened and oil consumption increased. A torque wrench can always be used to tighten connecting rod nuts.

WHEN TO REPLACE TIMING CHAINS

The life of a timing chain, Fig. E-33, is normally in excess of 100,000 miles. A worn timing chain will first be indicated by a whirring and rattling noise from the front of the engine. In cases of extreme wear, the tim-

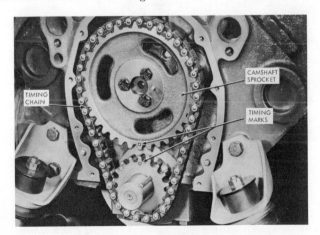

Fig. E-33. Typical timing chain installation.

ing chain may be so loose, it will jump from one position to another on the sprockets with the result that the timing of the ignition and camshaft will be altered. When this happens, the engine will fail to operate, or if it does operate, performance will be very poor.

HOW TO REPLACE TIMING CHAINS

The timing chain, as used on V-8 engines, is easily replaced after removing the radiator, hydraulic balancer, and timing case cover. Crank the engine until timing marks on the sprocket are in line, as shown in Fig. E-33. Remove the three camshaft sprocket to camshaft bolts. Then remove the camshaft sprocket and timing chain together. The sprocket is a light press fit on the camshaft. A light blow with a plastic faced hammer on the lower edge of the ridge of the sprocket should free it.

When installing the timing chain and sprocket, be sure the timing marks are in alignment, Fig. E-33. Do not drive the sprocket on the camshaft, as this will push on the sealing plug at the rear end of the shaft, causing an oil leak. Instead draw the camshaft sprocket into position by tightening the three bolts in rotation.

HOW TO REPLACE TIMING GEARS

Timing gears are used on all Chevrolet in-line engines, including the 153, 194, 230, 235 and 250 cu. in. engines, Fig. E-34. These gears seldom require replacement.

The camshaft gear is a press fit on the camshaft, and it is necessary to remove the camshaft from the cylinder block to remove the gear.

Fig. E-34. Typical timing gear installation. A method of checking gear lash with a feeler gauge is illustrated.

Fig. E-35. Installing oil seal in timing case cover.

FRONT COVER OIL SEAL

In case of oil leakage from the front cover, it is necessary to install a new oil seal and gasket. The procedure is to remove the cover, and pry out the old seal. Then install a new seal so the open end of the seal is toward the inside of the cover, and drive it into a position with a round drift of the diameter which fits the seal, Fig. E-35.

The replacement of the front cover oil seal can be made either with the cover removed, or with the cover still installed on the front of the engine. If the cover is still on the front of the engine, the procedure is to remove the crankshaft pulley and hub or torsional damper after which the seal can be pried from the cover with a large screwdriver, taking care not to damage the seal surface on the cover. The new seal is then installed in the same manner as previously described herein.

HYDRAULIC LIFTER CHECKS

Hydraulic valve lifters are available as either standard or optional equipment on all Chevrolet built engines, except the 409 cu. in. V-8. Hydraulic valve lifters seldom require attention, particularly if the engine oil is changed at frequent intervals. Fig. E-36 shows the details of hydraulic valve lifters used on recent model Chevrolet built engines.

It is normal for hydraulic valve lifters to be noisy when the engine is first started. That results from the oil having drained from the lifter, but as soon as the lifters are again filled with oil the noise will disappear. However, if the noise persists, servicing is required. An easy way to locate a noisy valve lifter is to use a piece of garden hose, approximately

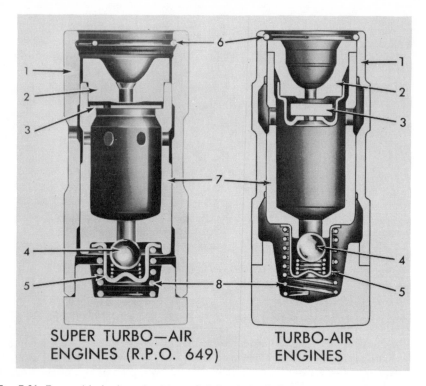

SUPER TURBO—AIR
ENGINES (R.P.O. 649)

TURBO-AIR
ENGINES

Fig. E-36. Types of hydraulic valve lifters. 1—Lifter body. 2—Push rod seat. 3—Valve. 4—Ball check. 5—Ball retainer. 6—Lock ring. 7—Plunger. 8—Check ball spring.

4 ft. long. Place one end of the hose near the end of each valve, with the other end of the hose being held to your ear. By following this procedure, noisy valve lifters can easily be located, as the garden hose acts as a stethoscope. Another method of locating a nosy lifter is to place a finger on the edge of the valve spring retainer on each valve in turn. Lifters not operating correctly will give a distinct shock each time the valve seats.

Each hydraulic lifter is a matched assembly. If the parts of one lifter are intermixed with those of another, improper valve operation will result and the lifter will be noisy. It is, therefore, necessary to keep the parts of each valve lifter separated so that they will not be mixed with the parts of other lifters. Also keep the lifter assemblies in proper sequence so they can be installed in their original position.

To disassemble a hydraulic valve lifter, grasp the lock ring, Fig. E-36, at the upper end of the lifter with a pair of long-nosed pliers to release it from the groove. It may be necessary to depress the plunger slightly in order to release the lock ring. After removing the lock ring, the other parts are easily removed from the lifter body.

In general, when hydraulic valve lifters have seen enough mileage so they are no longer operating quietly, it pays to install a complete new unit rather than to attempt to salvage the old ones. However, in cases where the cost factor is of major importance, by thoroughly cleaning the individual parts of the hydraulic lifters with solvent, they can be reassembled and placed back in service.

Instructions covering the adjustment of hydraulic valve lifters are given in the Chapter on Valve Tappet Adjustment.

DO NOT MIX PARTS

Regardless of what part of the engine is being assembled, it always pays to carefully observe the relative position of each part. Whenever possible the parts should be marked so they can be reassembled in their original position. This applies particularly to such parts as engine valves, hydraulic valve lifters, rocker arms, piston and rod assemblies, and engine bearings.

TROUBLE SHOOTING

See also Chapters on Fuel, Ignition and Electrical Systems.

LACK OF POWER

Incorrect valve lash. Sticking valves. Leaking valves. Valve springs weak or broken. Valve or ignition timing incorrect. Leaking cylinder head gasket. Worn pistons, rings and cylinder walls. Low compression.

Fig. E-37. Parts of a typical hydraulic valve lifter.

EXCESSIVE OIL CONSUMPTION

Oil leaks, check all gaskets and oil lines. Clogged oil return from rocker arm chamber. Clogged crankcase ventilating system. Leaking rear main bearing. Worn rings, pistons and cylinder walls. Worn valve stems and guides. Worn valve stem seals. Defective vacuum diaphragm on dual type fuel pumps.

HARD STARTING

Low engine compression. Excessive friction. Heavy engine oil. Valves holding open. Leaking manifold gasket. Loose carburetor mountings.

POPPING, SPITTING, DETONATION

Excessive carbon in combustion chamber. Valves sticking. Incorrect valve lash. Valves too thin and overheating. Weak valve springs. Incorrect valve timing. Clogged water jackets. Restricted exhaust ports in cylinder head. Cylinder head gasket blown between cylinders. Clogged muffler and exhaust system.

ROUGH ENGINE IDLE

Incorrect valve lash. Valve loose in guides. Valves not seating properly. Sticking valves. Leaking head gasket. Cracks in exhaust port.

MISSING ON ACCELERATION

Incorrect valve lash. Burned valves. Sticking valves. Leaking manifold gaskets. Low compression. Leaking head gasket.

ENGINE NOISE

Worn main bearings will give a heavy thumping noise, which is loudest on slow heavy pull. Worn rod bearings will give a sharp knock which is loudest at speeds of about 40 mph and as the engine goes from a pull to a coast. Worn pistons will give a sharp knock or slap which is worse when the engine is cold and decreases as the engine reaches operating temperature. Worn piston pins will act very much the same as a worn piston. Loose or worn engine mounts will cause a heavy thump particularly on sudden acceleration.

VALVE
ADJUSTING

In order to get maximum power from engines with mechanical lifters, it is essential that the valve lash of these lifters be accurately adjusted. Valve lash is the distance between the end of the rocker arm and the end of the valve stem.

MECHANICAL VALVE LIFTER ADJUSTMENT

Mechanical lifters are used on the 235 cu. in. Six and also as standard or special equipment on the 248, 302, 409 and 427 cu. in. V-8 engines. Correct valve lash on the Six is .006 in. for the intake valves and .015 in. for the exhaust. On the 348 and 409 cu. in. engines, the lash is .012 in. and .018 in. for the intake and exhaust respectively. On the 427 cu. in. engines the lash is .022 and .024 in. On the 302 cu. in. engines both valves are adjusted to .030 in.

On the 330 hp version of the 350 c.i.d. engine and 425 hp version of the 454 c.i.d. engine mechanical lifters are also used. In the case of the 350 c.i.d. engine the intake valve clearance is .024 in., and the exhaust is .030 in. The valve clearance for the 454 c.i.d. engine is .024 in. and .028 in. for the intake and exhaust valves respectively.

Before attempting to adjust valve lash, normalize the temperature of the engine. The best method of doing this is to drive the car for about 5 miles, or until the engine oil temperature remains the same for about 5 minutes.

Adjustment of the clearance between the end of the valve stem and the rocker arm is made by first loosening the lock nut on the rocker arm, Fig. F-1, and turning the adjustment until the proper clearance is obtained between the end of the rocker arm and the end of the valve stem. The clearance is measured by means of a feeler gauge.

MECHANICAL LIFTERS ON V-8 ENGINES

To adjust the mechanical valve lifters as used on V-8 engines, proceed as follows: Crank engine until mark on torsional damper lines up with the center or "O" mark on the timing tab and the engine is in the number one firing position. This may be determined by placing fingers on number one cylinder valve as the mark on the damper comes near the "O" mark on the front cover. If the valves are not moving, the engine is in the number one firing position. If the valves move as the mark comes up to the timing tab, the engine is in number six firing position and the crankshaft should be rotated one more revolution to reach the number one position.

Fig. F-1. Adjusting mechanical valve tappets on Chevrolet 235 cu. in. Six. Note feeler gauge in mechanic's left hand.

With the engine in number one firing position, as determined above, adjust the following valves to specifications with a feeler gauge, Fig. F-2: Exhaust valves 4 and 8, Intake valves 2 and 7. Turn the crankshaft one-half revolution clockwise and adjust the following valves to specifications with a feeler gauge: Exhaust valves 3 and 6, Intake valves 1 and 8.

Turn the crankshaft one-half revolution clockwise until the pointer

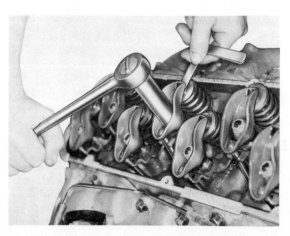

Fig. F-2. Adjusting valve lash on pivot type rocker arms.

Valve Adjusting

"O" mark and the torsional damper mark are again in alignment. This is number 6 line position. With the engine in this position, adjust the following valves to specifications with a feeler gauge: Exhaust valves 5 and 7, Intake valves 3 and 4.

Turn crankshaft one-half revolution clockwise and adjust the following valves to specifications with a feeler gauge: Exhaust valves 1 and 2, Intake valves 5 and 6.

The valve lash should be adjusted with the engine hot and running, and only after the engine has reached full operating temperature.

HYDRAULIC LIFTERS

A typical hydraulic valve lifter is shown in Figs. E-36 and F-3. Hydraulic valve lifters very seldom require attention. The lifters are extremely simple in design, the adjustments are not necessary and servicing of the lifters requires only that care and cleanliness be exercised in the handling of parts.

Locating noisy hydraulic valve lifters was discussed in the previous chapter. The general types of valve lifter noise are as follows:

Hard rapping noise: Usually caused by the plunger becoming tight in the bore of the lifter body to such an extent that the return spring can no longer push the plunger back up to the working position. Probable causes are: Excessive varnish or carbon deposit causing abnormal stickiness. Galling or pickup between plunger and bore of lifter body, usually caused by an abrasive piece of dirt or metal wedging between plunger and lifter body.

Moderate rapping noise: Probable causes are: Excessively high leakdown rate. Leaking check valve seat. Improper adjustment.

General noise throughout the valve train: This will in most cases be a definite indication of insufficient oil supply or improper adjustment.

Clicking noise; Intermittent clicking: Probable causes are: A microscopic piece of dirt momentarily caught between ball seat and check valve ball. In rare cases the ball itself may be out-of-round or have a flat spot. Improper adjustment.

In most cases where noise exists in one or more lifters, all lifter units should be removed, disassembled, cleaned in a solvent, reassembled and reinstalled in the engine. If dirt, corrosion, carbon, etc. are shown to exist in one unit, it probably exists in all units, thus it would on be a matter of time before all lifters cause trouble.

Hydraulic valve lifters can be removed after first removing the intake manifold. Then remove the rocker arms and push rods after which the valve lifters can be lifted from the engine.

TIPS ON HYDRAULIC LIFTER SERVICE

Thoroughly clean all parts in cleaning solvent, and inspect them carefully. If any parts are damaged or worn, the entire lifter assembly should be replaced. If the lifter body wall is scuffed or worn, inspect the cylinder block lifter bore; if the bottom of the lifter is scuffed or worn, inspect the camshaft lobe; if the push rod seat is scuffed or worn, inspect the push rod.

Note that the inertia valve and retainer in the hydraulic lifter installed in the turbo air engines should not be removed from the push rod seat. To check the valve, shake the push rod seat and inertia valve assembly and the valve should move.

Plungers and other parts of hydraulic lifters are not interchangeable; they are a selective fit at the factory. Should a plunger or lifter body become damaged, it is necessary to replace the entire unit. The plunger must be free in the lifter body. A simple test for this is to be sure the plunger will drop of its own weight in the body.

When disassembling a hydraulic valve lifter, be sure the parts are not mixed and are returned to the same unit. A unit is easily disassembled by removing the retainer, shown in Fig. E-36 and F-3, after which the other parts can be pulled from the body of the unit. When replacing a hydraulic valve lifter, be sure to fill the assembly with SAE 10 oil before completing the installation.

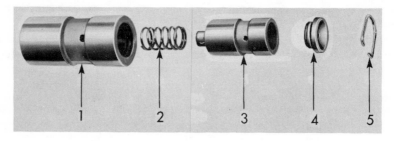

Fig. F-3. Parts of typical valve lifter. 1—Body. 2—Spring. 3—Plunger and ball check. 4—Push rod seat. 5—Retainer.

Hydraulic valve lifters are easily removed. In the case of V-8 engines, remove the rocker arm cover attaching screws and remove the rocker arm cover. Also remove the intake manifold. Back off the rocker arm nuts until the arms can be swung away from the push rods. Remove the push rods. The hydraulic valve lifters can then be lifted from their places in the cylinder block.

A similar procedure is to be followed when removing the hydraulic valve lifters from six cylinder engines.

ASSEMBLING HYDRAULIC LIFTERS

Place the ball check on small hole in bottom of plunger. Insert check ball spring on seat in ball retainer and place retainer over ball so spring rests on the ball. Carefully press the retainer into position in plunger with a blade of a small screwdriver.

Place the plunger spring over the ball retainer and slide the lifter body over the spring and plunger, being careful to line up the oil feed holes in the lifter body and plunger. Fill the assembly with SAE 10 oil, then insert the end of a 1/8 in. drift pin into the plunger and press down solid. At this point, oil hole in lifter body and plunger assembly will be in alignment. Do not attempt to force or pump the plunger.

Insert a 1/16 in. drift pin through both oil holes to hold the plunger down against the lifter spring tension. On the type illustrated as turbo-air in Fig. E-36, the drift pin must not extend inside the plunger. Remove the 1/8 in. drift pin. Refill assembly with SAE 10 oil. Install the metering valve and push rod seat or push rod seat and inertia valve, as the case may be, Fig. E-36. Install the push rod seat retainer, press down on the push rod seat and remove the 1/16 in. drift pin from the oil holes. Lifter is now completely assembled, filled with oil and ready for installation.

Before installing any new lifters, be sure to coat the bottom of the lifter with Molykote or its equivalent. This is necessary to prevent scoring of the lifter and rapid wear of the cam.

ADJUSTING HYDRAULIC VALVE LIFTERS

When rocker arm assemblies or valve lifters have been removed and replaced on an engine, it is then necessary to make an initial adjustment of each valve lifter. This adjustment must be made when the lifter is on the base circle of the cam, following this procedure:

Crank engine until mark on torsional damper aligns with center or "O" mark on the timing tab and the engine is in the number one firing position. This may be determined by placing fingers on the number one cylinder valve as the mark on the damper comes near the "O" mark on the front cover. If the valves are not moving, the engine is in the number one firing position. If the valves are moving, as the mark comes up to the timing tab, the engine is in the number six firing position and the crankshaft should be rotated one more revolution to reach the number one position.

Valve adjustment is made by backing off the adjusting nut, (rocker arm stud nut) until there is play in the push rod and then tighten nut to just remove all push rod to rocker arm clearance. This may be determined by rotating push rod with fingers as the nut is tightened, Fig. F-4. When the push rod does not readily move in relation to the rocker arm, the clearance has been eliminated. The adjusting nut should then be tightened an additional one turn to place the hydraulic lifter plunger in the center of the travel. No other adjustment is required.

With the V-8 engine in number one firing position, as determined above, the following valves may be adjusted: Exhaust 1, 3, 4, 8. Intake 1, 2, 5, 7. Crank the engine one revolution until the pointer and the "O" mark are again in alignment. This is number six firing position. With the engine in this position, the following valves may be adjusted: Exhaust 2, 5, 6, 7. Intake 3, 4, 6, 8.

On six cylinder engines the procedure for cranking the engine so that the engine is on the base circle of the camshaft's lobe is slightly different, and is as follows:

Mark distributor housing with chalk, at each cylinder position (plug wire) then disconnect plug wires at spark plugs and coil and remove distributor cap and plug wire assembly (if not previously done).

Crank engine until distributor rotor points to number one cylinder position and breaker points are open. Both valves on number one cylinder may now be adjusted.

Fig. F-4. Adjusting hydraulic valve lifter.

Back out adjusting nut until lash is felt at the push rod, then turn in adjusting nuts until all lash is removed. This can be determined by checking push rod side play while turning adjusting nut, Fig. F-4. When play has been removed, turn adjusting nut in one full additional turn in order to center lifter plunger.

Adjust the remaining valves, one cylinder at a time, in the same manner.

Firing order of the six cylinder engines is 1-5-3-6-2-4; V-8 engines 1-8-4-3-6-5-7-2; four cylinder engines 1-3-4-2.

COOLING SYSTEM
KINKS

Many of the troubles that occur in the engine cooling system can be eliminated by draining and flushing the system in the spring and again in the fall before antifreeze is installed. Always be sure that a rust inhibitor is used with the water, or that a high quality antifreeze, which contains a rust inhibitor, is used.

In that way rust formations within the cooling system will be kept to a minimum.

A pressure cooling system, Fig. G-1, is provided on all models by a pressure type radiator cap, Fig. G-2. The pressure type radiator cap is designed to hold a pressure in the cooling system. Since 1966 this pressure has been 15 psi, and from 1958 to 1965 the pressure was 13 psi. Excessive pressure is relieved by a valve within the cap that opens to radiator overflow. As shown in Fig. G-2, vacuum relief is also provided in the design of the radiator cap. With the 15 lb. pressure cap, coolant temperatures of up to 247 deg. F. are provided.

When the radiator cap is removed or loosened, the system pressure drops to atmospheric and the heat which had caused water temperatures to be higher than 212 deg. F. will be dissipated by conversion of water into steam. Inasmuch as the steam may form in the engine water passages it will blow coolant out of the radiator upper hose and top tank, necessitating coolant replacement. Engine operating temperatures higher than the normal boiling point of water are in no way objectionable as long as the coolant level is satisfactory when the engine is cool. The cooling system fluid level should be maintained one inch below the bottom of the filler neck of the down flow radiator when the cooling system is cold, or at the bottom of the filler neck when the system is warm. Coolant level in cross flow radiators should be maintained three inches below the bottom of the filler neck when the system is cold. It is very important that the correct fluid level be maintained. If there is repeated coolant loss, the pressure radiator cap and seat should be checked for sealing ability, also the cooling system should be checked for loose hose connections, defective hoses, gasket leaks, etc.

DRAINING THE COOLING SYSTEM

Every two years the cooling system should be serviced by flushing with clear water, then completely refilled with a fresh solution of water and a high quality permanent type glycol base antifreeze. This will help prevent the formation of rust and sludge in the system.

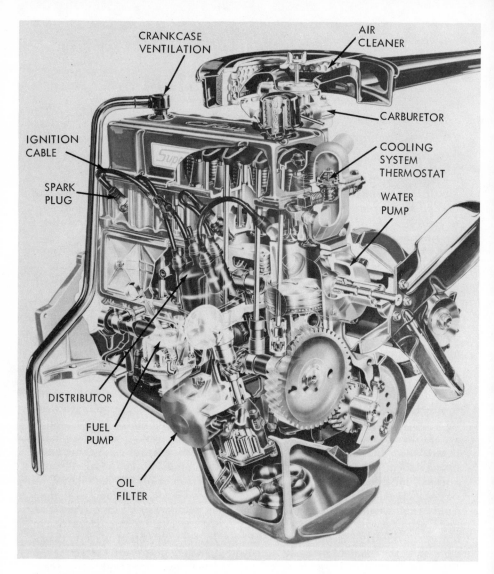

CRANKCASE
VENTILATION

AIR
CLEANER

CARBURETOR

IGNITION
CABLE

COOLING
SYSTEM
THERMOSTAT

WATER
PUMP

SPARK
PLUG

DISTRIBUTOR

FUEL
PUMP

OIL
FILTER

Fig. G-1. Details of 153 cu. in. four cylinder engine. Note location of cooling system thermostat, water pump and fan. Typical of other engines.

In order to drain the cooling system, the drain cock located at the bottom of the radiator, and the drain cocks in the cylinder block should be open. In the case of in-line engines, such as the Chevrolet Six and the Chevy II, there will be a single drain cock, but in the case of V-8 engines, there is a drain cock on each side of the engine block.

After the system has been drained, it should be thoroughly flushed to remove all traces of rust and old coolant. If a strong stream of water is available, it is advisable to reverse flush the system. That is done by disconnecting the upper hose, removing the thermostat, Figs. G-1 and G-3, then applying the water pressure at the bottom of the radiator so that the water flows from the bottom to the top. Also apply the water pressure at the top of the engine so that the water will flow from the top of the engine and out the bottom.

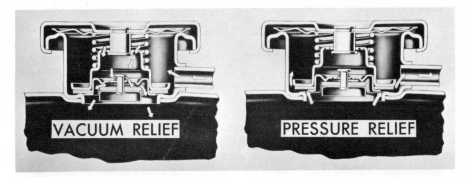

Fig. G-2. Sectional views of pressure type radiator cap. The vacuum relief relieves the vacuum created when the engine cools. The pressure relief allows excessive pressure to be relieved out the radiator overflow.

After flushing with clear water, the system should be filled with water and a permanent type antifreeze as explained later in this chapter. In addition, add a cooling system inhibitor and sealer of high quality. This will retard the formation of rust and scale.

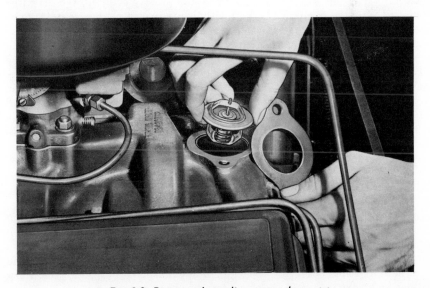

Fig. G-3. Removing the cooling system thermostat.

It is desirable to remove the cooling system thermostat from the system before flushing to insure a free flow of water. The cooling system thermostat is located at the forward end of the cylinder head, Fig. G-1 and Fig. G-3, where the hose connection for the radiator is located.

WHEN THE SYSTEM GETS CLOGGED

Tests for a clogged radiator can be made by warming the engine and then turning the engine off and feeling the surface of the radiator. The radiator should be hot at the top and warm at the bottom with an even temperature rise from bottom to top. Cold spots in the radiator indicate sections that are clogged. Water pump operation can be checked by running the engine while squeezing the upper radiator hose. A pressure surge should be felt.

A defective cylinder head gasket may allow exhaust gases to leak into the cooling system. This is particularly damaging to the cooling system as the gases combine with the water to form acids which are harmful to the radiator and engine. In addition, such a condition will result in severe overheating.

IF ANTIFREEZE GETS IN LUBRICATING SYSTEM

As the result of a defective cylinder head gasket, or a cracked water jacket, the coolant may get into the engine crankcase. If the coolant is of the ethylene glycol type, a heavy gummy substance will be formed in the engine crankcase and it will be necessary to clean the entire lubricating system. First the engine oil should be completely drained, the oil filter removed, and the crankcase filled with a mixture of approximately three quarts of SAE 10W motor oil and two quarts of butyl cellulose. That material can be obtained from a chemical supply company. The engine should be run at idling speed for thirty minutes, paying particular attention to the oil pressure and then immediately drained. A flushing solution of approximately three quarts of SAE 10W oil and two quarts of kerosene should then be circulated through the engine at idling speed for approximately five minutes and then completely drained. If the engine cannot be cranked because of the contaminated oil, run hot water from a steam Jennie through the cooling system which will soften the glycol in the oiling system so that the engine can be cranked.

QUICK CHECK FOR LEAKS

To check for exhaust leaks into the cooling system, drain the system until the water level stands just above the top of the cylinder head. Then disconnect the upper radiator hose and remove the thermostat and fan belt. Start the engine and quickly accelerate several times. At the same time note any appreciable water rise, or appearance of bubbles, which are indicative of exhaust gases leaking into the cooling system.

Small water leaks in the cooling system can be fixed by means of special preparations designed to stop such leaks. Instructions covering the use of such chemicals supplied by the manufacturer should be carefully followed.

In the case of leaking core plugs, Fig. H-4, these should be replaced. There are a number of these core plugs located throughout the engine water jacket and in some cases they are rather difficult to reach. To remove a rusted core plug, drive a screwdriver or other pointed tool into the center of the plug and pry it from the engine block. After carefully cleaning the recess, a new plug is installed by driving it into position with a drift approximately the same diameter as the plug. Before driving the plug into position, the recess is carefully coated with a suitable cement.

Fig. G-4. Applying pressure to the cooling system as a check for leaks.

Most water leaks in a cooling system are clearly visible to the eye. However, to locate some leaks it is necessary to apply pressure to the cooling system. Such pressure can be applied by means of special equipment such as is shown in Fig. G-4. If the pressure applied to the system as indicated by the gauge is maintained, there is no leak present and water is probably being lost through the radiator cap and overflow. But if the pressure is not maintained there is leakage somewhere and if it cannot be seen by the eye, it is probably at a defective cylinder head gasket.

1972 Nova Coupe.

CHECK RADIATOR CAP

It is important that the radiator cap be checked seasonally to be sure that it is operating correctly. Radiator caps used on Chevrolet built engines from 1958 to 1965 are designed to open at 13 lb. pressure and air conditioned cars at 15 lb. pressure. From 1966, the 15 lb. caps were used throughout.

The pressure at which these caps will open can be tested by using a special tester, Fig. G-5. Such a tester applies pressure to the cap and unless these caps open at the specified value, the pressure may become so great that the radiator will burst. This usually occurs at the seam of the radiator tank. If the caps open at a pressure lower than the specified value, coolant will be lost and overheating result.

Fig. G-5. Checking a radiator cap with special tester which applies air pressure.

CLEANING THE COOLING SYSTEM

When the coolant in the cooling system appears rusty, the system should be cleaned with one of the chemicals available for that purpose. Directions for using that particular cleaner should be carefully followed.

In the event that no special cleaning preparation is available, oxalic acid in crystal form can be used, but special care must be taken to thoroughly flush all traces of this from the system, and then use a good rust inhibitor. One-half pound of oxalic acid is usually sufficient to clean the cooling system.

In cases of persistent overheating it may be necessary to remove the radiator and have it cleaned by a specialist in such work. In such cases, it is usually advisable to remove the cylinder head also and have it reconditioned, which includes cleaning the water jacket. While the cylinder head is removed, the water jacket and cylinder block should be scrapped as

Fig. G-6. Cooling system thermostat marked with temperature at which it is designed to open.

clean as possible and flushed repeatedly to remove as much rust as possible. The interior of the water jacket can be reached through the openings in the top of the cylinder block and if necessary the core plugs can be removed from the side of the cylinder block which will also aid in reaching the interior of the water jacket with the scrapper.

CHECKING RADIATOR FLOW

If there is any doubt about the condition of the radiator, it can be checked by filling it with water after it is removed and then seeing how fast the water will flow from the lower outlet. A radiator in good condition will have water flowing from the outlet reach a height of approximately 6 in. If the water fails to come out in a strong stream, it is definite that the radiator passages are clogged and that the radiator should be reconditioned or replaced.

FILLING THE RADIATOR

Filling the radiator of a warm engine presents no difficulty, but when the engine is cold, the thermostat is closed and little coolant will reach the water jacket surrounding the engine. It, therefore, becomes necessary to fill the radiator as much as possible, then start the engine. When it has reached operating temperature, the thermostat will open permitting the coolant from the radiator to enter the water jacket. It will then be possible to add more coolant to the radiator so the system is filled completely.

WHAT TO DO ABOUT THERMOSTATS

Starting with the 1968 models, a 195 deg. thermostat was standard equipment on all Chevrolet water cooled engines. Prior to that time a 180 deg. thermostat was used. Alcohol and methanol antifreeze solutions are not recommended for use in the 1968 models. Such coolants would require

132

a thermostat operating at a lower temperature. As shown in Fig. G-6, the thermostat is marked to indicate the temperature at which it is designed to open.

Thermostats are located in the water outlets in the engine, Fig. G-1 and Fig. G-3. To remove a thermostat, first drain the system until the water level is below the thermostat. Then remove the water outlet elbow, or the elbow to which the radiator upper hose is connected. The thermo-

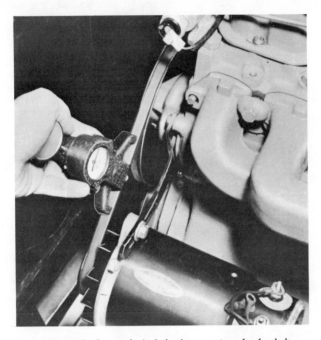

Fig. G-7. One method of checking tension of a fan belt.

stat can then be lifted from the engine, Fig. G-3. At room temperature the valve of the thermostat should be in the closed position. If there is any doubt regarding the condition of the thermostat, place it in a pan of water. The thermostat should be open when the water reaches the specified temperature.

CHECKING THE FAN BELT

Fan and accessory belts when properly adjusted will operate for at least 25,000 miles without giving any trouble. But it is well to anticipate their failure, as the belt not only drives the fan, but also the water pump and the generator. Accessory belts are also important. As a result, should the fan belt break, not only will the engine overheat but the battery will soon become discharged. In addition to checking the tension of the belts, examine the belt to be sure that there are no cracks at any point, or lumps which would indicate deterioration.

To adjust tension of the fan belt, loosen bolts at generator slotted bracket. Pull the generator away from the engine until the desired belt tension is obtained. Special testers are available, Fig. G-7, to check the tension of the belts, but when such equipment is not available, apply a light pressure midway between the water pump pulley and the generator pulley. The belt should deflect 5/16 in. on four cylinder and six cylinder models, and 13/16 in. on the V-8 models, Fig. G-8. Do not use a pry bar against the alternator case as this may distort or crack the case.

Fig. G-8. A simple method of checking tension is to measure the deflection of the belt.

WHICH TYPE ANTIFREEZE?

Regardless of whether freezing temperatures are expected, cooling system protection should be maintained at least to zero degrees F in order to provide adequate corrosion protection and proper temperature indicating light operation. Every two years the system should be serviced by flushing with water and then completely refilled with a high quality ethylene glycol type antifreeze. Add a high quality rust inhibitor and sealer. Also check and add inhibitor and sealer every year.

Alcohol and methanol types antifreeze or just plain water are not recommended for use in Chevrolet engines at any time.

The use of the ethylene glycol antifreeze permits the use of a 195 deg. thermostat and a 15 deg. radiator cap. This in turn permits safe engine operating temperature of 252 deg. F.

To make sure that there is sufficient antifreeze in the cooling system to provide protection against freezing, the coolant should be checked with a hydrometer, Fig. G-9. Such checks should be made several times during the winter driving season, particularly if nonpermanent type antifreeze is used.

Fig. G-9. Checking the antifreeze in the cooling system.

KINKS ON WATER PUMP SERVICE

Water pumps give good service for many thousands of miles of operation and need replacement only after they start to leak, as a result of failure of the seal and scoring of the shaft. While replacement parts are available for rebuilding water pumps, most mechanics prefer to install a new or rebuilt pump rather than take the time to rebuild the worn unit. To disassemble a water pump requires a puller to remove the hub and drive pulley from the shaft and a press, Fig. G-10, to push the shaft from the impeller.

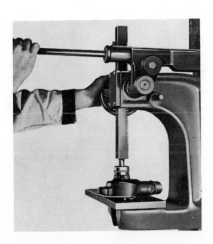

Fig. G-10. Pressing impeller and shaft from a water pump housing.

The procedure for removing the water pump is as follows: First drain the radiator and remove the water inlet hose from the pump. Remove the fan belt. On cars equipped with heaters, remove the hose from the pump housing. Remove the water pump to cylinder block attaching bolts and then remove the pump from the engine.

COOLANT RECOVERY SYSTEM

A coolant recovery system has been developed especially for recreational vehicles operating under severe conditions. This converts the conventional pressure vented system into one that is closed, but which compensates for coolant expansion and returns the coolant to the radiator when system cools. In that way the possibility of overheating is greatly reduced.

TROUBLE SHOOTING

CAUSES OF OVERHEATING

Restricted radiator passages. Restricted water jacket in engine. Restricted hose connections. Defective cooling system thermostat. Defective radiator cap. Lack of coolant. Loose fan belt. Water pump inoperative. Incorrect valve or ignition timing. Brakes dragging. Improper grade and viscosity of engine oil. Restricted exhaust system. Restricted air flow through radiator. Leaking cylinder head gasket. Radiator capacity too small for car equipped with air conditioning.

Towing a trailer or other vehicle, particularly in warm weather will often cause overheating, as will operation of the air conditioning system particularly for prolonged periods when the vehicle is not in motion.

LOSS OF COOLANT

Leaking radiator. Loose or damaged hose connections. Leaking water pump. Loose or damaged heater hose. Leaking heater unit. Leaking cylinder head gasket. Cracked cylinder head. Core plugs in cylinder and cylinder head loose or rusted. Wrong type or defective radiator cap.

CIRCULATION SYSTEM NOISY

Defective fan belt. Defective water pump shaft bearings. Fan blades loose or bent. Improper fan to shroud clearance.

OVERCOOLING

Defective thermostat.

EXHAUST SYSTEM
SERVICE

The exhaust system includes the muffler, exhaust manifold and connecting pipes and in some installations a resonator. The exhaust system used on all single exhaust passenger car models includes an exhaust pipe and muffler assembly, and a tail pipe that extends back to a point where the gases are discharged below the rear bumper on the left side of the vehicle. An exhaust crossover pipe is used on V-8 models to connect the two exhaust manifolds.

On dual exhaust systems, Fig. H-1, two exhaust pipe and muffler assemblies are used together with two resonators and two tail pipes. Each assembly is connected to its own exhaust manifold, Fig. H-2, and carries the exhaust gases to the rear.

The life of mufflers and pipes is dependent largely on the type of service in which the vehicle is used. If it is used mostly in city type stop-and-go driving, with few trips exceeding five miles, the muffler will soon be rusted out. In most cases on dual muffler installations on V-8 engines, the maximum mileage under such conditions is seldom in excess of 10,000 miles. On single muffler jobs, 20,000 to 25,000 miles may be expected.

The reason for such short muffler life is that on short trips, condensed moisture from the engine exhaust gases collects in the mufflers and pipes. This moisture is highly acidic and corrosive. As a result the pipes and mufflers are soon corroded and have to be replaced.

If the car is driven mostly on longer trips, the mufflers and pipes will get hot enough to evaporate this moisture. Consequently, corrosive action is retarded and exhaust system parts will last longer.

Mufflers and pipes used on single exhaust systems will last much longer than a dual muffler installation, because all the exhaust gases pass through the single muffler, and as a result its temperature reaches a higher value more quickly, and the corrosive moisture will be evaporated sooner.

Mufflers and pipes should be replaced before they are rusted completely through, for if there are any leaks in the system, the exhaust gases, which are poisonous, will escape into the interior of the car where they may cause the death of the occupants, or a serious accident if the driver becomes affected by the gas.

The different sections of the pipes and mufflers are telescoped together and supported by brackets, Fig. H-1. The removal of worn exhaust pipes and mufflers is not complicated, but it is sometimes difficult be-

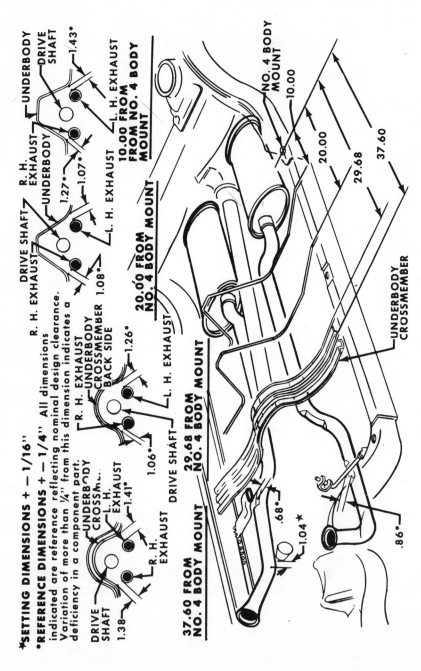

*SETTING DIMENSIONS + − 1/16″

*REFERENCE DIMENSIONS + − 1/4″ All dimensions indicated are reference reflecting nominal design clearance. Variation of more than ¼″ from this dimension indicates a deficiency in a component part.

DRIVE SHAFT

UNDERBODY

R. H. EXHAUST

1.43*

L. H. EXHAUST 10.00 FROM FROM NO. 4 BODY MOUNT

R. H. EXHAUST

DRIVE SHAFT

UNDERBODY

1.27*

1.07*

L. H. EXHAUST 1.08*

20.00 FROM NO. 4 BODY MOUNT

R. H. EXHAUST

UNDERBODY CROSSMEMBER BACK SIDE

1.26*

L. H. EXHAUST

R. H. EXHAUST

UNDERBODY CROSSMEMBER

1.06*

L. H. EXHAUST

29.68 FROM NO. 4 BODY MOUNT

DRIVE SHAFT

DRIVE SHAFT

1.38*

L. H. EXHAUST 1.41*

R. H. EXHAUST

37.60 FROM NO. 4 BODY MOUNT

NO. 4 BODY MOUNT

10.00

20.00

29.68

37.60

UNDERBODY CROSSMEMBER

.68*

1.04*

.86*

Fig. H-1. Checking dimensions of exhaust system (front half) Chevrolet.

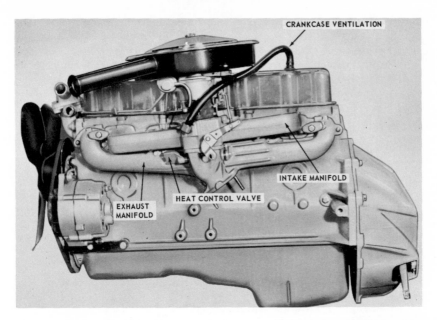

Fig. H-2. Exhaust manifold and heat control valve as installed on in-line six cylinder engine.

cause various sections are rusted together. To disassemble the system so that replacement can be made, it is usually necessary to cut them apart with a hacksaw or a chisel, as shown in Fig. H-3.

Before cutting at the rear exhaust pipe, measure service muffler exhaust pipe end, and make certain to allow 1-1/2 in. for engagement of the rear exhaust pipe into service muffler pipe.

The procedure for removing mufflers and pipes is as follows: First apply penetrating oil to all the bolts and nuts of the support brackets and

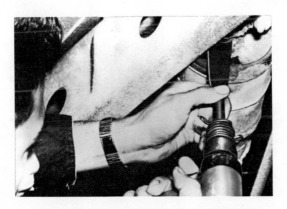

Fig. H-3. Cutting a tail pipe from a muffler.

clamps. Separate the pipes from the muffler either by cutting with a hacksaw or chisel after having jacked up the rear of the car with a bumper jack so as to provide as much clearance between the rear axle and the body as possible. Then remove the clamps from the exhaust pipes, mufflers and tailpipes, permitting removal of the various parts. The car should be jacked up as high as possible, to allow ample room between the rear axle and the lower side of the body, so that the long tail pipe can be maneuvered into position. When making the installation of new pipes and mufflers, the usual procedure is to first install the exhaust pipe, then the muffler, and finally the tail pipe.

All exhaust systems used on the Chevrolet from 1968 are of a split system in which all components (exhaust pipes, mufflers, resonators and tail pipes) can be separated by removing clamps. All other models have at least two components that cannot be separated by merely removing a clamp.

All V-8 single exhaust systems incorporate a cross-under exhaust pipe in which either the left or right exhaust pipe crosses under the engine oil pan to join the rest of the system.

Dual exhaust systems are available as regular production or optional equipment on all models. Chevrolet and Camaro offer an optional "deep-tone" system which eliminates the resonators.

MANIFOLD HEAT CONTROL VALVE

The manifold heat control valve, Figs. H-2 and H-4, is designed to provide a certain amount of heat to the intake manifold in order to improve the air-fuel mixture reaching the combustion chamber. It is controlled by

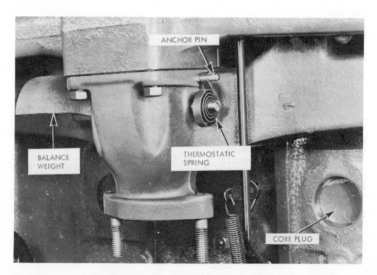

Fig. H-4. Manifold heat control valve.

Exhaust Systems

a thermostatic coil and counterweight and velocity of exhaust gas through the exhaust manifold. The thermostatic coil is installed in a manner which will maintain sufficient tension on the valve shaft to keep the valve in a closed position when the engine is cold.

In the cold position, hot gases from the exhaust circulate up and around the hot spot chamber in the intake manifold. This in turn helps vaporize fuel passing down through the intake manifold, resulting in smooth engine performance. Should the heat control valve become stuck in either the open or closed position, the car performance will be affected.

The operation of the heat control valve should be inspected at every lubrication and oil change, by moving the counterweights through the complete arc of its travel.

Note that in Fig. H-2 the manifold heat control valve for six cylinder in-line engines is placed immediately below the carburetor, and is on the left side of the engine. The manifold heat control valve for eight cylinder engines is located on the right side of the engine.

If the shaft of the heat control valve is sticking, it can be freed by applying special solvents, or penetrating oil, and also by tapping the shaft back and forth in the manifold.

Note that on eight cylinder engines it may be necessary to remove the heat control valve flange to free the inboard end of the valve shaft.

1972 Camaro Sport Coupe.

Quick Tests on
BATTERIES

If headlamps do not light to normal brilliance when engine is not running or when the engine is not cranked at normal speed, the first point to check is the starting battery.

First of all, the battery connections must be clean and tight. Corroded terminals or loose connections provide a high resistance in the circuit, so that full voltage is not available for lighting, starting and ignition.

The battery terminals and cable connections should be cleaned by scraping with a knife, or brushed with a wire bristle brush.

The top surface of the battery must also be kept clean and dry as any moisture and/or dirt will permit current leakage, and is a major cause of discharged batteries.

The level of the electrolyte should also be checked every 1000 miles and should never be permitted to get below the top of the battery plates. Use clean water, distilled if possible, to bring the electrolyte level up to the bottom of the filler necks.

COMMON CAUSES OF FAILURE

If the battery tests good but fails to perform satisfactorily in service for no apparent reason, the following are some of the more important factors that may point to the cause of the trouble.

Vehicle accessories inadvertently left on overnight cause a discharge condition. Slow speed driving of short duration, also causes an undercharged condition.

A vehicle electrical load exceeding the generator capacity. Defect in the charging system such as high resistance, slipping fan belt, faulty generator or voltage regulator.

ELECTROLYTE INDICATOR

The Delco battery which is used as standard equipment, and also in many cases as a replacement, features an electrolyte level indicator which is a specially designed vent plug with a transparent rod extending through the center. When the electrolyte is at the proper level, the lower tip of the rod is immersed, and the exposed top of the rod will appear very dark; when the level falls below the tip of the rod, the top will glow.

The indicator reveals at a glance if water is needed without the necessity of removing the vent plugs. The level indicator is used only in one cell, the second cell cap from the positive battery post, because when the electrolyte level is low in one cell, it is normally low in all cells.

Fumes from a starting battery are highly explosive; therefore never use an open flame to see the level of the electrolyte in the battery. Use only a flashlight to check the level.

HOW TO TEST THE BATTERY

In the past one of the most popular methods of testing the condition of the battery was by means of a voltmeter. However, since all modern starting batteries have a hard cover over the entire surface of the top of the battery, a hydrometer is now the preferred method, as it permits testing the condition of each cell of the battery. This is a reliable test and the hydrometer is low in price.

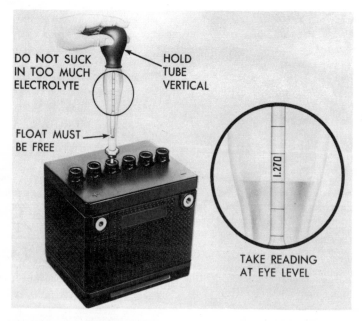

Fig. J-1. Using hydrometer to check the condition of the battery.

A hydrometer, Fig. J-1, should be used only when there is sufficient electrolyte above the battery plate to fill the hydrometer tube. Do not take hydrometer readings immediately after filling a battery with distilled water. Instead place the battery on charge or drive the car for about an hour or two. Normal battery activity will then disburse the water to the electrolyte.

Batteries

To check the condition of a battery with a hydrometer, the tube of the instrument is placed in the opening of the filler plug and electrolyte is drawn into the instrument by means of the suction bulb, as shown in Fig. J-1.

Draw the electrolyte into the tube and force it out several times to bring the temperature of the hydrometer float to that of the electrolyte. Then draw in just enough electrolyte to lift the float. Read the specific gravity of the electrolyte on the float, Fig. J-1. A specific gravity of 1.275 to 1.285 indicates a full charged battery. A reading of 1.230 to 1.240 inicates approximately 60 percent charge. If the specific gravity varies more than .025 between cells of the battery, the battery should be replaced.

Some batteries supplied to warm climates have a specific gravity reading of 1.260 when fully charged. In such cases, the battery is plainly marked.

Batteries that are not fully charged will freeze at low temperatures, while a fully charged battery will not freeze until the temperature reaches -90 deg. F.

Specific Gravity	Freezing Temperature
1.280	-90 deg.
1.250	-62 deg.
1.200	-16 deg.
1.150	+ 5 deg.
1.100	+19 deg.

CHARGING BATTERIES

If the car owner lives in an isolated area, where service stations are at some distance, it pays to have a battery charger of some type available for charging batteries in an emergency. Battery chargers are available for charging a single battery. Instructions for charging the battery, which accompany the charger, should be carefully followed.

EVIDENCE OF OVERCHARGING

If it is necessary to add water to the battery at frequent intervals, it is an indication that the battery is being overcharged. In such cases, a careful check of the voltage regulator should be made and it should be either readjusted or a new unit installed.

INSTALLING THE BATTERY

When installing a battery, it is particularly important that only the negative terminal of the battery be grounded. A battery that is installed backwards (with positive terminal grounded) will burn out the rectifiers on alternating current systems. Also, the battery will be quickly ruined because of the reversal of the charge.

The positive terminal is indicated with a plus sign, and the negative terminal with a minus sign, Fig. J-2. These markings are either placed directly on the top of the battery posts or on the battery case adjacent to the terminal.

When it is difficult to start an engine, it is sometimes desirable to use an additional battery for a quick start. In such cases, the positive terminal of the additional battery should be connected to the positive terminal of the car battery, and the negative terminal of the additional battery to the negative terminal of the car battery. The starting switch is then used in the usual manner.

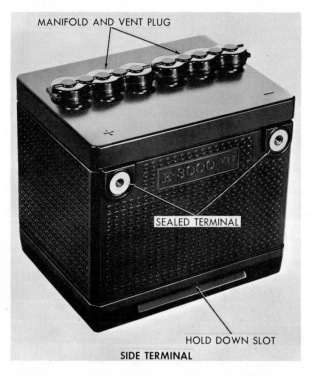

MANIFOLD AND VENT PLUG

SEALED TERMINAL

HOLD DOWN SLOT

SIDE TERMINAL

Fig. J-2. While late model cars are equipped with side terminal starting batteries, older models have the terminal on the top of the battery.

Simplified
GENERATOR SERVICE

The following instructions are limited primarily to determining whether trouble exists in the generator (alternator), regulator or battery.

Knowing the location of the trouble, a new unit, as needed, can then be obtained and installed and properly adjusted. This same policy is followed by many service shops.

Fig. K-1. Showing location of alternator on V-8 engine.

Before making any tests on a generator (alternator), or regulator, the battery should be carefully checked as outlined in the Chapter on Quick Tests on Batteries. If the battery and its connections prove to be in good condition, and the generator (alternator) drive belt is also correctly adjusted, then tests on the generator (alternator) and regulator should be made.

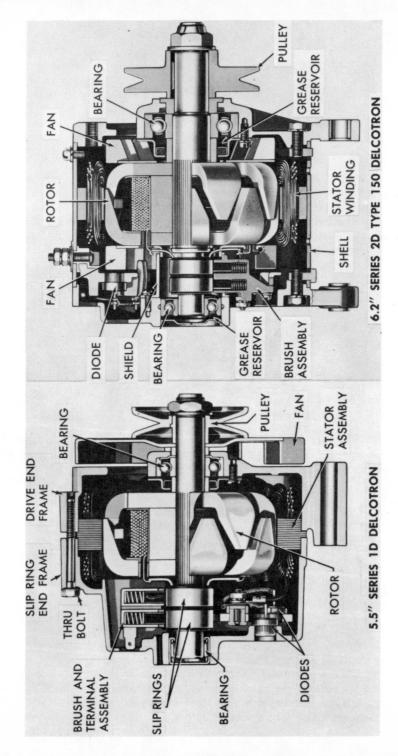

BEARING

FAN

ROTOR

FAN

DIODE

SHIELD

BEARING

GREASE RESERVOIR

BRUSH ASSEMBLY

PULLEY

GREASE RESERVOIR

STATOR WINDING

SHELL

6.2″ SERIES 2D TYPE 150 DELCOTRON

SLIP RING END FRAME

DRIVE END FRAME

BEARING

THRU BOLT

BRUSH AND TERMINAL ASSEMBLY

SLIP RINGS

BEARING

DIODES

ROTOR

STATOR ASSEMBLY

FAN

PULLEY

5.5″ SERIES 1D DELCOTRON

Fig. K-2. 1968–1970 types of Delcotron alternating current generators. Previous models were similar.

148

THE ALTERNATOR

The Delcotron alternator was first provided as optional equipment on the 1962 models, and in 1963 was adopted for all models.

The alternator is mounted on the side of the engine, and a typical installation is shown in Fig. K-1.

Two types of alternators are shown in Fig. K-2, and diagrams of connections are shown in Fig. K-3 and Fig. K-4. Another alternator with a built-in solid state regulator, which requires no adjustment, was introduced as standard equipment on the 1969 Corvette, Fig. K-2a.

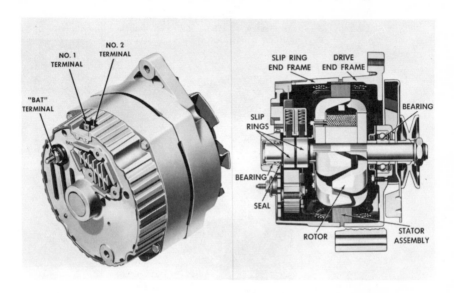

Fig. K-2a. Delcotron with built-in solid regulator is standard equipment on 1971 models and was also used on 1970 and 1969 models. The 1972 installation is similar.

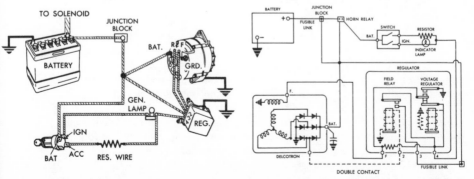

Fig. K-3. Left. Typical alternator wiring diagram. Fig. K-3a. Right. Voltage circuitry of double contact voltage regulator (1970).

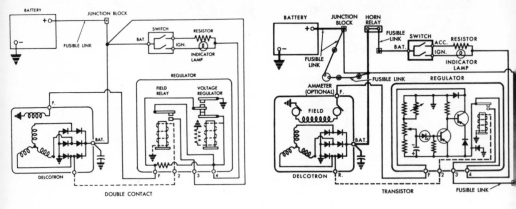

Fig. K-4. Circuitry of voltage regulators, 1968–1969. Left—Double contact system.
Right—Transistor system.

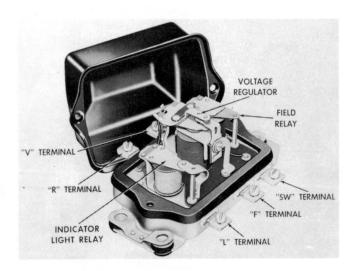

Fig. K-5. Regulator with light indicator relay as used with Delcotron on 1962 models.

The alternator, Fig. K-1 and Fig. K-2, generates alternating current and is provided with six rectifier diodes, located in the slip ring end frame. The diodes change the alternating voltage to direct voltage, which appears at the outlet terminal of the alternator. Conventional direct current instruments can be used for testing the output of the alternator.

The system used in 1962 was provided with a regulator, Fig. K-5, which included an indicator light relay. Starting with the 1963 models, a two unit, double contact regulator was used, Fig. K-6, and some installations were provided with a transistor type voltage regulator, Fig. K-7. The double contact regulator is used on all models of the Delcotron up to and including the 52 amp. model, while a transistorized regulator is used on the 62 amp. system.

SPECIAL PRECAUTIONS NECESSARY

There are several precautions which must be emphasized when working on the alternator system. First of all, in installing a battery, always make sure the ground polarity of the battery, alternator and regulator are the same. On the Chevrolet models, the negative terminal of the battery must be grounded.

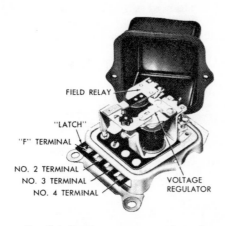

FIELD RELAY

"LATCH"

"F" TERMINAL

NO. 2 TERMINAL
NO. 3 TERMINAL
NO. 4 TERMINAL

VOLTAGE
REGULATOR

Fig. K-6. Double contact, two unit regulator.

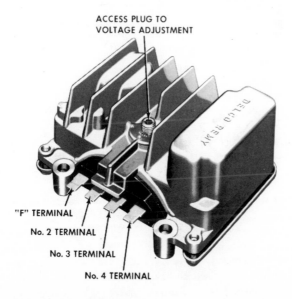

ACCESS PLUG TO
VOLTAGE ADJUSTMENT

"F" TERMINAL

No. 2 TERMINAL

No. 3 TERMINAL

No. 4 TERMINAL

Fig. K-7. Note location of voltage adjustment on this transistor type regulator.

Fix Your Chevrolet

When connecting a booster battery, make certain to connect the correct battery terminals together. That is, the positive terminal of the booster battery must be connected to the positive terminal of the battery in the car, and the two negative terminals will be connected together. Also when connecting a charger to the battery, connect positive terminal of the charger to the positive terminal of the battery and the negative terminal of the charger to the negative terminal of the battery.

Never operate the alternator on open circuit. Make certain that all connections in the system are tight and clean. Never short across or ground any of the terminals on the alternator or the regulator. Do not attempt to polarize the alternating current Delcotron.

PINPOINTING TROUBLE IN THE ALTERNATOR

It is a simple matter to determine whether failure to generate voltage lies in the alternator or the regulator. Unplug the connector from the alternator which will expose the relay (R) terminal and the field (F) terminal. Connect a jumper from the generator (F) terminal to the BAT terminal, and in this way full field current will be applied to the alternator. Turn on all possible accessory loads, such as headlights, etc. Then with the en-

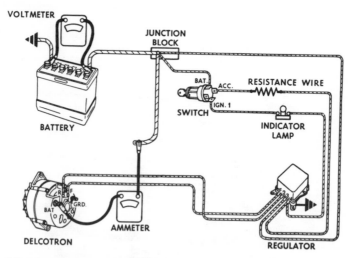

Fig. K-8. Note connections of voltmeter and ammeter when checking output of Delcotron.

gine at a fast idle, if the indicator lamp or ammeter on instrument panel shows a charge, the regulator is defective. If no charge is shown, then the alternator is probably defective. Knowing which of these two units is defective, a new part is then easily substituted.

A more accurate test is shown under the paragraph headed Output Check.

Generator Service

Another test, which may be used to isolate the Delcotron, its companion regulator, and the wiring harness for testing, is known as the "Dynamic Test." After checking for a loose drive belt and a defective battery, proceed as follows:

Start the engine and operate at a fast idle of approximately 1500 to 2000 rpm. Make sure that all accessories, lights, etc. are disconnected from the circuit. With the engine still operating, disconnect the battery ground cable. If the engine stops, the alternator is probably defective. If the engine continues to operate, either the regulator or wire harness is defective.

To determine if harness or regulator is defective, remove wiring push-on connector from the regulator and install a known good regulator. Be sure to ground the regulator to the vehicle.

Repeat the previous check of disconnecting the battery ground cable. If indicator lamp remains on with the engine idling, check for open resistor. If indicator lamp operates normally, regulator is shown to be defective.

OUTPUT CHECK

To make a complete current output test of an alternator, first make sure the drive belt is adjusted to the proper tension. Then disconnect the battery ground cable from the battery. Connect an ammeter between alternator BAT terminal and disconnect lead as shown in Fig. K-8. Connect a tachometer from distributor terminal of coil to ground. Reconnect battery ground cable. Connect a voltmeter across battery.

Turn on all possible accessory loads. Apply parking brake firmly. Start engine. Adjust engine idle to approximately 500 rpm with the transmission in drive position. At this engine speed, generator output should be approximately 10 amp. or over. Shift transmission to park and increase engine speed to approximately 1500 rpm and output should be 30 amp. or over.

If output is low in either of the preceding tests, try supplying field current directly to cause full generator output. This is done by unplugging the connector from the generator and connecting a jumper from the generator (F) terminal to BAT terminal. Retest at 500 rpm and 1500 rpm as described previously. If output is still low, generator is faulty and should be replaced. If output is now O.K. when using the field jumper, trouble is in the regulator or wiring harness.

DELCOTRON DIODE AND FIELD TEST

A diode is a device which rectifies the alternating current to direct. Diodes can be easily tested without special equipment, other than a 12V battery and a small lamp bulb. These are used as a test set to see if current will flow through the diodes. First separate the three stator leads at the (Y) connection. Test the rectifiers with the 12V battery and a test

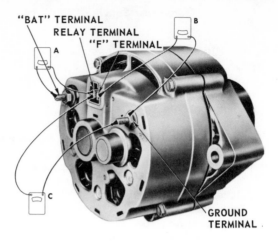

"BAT" TERMINAL
RELAY TERMINAL
"F" TERMINAL
A
B
C
GROUND
TERMINAL

Fig. K-9. Meter connections for checking diodes and field.

lamp by connecting one side of the test lamp to the positive battery post. Connect the other side of the lamp to a test probe with the other test probe connected to the negative battery post.

Contact the outer case of the diode with one probe, and the other probe to the wire at the center of the rectifier. Reverse the probes, moving the probes from rectifier outer case to the rectifier wire, and the probe from the rectifier wire to the rectifier outer case. If the test lamp lights in one direction, but does not light in the other direction, the rectifier is satisfactory. If the lamp lights in both directions, the rectifier is shorted and should be replaced. If the test lamp does not light in either direction, the rectifier is open and will also have to be replaced.

Another method of testing the diodes is to use an ohmmeter. This naturally is a much more accurate test. The procedure is as follows: First disconnect the battery ground cable at battery. To test the positive diodes, connect the ohmmeter as shown at A in Fig. K-9, that is between the (R) terminal and the BAT terminal, and note the reading. Then reverse the leads at the same terminal and note this reading. The meter should read high resistance in one direction and low in the other.

To test the negative diodes connect the ohmmeter as shown at C in Fig. K-9, that is between the (R) terminal and the GRD terminal, and note the reading, then reverse the leads and note this reading. Meter should read high in one direction and low in the other.

A high or low reading in both directions indicates a defective diode.

DELCOTRON OPEN FIELD CHECK

To check for an open field in a Delcotron alternator, connect the ohmmeter as shown at B in Fig. K-9. That is from the (F) terminal to the GRD terminal stud and note the reading on the lowest scale of the ohmmeter. The meter should read 7 to 20 ohms. If the meter reads zero or excessively high resistance, the Delcotron is faulty.

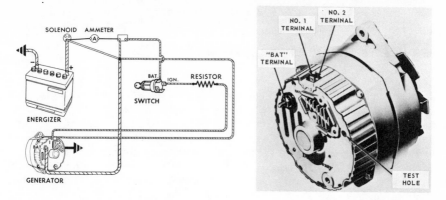

Fig. K-10. Left. Basic wiring diagram of series 10–S1 alternator. Fig. K-11. Right. Showing location of test hole in 10–S1 alternator.

ADJUSTING ALTERNATOR REGULATOR VOLTAGE

Regulators used on recent model cars with Delcotrons are shown in Figs. K-6 and K-7. To adjust these types of regulators proceed as follows: Connect a 1/4 ohm 25 watt fixed resistor into the charging circuit at the junction block as shown in Fig. K-12.

Operate the engine at about 1500 rpm, or above for at least 15 minutes of warmup. Then cycle the regulator voltage control (by disconnecting and reconnecting regulator connector) and read the voltage.

If the voltage is 13.5 to 15.2 volts, the regulator is in good condition. If the voltage is not within those limits, leave engine running at 1500 rpm and disconnect four terminal connector, Fig. K-6, and adjust the voltage to 14.2 to 14.6. This is done with the high beam headlights and heater blower on for five to ten minutes. Then disconnect four terminal connector and reinstall regulator cover and reinstall connector. Cycle regulator voltage by disconnecting and reconnecting regulator connector. Read voltage. A reading between 13.5 and 15.2 volts indicates a good regulator.

Caution: Be sure four terminal regulator connector is disconnected when removing or installing cover. This is to prevent regulator damage by short circuit.

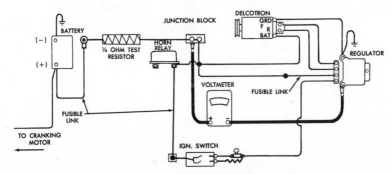

Fig. K-12. Diagram of connections for voltage setting on alternators.

SERVICE TIPS ON 10-S1 DELCOTRON

The 10-S1 series Delcotron alternator shown in Fig. K-2a features a solid state regulator that is mounted inside the generator slip ring and frame. This Delcotron is used as standard equipment on the 1969 Corvette and on some of the 1970 Corvettes. All regulator components are enclosed in a solid mold and this unit along with the brush holder is attached to the slip ring end frame. The regulator voltage setting never requires adjustment and no provision for adjustment is provided. Rotor bearings contain an adequate supply of lubricant, eliminating the need for periodic lubrication.

A basic wiring diagram of the series 10-S1 Delcotron is shown in Fig. K-10. If engine cranks slowly and specific gravity readings of battery are low, the trouble may be determined by making the following checks after making sure all wiring is in good condition, and fan belt is tight. Then connect a voltmeter in the circuit at the "BAT" terminal of the alternator. Operate engine at approximately 1500 to 2000 rpm and then turn on all electrical accessories. If voltmeter reading is more than 12.8 volts, alternator is not defective. If reading is less than 12.8 volts, ground the field winding by inserting a screwdriver into test hole (not more than 1 in.) in end frame to depress tab, Fig. K-11. If voltage increases to more than 13.0 volts, the regulator is defective.

Fig. K-13. Typical direct current generator.

DIRECT CURRENT GENERATOR SERVICE

The direct current system was used on Chevrolet cars up to 1962. A typical generator installation is shown in Fig. K-13, and a three unit regulator is shown in Fig. K-14. The regulator is designed to maintain the

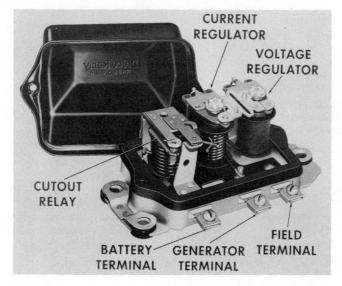

Fig. K-14. DC three unit regulator as used on 1962 and earlier direct current systems.

starting battery in a fully charged condition. The design is such that when the battery is fully charged, the charging rate is reduced to a minimum. When the battery is low in charge, the voltage regulator will automatically increase the current flowing into the starting battery to restore it to a

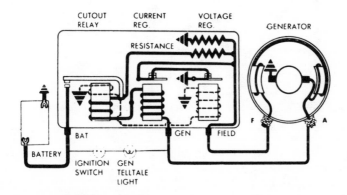

Fig. K-15. Circuitry of single contact direct current regulator.

fully charged condition. A simplified wiring diagram of a generator, voltage regulator and starting battery is shown in Fig. K-15. Some of the early cars were equipped with a voltage regulator of a double contact type, Fig. K-16.

157

Adjustment of a voltage regulator should not be attempted unless the necessary equipment is available. However, there are a number of tests which can be made without equipment, which will quickly determine whether or not the units are operating normally. If not, the test will indicate whether the generator or regulator is at fault so the defective unit can be replaced or repaired.

A fully charged battery at a low charging rate, as indicated by the ammeter on the instrument panel, indicates that the generator and voltage regulator are correctly operating. As a further check, crank the engine with the starting motor with the ignition switch in the off position for about 30 seconds, or pull the high tension lead out of the ignition coil so that the engine will not start. After cranking the engine for about 30 seconds, start the engine and with it operating at medium speed, turn on the lights and other electrical accessories and note the generator output as indicated by the ammeter on the instrument panel. The ammeter should be indicating in excess of 25 amperes if the system is in good condition. Turn off the lights and other electrical accessories, and allow the engine to continue running at a fast idle, and if the system is in good condition, the reading on the ammeter will gradually decrease to a few amperes.

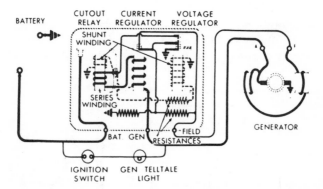

Fig. K-16. Generator circuit of double contact regulator installed as special equipment on direct current circuits.

On cars which do not have an ammeter on the instrument panel, it will be necessary to connect an ammeter in series with the generator. To do this, disconnect the wire attached to the armature terminal of the generator, Fig. K-13, and connect that wire to one terminal of the ammeter and the other terminal of the ammeter to the armature terminal on the generator.

If the starting battery is fully charged and the ammeter on the instrument panel, or the test ammeter, always shows a high rate of charge, start the engine and run it at a medium speed. Then disconnect the wire from (F) terminal on the voltage regulator. The (F) terminal is indicated

1972 Kingswood Estate Wagon.

in Fig. K-13. With the field wire disconnected, the output should immediately drop to zero. If it does not, the generator field circuit is grounded either inside the generator or in the wiring harness. If the output drops off to zero with the field lead disconnected, the trouble is in the regulator. Reconnect the field lead on the field terminal of the regulator.

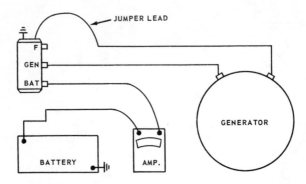

Fig. K-17. Quick test for generator and regulator.

Remove the cover on the voltage regulator and depress the voltage regulator armature to open the points. If the output now drops off, the voltage regulator should be readjusted or replaced. If opening the voltage regulator contact points does not cause the output to drop off, the field circuit within the regulator is defective and the regulator should be replaced. If tests show that the battery is low in charge and the ammeter on the instrument panel, with the engine running, shows little or no charge, the first step is to check all of the connections of the regulator, generator and battery to make sure they are all clean and in good electrical condition. Any loose or high resistant connections at those points will prevent normal charge from reaching the battery.

Another method of checking to see whether the failure to charge is in the generator or in the regulator can be made by disconnecting the field lead from its regulator terminal and clipping a jumper lead from the disconnected lead terminal to the ground, Fig. K-17. This will complete the generator field circuit without making it pass through the regulator.

If an ammeter is available, it should be connected as shown in the illustration. If not, the ammeter or indicator light on the instrument panel can be used as an indication as to whether the system is charging or not.

Increase the engine speed to approximately 1500 rpm and if the output increases, the regulator is defective. On the other hand if the generator output remains at a few amperes with the generator field terminal grounded, the generator is at fault.

If the generator does not show any output at all, either with or without the field terminal grounded, quickly disconnect the generator leads from the generator terminal on the voltage regulator and strike it against a convenient ground with the generator operating at a medium speed. If a spark does not occur, the generator is defective and should be replaced. If a spark does occur, the circuit breaker in the voltage regulator is not operating.

Be very careful not to operate the generator with the generator lead disconnected for an appreciable time, as the generator or regulator will be damaged.

POLARIZING THE GENERATOR

Whenever a direct current generator has been replaced, or a new regulator installed, it is necessary to polarize the generator. To do this, after reconnecting the leads, momentarily connect a jumper lead between the GEN and the BAT terminals of the regulator. This allows a momentary surge of current to flow through the generator, which correctly polarizes it. Failure to do this may result in severe damage to the equipment, since reverse polarity causes vibration, arcing and burning out of the relay contacts. Do not attempt to polarize alternating current generators.

SPECIAL CAUTIONS

As previously pointed out, it is important that all connections at the generator be clean and tight. In addition, it is important that the commutator and brushes should be in good condition. Commutators in good condition will have a slightly purplish color and will be smooth and without ridges. Commutators that are slightly scratched or grooved should be sanded with fine sand paper. To do this, remove the cover band from the generator. Then pass a strip of abrasive paper over the end of a flat piece of wood. With the armature revolving, the abrasive paper is pressed against the commutator. Never use emery paper to clean a commutator. At the same time, the generator brushes should be examined and if they are worn to one-half of their original length, they should be replaced. To determine the extent of the wear, the old brushes can be compared with the new ones. Generator brushes will usually last from 25,000 to 30,000 miles before replacement is necessary.

On newer type generators, Fig. K-13, that do not have a cover band, it will be necessary to disassemble the generator in order to service the commutator.

On cars with an indicator light, the following checks can be made: If the indicator light stays on after the engine is started and run above idle speed, the generator should be checked. If light stays on at idle only, check for a low idle speed. Also check to see that the generator field is properly grounded by connecting a jumper wire from the generator field terminal to the ground with the engine running at medium speed. If the light goes out after connecting the jumper wire, the cause of trouble is an improperly grounded generator field circuit.

Be careful not to ground the field terminal on double contact voltage regulator. Instead remove the leads from the field terminal and ground those leads.

If the light does not go out with the ignition switch on, and the engine off, the indicator bulb should be checked as a telltale light circuit and inspected for the possibility of an open circuit or loose connection.

TROUBLE SHOOTING

LOW CHARGING RATE

This is a normal condition if battery is fully charged. If battery is not fully charged, the low charging rate may be caused by "slipping fan belt." Dirty generator commutator. High resistance in charging circuit. Voltage regulator incorrectly adjusted. Partly shorted field coil. On Delcotron, also check faulty field relay and faulty resistor.

HIGH CHARGING RATE

Voltage regulator set too high. Voltage regulator points stuck. Regulator unit improperly grounded. Generator field circuit to regulator short circuited. Shunt field circuit shorted with regulator.

LOW BATTERY AND NO CHARGING RATE

Fan belt broken or loose. Charging circuit broken between regulator and battery. Cut out voltage winding open. Corroded points in current and voltage regulator. Open circuit between generator and regulator. Internal trouble in generator. Faulty indicator lamp operation. Burned out bulb. Defective socket. Defective wiring. Positive diodes. Failure on Delcotron. Loose fan belt. Low voltage setting.

STARTER
SERVICE

Two types of starting motors are used on Chevrolet built cars. One type has four field coils, all of which are connected in a series from the motor terminal of the solenoid to the insulated brush. The other type has three field coils connected in series, plus one shunt coil connected from the solenoid motor terminal to the ground. A view of the starting motor is shown in Fig. L-1 and a detailed view is shown in Fig. L-2.

No periodic lubrication of the starting motor or solenoid is required. Since the starting motor and brushes cannot be inspected without disassembly of the unit, no service is required on these units between overhauls.

CHECKS AND ADJUSTMENTS

Although the starting motor cannot be completely checked against specifications while on the car, a check can be made for excessive resistance in the starting circuit.

Place a voltmeter across points in the cranking circuit, Fig. L-3, as outlined below and observe the reading with the starting switch closed and the motor cranking (distributor primary lead grounded to prevent engine firing):

1. From battery positive post to solenoid battery terminal.
2. From battery negative post to starting motor housing.
3. From solenoid battery terminal to solenoid motor terminal.

If the voltage drop in any of the above checks exceeds 0.2 volts, excessive resistance is indicated in that portion of the starting circuit, and the cause of the excessive resistance should be located and corrected in order to obtain maximum efficiency in the circuit.

Caution: Do not operate the starting motor continuously for more than 30 seconds in order to prevent overheating.

When the solenoid, Fig. L-1, fails to pull in, the trouble may be due to excessive voltage drop in the solenoid control circuit. To check for this condition, close the starting switch and measure the voltage drop between the battery terminal of the solenoid and the switch (S) terminal of the solenoid.

1. If this voltage drop exceeds 3.5 volts, excessive resistance in the solenoid control circuit is indicated and should be corrected.

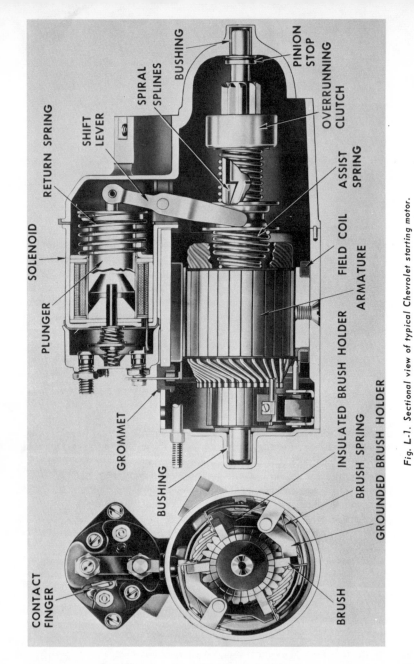

Fig. L-1. Sectional view of typical Chevrolet starting motor.

2. If the voltage drop does not exceed 3.5 volts, and the solenoid does not pull in, measure the voltage available at the switch terminal of the solenoid.

3. If the solenoid does not feel warm, it should pull in whenever the voltage available at the switch terminal is 7.7 volts or more. When the solenoid feels warm, it will require a somewhat higher voltage to pull in.

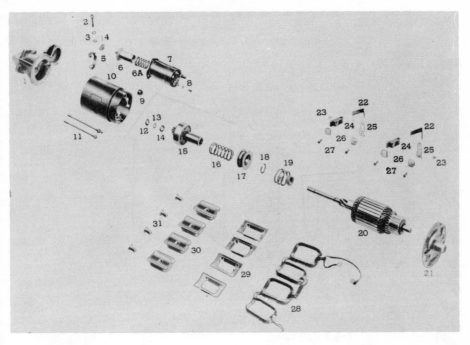

Fig. L-2. Exploded view of starting motor.

1—Drive housing.	12—Thrust collar.	24—Insulated brush holders.
2—Shift lever bolt.	13—Snap ring.	25—Grounded brush holders.
3—Shift lever nut and lock washer.	14—Retainer.	26—Brushes.
4—Pin.	15—Overrunning clutch assembly.	27—Screws.
5—Shift lever.	16—Spring.	28—Field coils.
6—Solenoid plunger.	17—Collar.	29—Insulators.
6A—Solenoid return spring.	18—Snap ring.	30—Pole shoes.
7—Solenoid case.	19—Assist spring.	31—Screws.
8—Screw and lock washer.	20—Armature.	
9—Grommet.	21—Commutator end frame.	
10—Field frame.	22—Brush springs.	
11—Through bolts.	23—Washer.	

STARTING MOTOR AND SOLENOID CHECK

The following checks may be made if the specific gravity of the battery is 1.215 or higher:

1. If the solenoid does not pull in, measure the voltage between the switch (S) terminal of the solenoid and ground with the starting switch closed.

Caution: If the solenoid feels warm, allow to cool before checking.

If the voltage is less than 7.7 volts, check for excessive resistance in the solenoid control circuit. If the voltage exceeds 7.7 volts, remove the starting motor and check:

1. Solenoid current draw; starting motor pinion clearance; and freedom of shift lever linkage.

2. If the solenoid chatters but does not hold in, check the solenoid for an open "hold-in" winding. Whenever it is necessary to replace the starting motor solenoid, always check starting motor pinion clearance.

3. If the motor engages but does not crank or cranks slowly, check for excessive resistance in the external starting circuit, trouble within the starting motor, or excessive engine resistance to cranking.

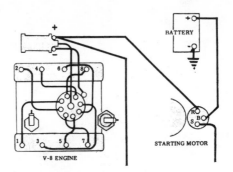

Fig. L-3. Starting circuit diagram for V-8 engines.

STARTING MOTOR REMOVAL

The following procedure is a general guide for all vehicles, and will vary slightly depending on series and model.

Disconnect battery ground cable at battery. Raise vehicle to a good working height. Disconnect all wires at solenoid terminals. Reinstall the nuts as each wire is disconnected, as thread size is different but may be mixed and stripped.

Loosen starter front bracket (nut on V-8 and bolt on L-6), then remove two mount bolts.

Remove the front bracket bolt or nut and rotate bracket clear of work area, then lower starter from vehicle by lowering front end first (hold starter against bell housing and sort of roll end over end).

Reverse the removal procedure to install. Torque the mount bolts to 25-35 ft. lb. first, then torque brace bolt.

TROUBLE SHOOTING

SLOW ENGINE CRANKING SPEED

Partly discharged battery, defective battery, loose or corroded battery terminals. Under capacity cables. Burned starter solenoid switch contacts. Defective starting motor. Heavy oil or other engine trouble causing undue load.

STARTER ENGAGES, BUT WILL NOT CRANK

Partly discharged battery. Bent armature shaft or damaged drive mechanism. Faulty armature or field.

STARTER WILL NOT RUN

Battery discharged. Shorted or open starter circuit. Defective starting motor. Defective solenoid switch.

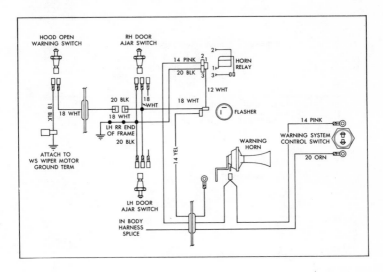

Anti-theft alarm circuit.

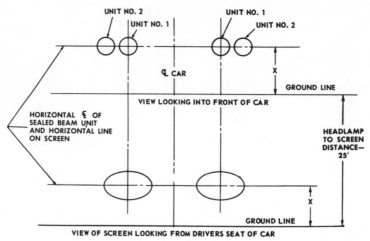

UNIT NO. 2
UNIT NO. 1
UNIT NO. 1
UNIT NO. 2

₵ CAR

X

GROUND LINE

VIEW LOOKING INTO FRONT OF CAR

HORIZONTAL ₵ OF
SEALED BEAM UNIT
AND HORIZONTAL LINE
ON SCREEN

HEADLAMP
TO SCREEN
DISTANCE—
25'

X

GROUND LINE

VIEW OF SCREEN LOOKING FROM DRIVERS SEAT OF CAR

UPPER BEAM ADJUSTMENT

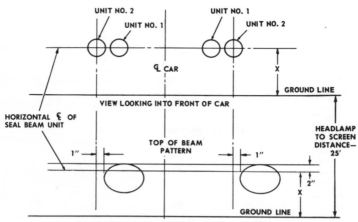

UNIT NO. 2
UNIT NO. 1
UNIT NO. 1
UNIT NO. 2

₵ CAR

X

GROUND LINE

VIEW LOOKING INTO FRONT OF CAR

HORIZONTAL ₵ OF
SEAL BEAM UNIT

HEADLAMP
TO SCREEN
DISTANCE—
25'

TOP OF BEAM
PATTERN

1"
1"

2"

X

GROUND LINE

VIEW OF SCREEN LOOKING FROM DRIVERS SEAT OF CAR

WHEN LOWER BEAM ADJUSTMENT
IS COMPLETED ON NO. 2 UNITS
THE UPPER BEAMS IN THESE UNITS
ARE CORRECTLY MADE AUTOMATICALLY.

LOWER BEAM ADJUSTMENT

THE ABOVE ARE THE RECOMMENDED SETTINGS. FOLLOW STATE
OR LOCAL RECOMMENDATIONS WHEN IN CONFLICT WITH ABOVE.

Fig. M-1. Head lamp aiming chart.

LIGHTING SYSTEM SERVICE

In order to get maximum light from headlights, or any other light on the vehicle, it is important that there be no resistance in the circuit. This can be easily checked by means of a voltmeter. To make a check, remove the head lamp rim, and with the sealed beam unit partly removed from its mounting seat, attach the leads of a low reading voltmeter to the prongs of the sealed beam unit, while it is still inserted in the connector socket.

With the sealed beam connected to the circuit, and after the engine has been stopped and the lights have burned for approximately five minutes, the voltage at the head lamp should not be less than 5.25 volts on 6 volt systems, and 11.25 volts on 12 volt systems. With the lamps burning and the engine warmed up, running at an approximate speed of 20 mph, the voltage at the head lamp should not be less than 6.3 volts, or more than 6.9 volts on 6 volt systems, and 12.3 and 12.5 volts for 12 volt systems. If the voltage is less than indicated, check the condition of the battery, and also clean and tighten all the battery terminals and ground cable. Also check the wires and connections to all lamps, and also at the main headlight switch for high resistance. All connections must be clean and tight.

If the voltage is more than the specified amount, check the adjustment of the voltage regulator.

Fig. M-2. Location of vertical and horizontal adjustments on sealed beam head lamp.

CHANGING SEALED BEAM HEADLIGHTS

Because of the construction of the sealed beam headlight, it is hardly possible to install the lamp incorrectly. These lights do not require focusing, and the only adjustment required is to aim them correctly so the light is directed along the road and will not blind oncoming drivers.

While specialized equipment is available for accurately aiming headlights, a satisfactory job can be done by using a screen or wall. The details for laying out such a screen, and aiming the lights are shown in Fig. M-1. Make sure the car is on a level floor and 25 ft. from the screen.

With the car in front of the aiming screen, remove the head lamp rim.

Fig. M-3. Removing retaining ring spring.

Fig. M-4. Removing retaining ring attaching screws.

Fig. M-5. Removing retaining ring, sealed beam unit and mounting ring.

Adjust the top adjusting screw, Fig. M-2, for vertical position of the beam and the side adjusting screw for horizontal position as required. Adjust one head lamp at a time. While adjusting one lamp, cover the other lamp with an opaque cloth so that there will be no confusion.

SEALED BEAM UNIT REPLACEMENT

Remove the screws holding the head lamp bezel in place. With long nosed pliers, remove the retaining spring, Fig. M-3, from the retaining ring. Then remove the retaining ring attaching screws, Fig. M-4. Do not disturb the adjusting screws unless it is necessary to reaim the light after the installation of a new lamp. The retaining ring may now be removed and the sealed beam unit and mounting ring pulled forward, Fig. M-5. Disconnect the connector plug from the sealed beam unit, and remove the unit, Fig. M-6. Install the mounting ring on the new head lamp and attach connector to new sealed beam unit. Make sure that the number or word "top" molded into the lens face is at the top after installation is completed.

In the dual head lamp installations, the inboard unit (No. 1) takes a double connector plug, the outboard unit (No. 2) takes a triple connector plug.

LIGHTING SWITCH

To remove a lighting switch, first disconnect the battery ground cable. Note: On the factory air conditioned Chevy II models, it is necessary to remove the parking brake and the air conditioning control head before proceeding further. On some 1970 models remove left radio speaker.

171

1971 line of Chevrolet cars, from top: Nova Coupe, Camaro SS Coupe, Chevrolet Caprice Coupe, and Corvette Convertible.

Fig. M-6. Disconnecting sealed beam unit.

Pull control knob of head lamps to "On" position. Note: On the Corvette only, remove screws at top and left sides of instrument panel, and pull panel forward for access to light switch.

Reach up under instrument panel and depress the switch shaft retainer, Fig. M-8, then remove knob and shaft assembly. Remove ferrule nut and switch assembly from instrument panel.

Remove vacuum hoses from Corvette, also Camaro and Chevrolet, optional head lamp switches. Tag location of hoses for reassembly.

Disconnect the multi-contact connector from the lighting switch. A screwdriver may be inserted in the side of the switch to pry the connector from the switch.

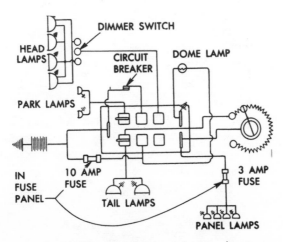

Fig. M-7. Typical lighting switch wiring diagram.

Connect the multicontact connector to the replacement switch. Connect vacuum hoses to head lamp switches and complete switch replacement in the reverse order of removal.

A typical lighting switch wiring diagram, as used on recent model Chevrolet built cars, is shown in Fig. M-7.

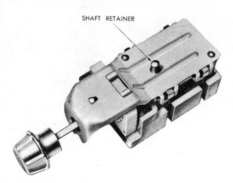

Fig. M-8. *Typical lighting switch. Note shaft retainer which must be pressed in to remove switch.*

Fig. M-9. *Rear of instrument panel cluster — warning devices. Typical.*

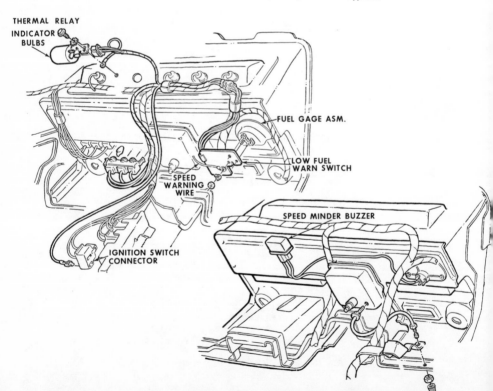

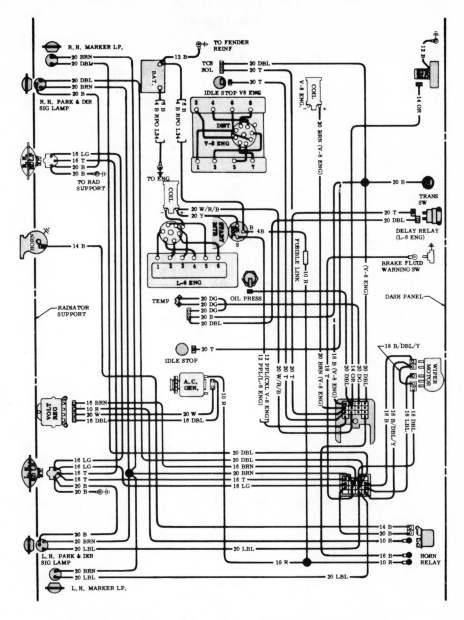

Fig. M-10. 1972 Chevelle and Monte Carlo engine compartment wiring diagram.

WIRING DIAGRAM

The standard instrument cluster for a typical Chevrolet is shown in Fig. M-9 and the wiring diagram of the front lighting and engine compartment of the 1972 Chevrolet is shown in Fig. M-10.

DIMMER SWITCH REPLACEMENT

To replace the headlight dimmer switch, first hold back the upper left corner of the front floor mat. Then disengage the connector lock fingers and disconnect multiplug connector from the dimmer switch, Fig. M-11.

Remove the two screws retaining dimmer switch to toe pan. Connect multiplug connector to new switch and check operation. Then install new switch to toe pan with two screws and replace the floor mat.

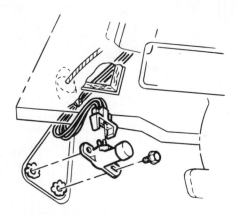

Fig. M-11. Typical dimmer switch installation.

BACKUP LAMP SWITCH REPLACEMENT

There are two types of backup lamp switches used on Chevrolet built cars. One is mounted on the mast jacket, and the other on the transmission.

To remove the switch located on the mast jacket (steering column), first disconnect wiring connector at switch terminal. Remove switch at-

Fig. M-12. Backup lamp switch installation on mast jacket.

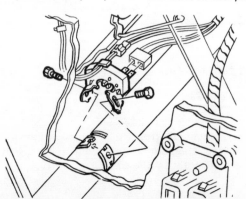

taching screws and switch from the mast jacket. Position the new switch on the mast jacket, install retaining screws and reconnect wire connector to switch.

Position gear shift in neutral before assembling switch to mast jacket.

When the backup lamp switch is located on the transmission, first raise the vehicle and then disconnect the switch wiring from the harness wiring at the in-line connector. Remove bolt retaining wiring attaching clip to transmission. Remove wire clip retaining reverse lever rod to switch. Remove screws retaining switch and shield assembly to transmission and remove the switch.

Do not remove transmission to bracket retaining bolts. To install the backup switch, reverse the procedure and check for operation.

To remove the instrument cluster (speedometer and fuel gauge and park assembly), the console must be removed from the vehicle. It is not necessary to remove the speedometer cluster from the console to remove individual units.

TROUBLE SHOOTING

HEADLIGHTS DIM

If the headlights are dim with the engine idling or shut off, the trouble may be: Partly discharged battery. Defective battery. Loose connection in the light circuit. Loose or dirty connections at battery and battery ground. Faulty sealed beam units. High resistance in circuit.

If the headlights are dim with the engine running well above idling speed, check the following: High resistance in lighting circuit. Faulty voltage control unit. Faulty sealed beam units.

LIGHTS FLICKER

Loose connections. Damaged wires in lighting circuit. Light wiring insulation damage, producing momentary short.

LIGHTS BURN OUT FREQUENTLY

Voltage regulator set too high. Loose connections in lighting circuit.

LIGHTS WILL NOT LIGHT

Discharged battery. Loose connections in lighting circuit. Burned out bulbs. Open or corroded contacts in lighting switch. Open or corroded contacts in dimmer switch. Burned out fuse.

CIRCUIT BREAKER CAUSING CURRENT INTERRUPTION

Short in headlight wiring. Short within some light or instrument in use.

HEADLAMP PANEL ADJUSTMENT

The headlamp panel adjustment (not to be confused with the headlamp adjustment) is made as follows:

1. "in-out" loosen screws fastening slotted bracket to underside of headlamp housing assembly, Fig. M-13.

2. "Down" lamp cover top to opening; by turning hex head screw fastened to top of pivot link.

3. "Open" fully extended actuator with rod. (a) remove spring from actuator rod pin. (b) remove cotter pin from rod pin. (c) turn actuator

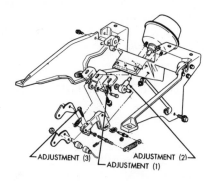

ADJUSTMENT (3) ADJUSTMENT (2)
ADJUSTMENT (1)

Fig. M-13. Headlamp panel adjustment (Corvette).

rod until bushing hole aligns to forward end of slot in connecting link extended position, with engine idling for vacuum. (d) shut off engine, retract actuator rod and unscrew rod one-half turn to preload actuator rod in link.

4. "Up" (bezel to opening alignment). Loosen jamb nut and turn bumper covered screw up or down to touch, then up one and one-half turns more. Micro switch on linkage must shut off warning lamp when lights are fully extended. Note: The headlamp housing must be properly aligned before headlamps are aimed.

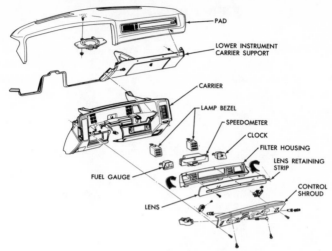

PAD

LOWER INSTRUMENT CARRIER SUPPORT

CARRIER

LAMP BEZEL

SPEEDOMETER

CLOCK

FILTER HOUSING

LENS RETAINING STRIP

FUEL GAUGE

CONTROL SHROUD

LENS

Fig. N-1. Chevrolet instrument panel. (Typical)

ACCESSORY AND INSTRUMENT SERVICE

All instruments and gauges on recent model Chevrolet vehicles are installed on the instrument panel or console, Fig. M-9, and the entire panel is removable so the individual instrument can be serviced. In general, all indicator or cluster illuminating lamp bulb sockets are clip retained and may be quickly snapped in or out of position.

On some models, when removing the console on which the instruments are mounted, it is also necessary to loosen the upper mast jacket retaining clamp and slide it upward, thus releasing the steering mast jacket. Then loosen the lower mast jacket retaining clamp. Loosen the mast jacket and steering wheel. Unscrew the speedometer cable from the speedometer and unsnap all wiring connectors. Remove the screws attaching the console to the instrument panel and the console can then be removed.

INSTRUMENT PANEL

The instrument panel, Fig. N-1, on recent model Chevrolets incorporates an instrument cluster carrier with controls for the various accessories. Tell-tale lights are in the cluster carrier. Access to those bulbs is from the front of the carrier. After four screws are removed, the shroud comes free of the carrier. Then three screws free the lens, giving access to the bulbs. The bulb has a wedge base and pushes straight in.

Access to cluster illumination bulbs, wiper washer switch, headlamp switch bezel nut, cigar lighter housing, rear window defogger switch, convertible top or rear window switch and left vent control lever assembly is as follows:

1. Disconnect battery ground cable.

2. Remove cigar lighter knob and remove hidden screw in shroud where knob was.

3. Pull on headlight switch, then remove hidden screw above middle of shaft.

4. Remove 2 screws at bottom corners of shroud and lift off shroud. Bulbs can then be pulled out. The far left illumination bulb will require wiper switch loosening for bulb access.

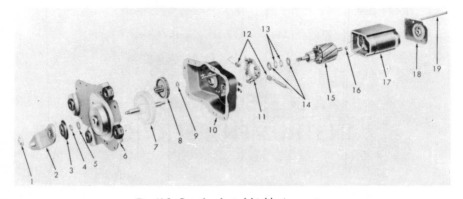

Fig. N-2. Details of windshield wiper motor.

1. Nut.	8. Intermediate gear.	14. Flat washers.
2. Crank arm.	9. Wave washer.	15. Armature.
3. Seal cap.	10. Gear box housing.	16. Thrust plug.
4. Retaining ring.	11. Brush plate assembly and	17. Frame and field.
5. Washer.	mounting brackets.	18. End plate.
6. Gear box cover.	12. Brushes.	19. Tie bolts, two required.
7. Output gear and shaft assembly.	13. Wave washers.	

WINDSHIELD WIPER SERVICE

Regular production Chevrolet cars are equipped with a two-speed electric windshield wiper.

Details of wiper motor and gear box used on recent models are shown in Fig. N-2. While instructions covering the removal of the windshield wiper motor varies with different models, in most cases they can be removed as follows:

Make sure wiper motor is in the Park position. Disconnect washer hoses and electrical connectors from the wiper motor assembly. Remove plenum chamber grille on Chevy II, Nova, Camaro and Corvette models. On Chevrolet models remove the plastic recess cover. Loosen the nuts which retain the drive link to the crank arm ball stud on Chevrolet models. On all other models remove the nut which retains the crank arm to the motor assembly. On Corvette models, it is necessary to remove the ignition shield and distributor cap to gain access to the motor retaining screw assemblies or nuts. Remove the three motor retaining screw assemblies or nuts and remove the motor.

To remove the transmission wiper assembly, Fig. N-3:

Make sure wiper motor is in Park position. Open hood. On Corvettes only, remove rubber plug from front of wiper door actuator, then insert a screwdriver, pushing internal piston rearward to actuate wiper door open. On all models, remove wiper arm and blade assemblies from the transmission. On articulated left-hand arm assemblies, remove carburetor type clip retaining pinned arm to arm blade. Remove plenum chamber air intake grille or screen, if so equipped. Loosen nuts retaining drive rod ball stud to crank arm and detach drive rod from crank arm. Remove transmission retaining screws, or nuts, then lower and drive rod assemblies into plenum chamber. Remove transmission and linkage from plenum chamber through cowl opening.

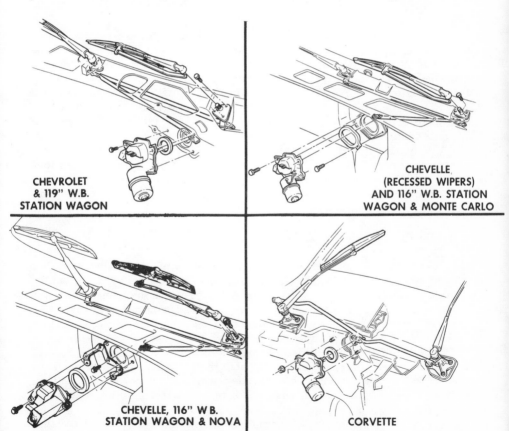

CHEVROLET & 119" W.B. STATION WAGON

CHEVELLE (RECESSED WIPERS) AND 116" W.B. STATION WAGON & MONTE CARLO

CHEVELLE, 116" W.B. STATION WAGON & NOVA

CORVETTE

Fig. N-3. Windshield wiper and linkage details. Typical.

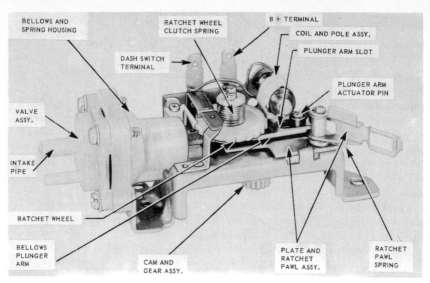

Fig. N-4. Windshield washer pump mechanism.

When trouble is experienced, it is usually advisable to first disconnect the linkage from the motor, and see if the motor will operate without the linkage. If motor does not operate, the trouble is either in the motor, the wiring or switch. Disconnect wiring and run a separate line directly from battery to motor. If motor now operates, the trouble is in the wiring. If the wiper will not shut off, disconnect wiring from dash switch. If motor now shuts off, a defective switch is now indicated. However, if wiper continues to operate, disconnect wiring from the wiper and connect a 12V battery direct to wiper terminal No. 2. Do not connect a jumper wire to terminal No. 1. If wiper now shuts off, check for grounded lead that extends between wiper terminal No. 1 and dash switch.

In case of intermittent operations, check for loose connections and sticking motor brushes.

WINDSHIELD WASHER SERVICE

Details of a current positive type displacement windshield washer pump are shown in Fig. N-4. Area pumps differ in appearance, but the basic pumping action and valve arrangement remain the same. The pump mechanism consists of a small bellows, bellows spring and valve arrangement, driven by a three lobe nylon cam and gear assembly. The wiper motor, Fig. N-2, drives the cam and gear, Fig. N-4.

The most frequent difficulty encountered in the operation of a windshield washer is clogged nozzles, which in most cases can be cleaned by means of a fine wire inserted into the opening of the nozzle. In addition, make sure the jar has an adequate supply of water solution, that hoses are not damaged, and connections are tight, that the screen at end of jar cover hose is not plugged, and that all electrical connections to washer pump and dash switch are tight.

HIDDEN HEAD LAMPS

The hide-away head lamps on the 1968 models are vacuum operated. The system is controlled by the light switch which controls not only the head lamp electrical circuit, but also the vacuum circuit which operates the head lamp doors. The vacuum source is the intake manifold with a reserve tank so the lamp doors can be operated through one cycle without the engine operating. A relay valve routes vacuum to the actuators. In case of malfunction of the system, there is an over center spring in the linkage to keep the door open or closed. The door can be manually operated from the front of the car by pushing on the housing until the housing locks in the open position. It may not be closed without pushing on the linkage inside the engine compartment.

When aiming these head lamps, operate the engine for one to two minutes after the light has been turned on to insure there is at least 20 in. of vacuum in the system.

A manual valve is incorporated in the system to operate the doors independently of the head lamp (through the head lamp switch) for purposes of bulb replacement, cleaning, etc. The manual valve must be pushed in before the doors will close or operate to the normal light switch circuit.

In case the doors fail to open or close, carefully check the entire vacuum circuit, including the reserve tank for leakage.

To replace the actuator assembly, Fig. N-5, the following procedure on Chevrolet cars is followed:

Actuate doors open by lifting upper cover lid up and back, then lifting lower cover up and back. Remove battery for right side actuator, or remove washer jar and bracket for left side actuator removal. Remove

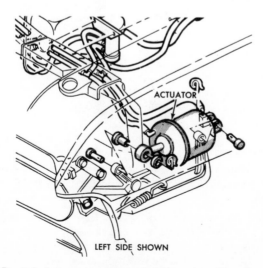

LEFT SIDE SHOWN

Fig. N-5. Actuator assembly for head lamp door, Chevrolet.

front and rear hoses on actuator. Remove front pivot pin retaining washers and pivot pin. Remove actuator rear pivot pin retainer with pin and lift actuator out of vehicle. To replace the actuator, reverse the procedure.

QUICK CHECK ON TURN SIGNAL

The turn signalling lever and cancelling mechanism, Fig. N-6, are located in the turn signal housing adjacent to the steering wheel. The switch requires no adjustment, but in case of malfunction, the steering wheel may be removed and the mechanism checked for defective parts.

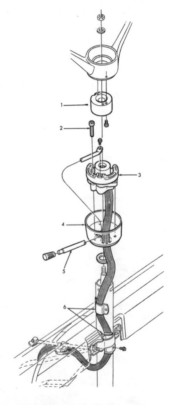

Fig. N-6. Direction signal assembly (Chevrolet). 1—Cancelling cam. 2—Control attaching screw. 3—Control unit. 4—Control housing. 5—Lever. 6—Harness clamps.

A two-bulb flasher is used on the Biscayne and Bel Air passenger cars, and in the Brookwood and Parkwood station wagons. This type flasher operates only two bulbs, the front parking lamp and the tail lamp. A three-bulb flasher is used on Impala cars and Nomad station wagons. The three-bulb flasher operates the front parking lamp and two tail lamps. When installing new flashers, it is important that the correct type be installed. If, when signaling a turn, the indicator light comes on but does not flash, the difficulty may be caused by a burned out parking lamp on that side. The flasher should also be checked.

If, when signalling a turn, the indicator light operation is very rapid, make sure that the correct flasher is installed and that it is in good condition. If, when signaling a turn, both turn indicators come on and stay on, or neither turn indicator turns on, and in either case no clicking is heard, then replace the flasher. Be sure to install the proper type flasher.

If, when signaling a turn, a clicking noise is heard, but the indicator light does not flash, the trouble is probably caused by a defective indicator bulb.

If the horn blows while direction signals are operating, this could most likely be a result of interference between the current signal cancelling pawl and the horn connector assembly which would ground the horn circuit.

If the flashing and cancelling of light is erratic, the trouble is probably caused from the turn signal switch heater being damaged or out of adjustment, and can be eliminated by correct adjustment.

In 1968-1969 models, directional signal assemblies provide as standard production equipment, a lane changing feature and hazard warning system on all model applications. Two different design switches are used. Major difference between the two units is that one type has cancelling and detent springs which are serviceable, otherwise both units are not repairable and must be replaced as an assembly in service.

Due to the integral design relationship of the signal switch and the energy absorbing steering column, which is illustrated in the Chapter on Steering, the switch is involved whenever any service operations are performed on the steering column. The hazard warning unit, even though an integral component of the directional switch assembly, requires the installation of an additional flasher unit in the fuse panel capable of operating six lamps simultaneously, depending upon the vehicle series and model.

TAIL-STOPLIGHT AND BACKUP LIGHT

To remove bulb: Unsnap the socket from the rear of the lamp unit. Replace bulb and snap socket back into place. On station wagon installations, replace bulb by removing lens retaining screws, remove lens and replace bulb.

The stoplight switch is located under the instrument panel and adjacent to the brake panel, Fig. N-7. If the stoplight does not operate when the brakes are applied, the switch can be checked by shorting across the switch terminals. If the bulb is not turned out, the light should light. To replace the switch, disconnect wiring. Remove the lock nut from the plunger end of switch and remove switch. The new switch should be installed in approximately the same position. Adjust switch for proper operation. Electrical contacts should be made when the brake pedal is depressed 5/8 in. from the fully released position.

THEFT DETERRENT SYSTEM

The horn relay-buzzer operates when the driver's door is opened to remind the vehicle driver that the ignition key has been left in the switch. A schematic wiring diagram of this theft deterrent system is shown in Fig. N-8.

With the key fully inserted into the ignition switch, the number four terminal on the horn relay buzzer is connected to the ground through the door switch when the driver's door is opened. Current then flows from the battery through the coil winding, the buzzer contacts, the ignition switch, and the door switch to the ground. Closing the door or removing the key will stop the buzzer action.

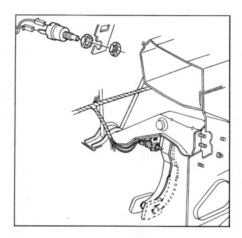

Fig. N-7. Location of stop light switch on Chevrolet. Typical.

When the horn switch is closed, the coil winding is connected to the ground and the armature moves toward the core to close the horn relay contacts. The horns are then connected to the battery and operate accordingly. With the horn switch closed, the buzzer contacts remain separated.

The system can be checked as follows: First be sure that the key is fully inserted into the ignition switch. Then open the driver's door, and observe the dome lamp. If both the dome lamp and buzzer fail to operate, check the door switch for defects. If the dome lamp is on, but the buzzer fails to operate, remove the horn relay buzzer from its mounting and identify the number one and number four terminals. Connect a jumper lead from number four terminal to ground. Slide a probe into the wiring harness connector to make contact if the terminals are of the slip-on type. If the buzzer now operates, check ignition switch wiring and ignition switch for defects. If buzzer does not operate, connect a volt-

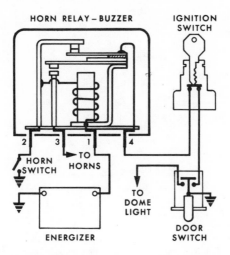

HORN RELAY – BUZZER

IGNITION SWITCH

2 3 1 4

HORN SWITCH

TO HORNS

TO DOME LIGHT

ENERGIZER

DOOR SWITCH

Fig. N-8. Wiring diagram of theft deterrent system.

meter from the No. 1 terminal to the ground. If the reading is zero, the circuit is open between this point and the battery. If a voltage reading is obtained, replace the horn relay-buzzer.

CARE OF SPEEDOMETERS

Speedometers ordinarily require very little attention. Some instruments, however, are provided with a lubrication belt or wick in the speedometer head. In such cases the wick should be saturated with special speedometer oil every 10,000 miles.

Speedometer cables should be lubricated every 10,000 miles. To lubricate, disconnect the cable at the instrument and draw the cables from the casings. Coat the cable with special lubricant and replace in the casing.

Most difficulty encountered in the operation of speedometers usually originates in the drive cable. The cable may be broken, kinked or in need of lubrication.

To determine what may be the cause of speedometer failure, the easiest method is to remove the cable. If the cable is in good condition, the difficulty is then in the speedometer head. In that case, the usual procedure is to remove the speedometer head and have it repaired by a specialist.

To remove a speedometer cable, disconnect the cable from the back of the speedometer head. This is done by turning back the coupling nut on the speedometer cable casing. The cable can then be withdrawn from the casing.

If the cable has broken, it will be necessary to disconnect the casing at the transmission in order to withdraw the lower portion of the cable.

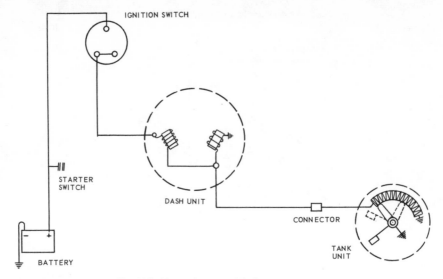

Fig. N-9. Wiring diagram of fuel gauge system.

Cables in good condition should be free from kinks and should not have any frayed or broken wires.

One method of testing a cable for kinks is to hold an end in each of your hands with the cable looped down in front. Then slowly rotate the end of the cable between your fingers. If it is kinked, the cable will "flop" and will not turn smoothly.

Some replacement speedometer cables are cut to the exact lengths and have the necessary fittings secured firmly at each end. In such cases, all that is necessary is to spread a thin coat of speedometer cable lubricant evenly over the lower two-thirds of the cable and insert it into the upper end of the casing, lower end first. Then, connect the upper end of the casing to the speedometer case, making sure the cable tip engages correctly in the speedometer drive member. Tighten the ferrule nut on the casing. Twist the lower end of the cable with your fingers to make sure it turns freely. A sharp twist of the cable should cause the speedometer and needle to register. Finally, connect the lower end of the casing to the transmission making sure that the cable engages in the speedometer driven gear.

When a speedometer cable kit is being used as a replacement, it will be necessary to cut the cable to the desired length and attach the tips. Complete instructions for measuring the cable and attaching the tips are included with the kit.

AIR CONDITIONING SERVICE

Inspect condenser and radiator cores at 2000 mile intervals to be sure they are not plugged with leaves or other foreign material. Check evaporator drain tubes at 2000 mile intervals for dirt or restrictions. At least once a year check the system for proper refrigerant charge and the flexible hoses for brittleness, wear or leaks. Every 2000 miles check sight glass for low freon level. Check tension of the drive belts regularly.

When replacing any of the air conditioning components, the system must be completely purged or drained of refrigerant. The purpose is to lower the pressure inside the system so that the component part can be removed safely. To do this, special equipment is required and the necessary instructions for using the equipment are included with the apparatus.

This same equipment is used when refilling the system with refrigerant.

GENERATOR CHARGE INDICATOR

Instead of an ammeter, some recent model Chevrolet cars are equipped with a charge indicator. If the telltale lamp does not light when the ignition switch is turned on, and the engine not running, the indicator lamp is burned out or the wiring is defective. If the telltale lamp stays on after the engine is started, check generator output. If the lamp stays on at idle speed only, check for low speed idle.

OIL PRESSURE INDICATOR

If the oil pressure indicator light does not come on when the ignition switch is turned on, or if the light stays on after engine is started, either the oil pressure is low, the oil level is low, the wiring or a unit in this circuit is defective.

If telltale light remains on with the engine running, the oil pressure is low. First check oil level, then if pressure is still low remove pressure switch and check oil pressure with a reliable pressure gauge. Another cause might be the electric circuit grounded between telltale light and pressure switch, or oil pressure switch is not operating correctly.

If the telltale lamp is off with the ignition switch on, and the engine not running, then the telltale lamp may be burned out, or there may be an open circuit between light and ignition switch, between light and pressure switch, pressure switch stuck, or the pressure switch not grounded.

FUEL GAUGE

The most common cause of fuel gauge trouble is high resistance in the circuit. Make sure all connections are tight and free from dirt, paint or corrosion.

Since the fuel gauge consists of two remotely located units, and the connecting wires, it is sometimes difficult to determine which unit is at fault.

The easiest way to determine where difficulty is located is to replace the units with new units until the trouble is located. A diagram of connections is shown in Fig. N-9.

TEMPERATURE INDICATOR

The temperature indicator requires very little attention other than making sure all connections are tight and free from dirt. Since the temperature gauge consists of two remotely located units, and the connecting wires, it is sometimes difficult to determine which unit is at fault. Make sure the unit is properly grounded by connecting one lead from a 12 V test lamp to the battery terminal on the starter and the other to the body of the engine unit. If the bulb lights, the unit is properly grounded. Remove test lead from body of the unit and connect lead to terminal of unit. If the bulb lights, the engine unit is internally short circuited and should be replaced.

POWER OPERATED FRONT SEATS (TYPICAL)

Seat adjusters are operated by a 12 volt reversible shunt wound motor. To remove seat for servicing the operating mechanism, first operate seat to full forward position. On four-way or six-way power seats, operate seats to full "up" position. Where front seat safety belts go through seat assembly, remove seat belt floor pan inner anchor plate attaching bolts. Where necessary, remove sill plates, and turn back floor mat and remove seat adjuster to floor pan rear attaching bolts, Fig. N-10. Operate seat

Fig. N-10. Four-way power operated seat. 1—Motor and transmission support. 2—Motor control relay. 3—Adjuster to floor pan front attaching bolt. 4—Ground strap. 5—Adjuster to floor pan rear attaching bolt. 6—Adjuster rear carpet retainer. 7—Adjuster to seat frame attaching bolt. 8—Adjuster track rear lower cover. 9—Adjuster track upper cover. 10—Four-way switch assembly. 11—Motor support attaching screws. 12—Adjuster track cover retainers. 13—Horizontal drive cable (black). 14—Vertical drive cable (blue). 15—Transmission assembly. 16—Motor to transmission coupling. 17—Motor assembly.

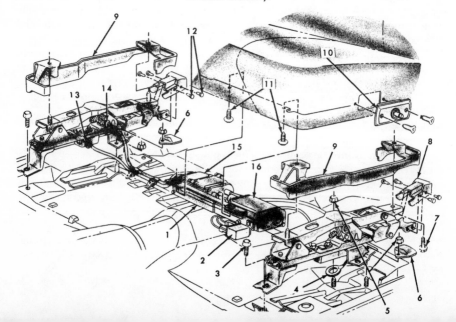

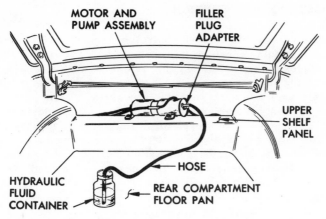

MOTOR AND
PUMP ASSEMBLY

FILLER
PLUG
ADAPTER

UPPER
SHELF
PANEL

HOSE

HYDRAULIC
FLUID
CONTAINER

REAR COMPARTMENT
FLOOR PAN

Fig. N-11. Motor and pump assembly of folding top mechanism.

to full rearward position. Remove adjuster-to-floor pan front adjusting bolts. Tilt seat assembly rearward sufficiently to disconnect seat harness feed connector and detach harness from floor pan. Disconnect any wiring. Then lift seat assembly from car.

FOLDING TOP

The hydraulic-electric system used to operate the Chevrolet folding top consists of a 12V reversible type motor, a rotor type pump, two hydraulic lift cylinders and an upper and lower hydraulic hose assembly. The unit is installed in the body directly behind the rear seat back, Fig. N-11.

When filling and bleeding this system, a filler plug adapter is needed. This can be made from a spare reservoir filler plug by drilling a quarter inch hole through the center of the plug. Then install two inch lengths of metal tubing, 3/16 in. i.d. into the center of the filler plug and solder tubing on both sides of the filler plug to form airtight connections.

To fill and bleed the reservoir, place the top in the raised position. Remove pump and motor shield. Place absorbent rags below reservoir at the filler plug. Using a straight-bladed screwdriver, slowly remove filler plug from reservoir, Fig. N-11. Install filler plug adapter to reservoir and attach four or five lengths of 3/16 in. rubber tubing or hose to filler plug tubing. Install opposite end of hose into a container of heavy-duty brake fluid. The container should be placed in the rear compartment body below the level of the fluid in the reservoir.

Operate top to down or stacked position. After top is fully loaded, continue to operate motor and pump assembly approximately 15 to 20 seconds, or until noise level of pump is noticeably reduced. Reduction in pump noise level indicates the hydraulic system is filling with fluid.

Operate top several times, or until operation of top is consistently smooth in both up-and-down cycles.

CRUISE MASTER SPEED CONTROL

The Cruise Master is a speed control system, Fig. N-12, which employs engine manifold vacuum to power the throttle servo unit, Fig. N-13. The servo moves the throttle when speed adjustment is necessary, by receiving a varying amount of bleed air from the regulator unit, Fig. N-14. The regulator varies the amount of bleed air to a valve system, which is linked to a speedometer-like mechanism. The speedometer cable from the transmission drives the regulators, and a cable from the regulator drives the instrument panel speedometer. The engagement of the regulator unit is controlled by an engagement switch located at the end of the turn signal lever. Two brake release switches are provided. An electric

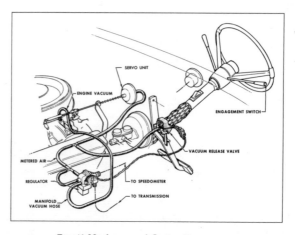

Fig. N-12. Layout of Cruise Master system.

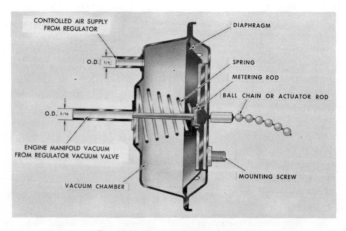

Fig. N-13. Sectional view of servo unit.

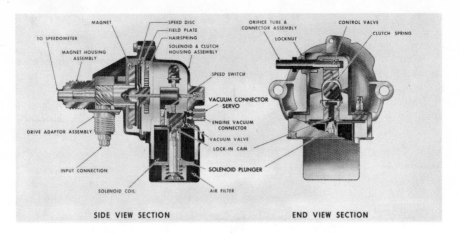

Fig. N-14. Details of Cruise Master regulator.

switch disengages the regulator unit, and a vacuum switch decreases the vacuum in the servo unit to quickly return the throttle to idle position. Fig. N-12 shows the location of the system components within the vehicle.

The components of the Cruise Master system are designed to be replaced should they become inoperative. The air filter mounted on the regulator must be replaced at 12,000 mile intervals.

CRUISE MASTER SYSTEM CHECKS

When system will not engage or is otherwise inoperative, check for the following: Brake switch circuit open. Clutch switch circuit open. Blown fuse. Defective engage switch. Vacuum leaks. Vacuum release switch misadjusted. Crossed vacuum and air hose at regulator. Open end wiring. Defective regulator.

Does not cruise at engagement speed, check for orifice tube misadjustment.

System shunts pulses or surges, check for the following: Bead chain loose. Hoses reversed at servo. Kinked or deteriorated hoses. Dirty air filter. Defective and/or improperly positioned drive cables and/or casing assemblies. Defective regulator.

System does not disengage with brake pedal: Brake and/or vacuum switch misadjusted or defective. Defective wiring.

System steadily accelerates or applies full throttle when engaged: Hose interchanged at servo. Manifold vacuum connected directly to outboard tube or servo. Defective regulator. Pinched or plugged air hose that is connected to the outboard tube of servo.

Cannot adjust speed downward with engage button: Defective engagement switch or wiring.

Does not engage or engages at lower than desired speeds: Defective regulator.

Slow throttle return to idle after brake is depressed: Pinched air hose at vacuum release switch.

High engine speed independent of carburetor adjustments, constant air bleed through system: May be caused by: Tight servo chain. Manifold vacuum connected directly to center tube of servo.

System can be engaged at idle by depressing switch but will drop out when switch is released: May be caused by wires reversed at regulator.

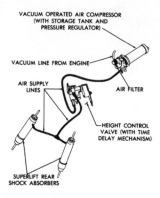

Fig. N-15. Automatic level control system.

AUTOMATIC LEVEL CONTROL

The automatic level control system is optional equipment and is designed to automatically maintain correct rear trim height of a car under varying load conditions. It is used only in conjunction with the super lift shock absorber which consists of two shock absorbers with pressure lines to a "T" where a fill valve is located. The shocks are inflated with or deflated of compressed air to obtain the vehicle level desired with any given load change.

The automatic leveling system is added to the super lift shock absorbers and supplies its own compressed air. Fig. N-15 consists of a vacuum operated air compressor with pressure regulator and integral storage tank, vacuum line to engine, air intake cylinder, air lines and height control valves.

After completion of work on this system or when servicing other parts of the car and the system is deflated, inflate the reservoir to 140 psi or maximum pressure available through the compression valve.

To make a quick check on the system of the automatic level control, fill the fuel tank. Turn off the engine and add a two passenger load to the rear bumper or tail'gate. Maintain the load until the car lifts or at least 20 seconds. After the car lifts remove the load and observe until the car lowers, which it should do in about twenty seconds.

Quick
CLUTCH SERVICE

Two designs of the diaphragm spring clutch are used with the different engine-transmission combinations. A third design is a dual plate, heavy-duty clutch option, which is available for all models with higher performance optional V-8 engines.

The clutch assembly is enclosed in a 360 deg. bell housing, which must be removed to gain access to the clutch.

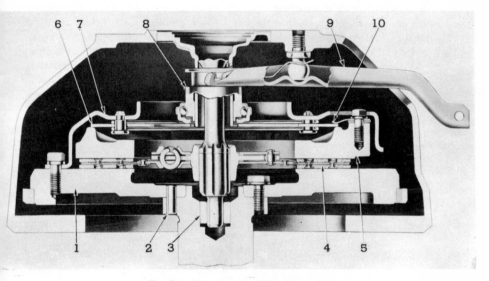

Fig. O-1. Cross section of flat finger clutch.

For engines of lower output, the clutch illustrated in Fig. O-1 is used as standard equipment. V-8 engines equipped with a 4-speed transmission use a bent-finger, centrifugal diaphragm type clutch, Fig. O-2. While the new dual plate heavy-duty clutch option which is available for all models of high performance V-8 engine is shown in Fig. O-3. This new heavy-duty clutch option combines the semicentrifugal bent-finger design and diaphragm type spring, used in regular Chevrolet high capacity clutches, with two conventional dry driven discs separated by a ring type intermediate pressure plate, Fig. O-3. The total disc facing area is 201 sq. in. compared to 123.7 sq. in. for the conventional regular production

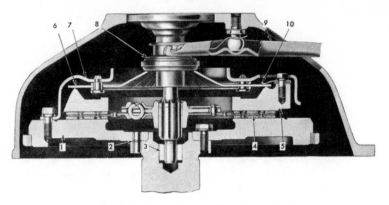

Fig. O-2. Sectional view of bent finger clutch.

unit. The greater total working area of the dual unit permits a reduction of plate load with no loss in efficiency. As a result, pedal effort to disengage the dual unit is approximately one-half of the comparable single disc unit, and clutch life is more than double. In addition, abuse capacity is always measurably greater. A new engine flywheel with a recessed contact area provides the space required to accommodate the second clutch disc and intermediate plate.

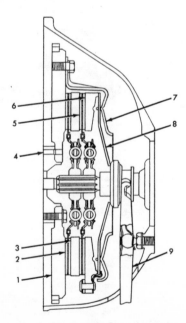

Fig. O-3. Dual plate clutch assembly. 1—Flywheel. 2—Front driven disc. 3—Front pressure plate. 4—Dowel hole. 5—Rear driven disc. 6—Pressure plate. 7—Cover. 8—Retracting spring. 9—Clutch fork.

Clutch Service

Clutch linkage on each of these clutches should be adjusted, unless otherwise specified, so there is one inch free travel, as measured at the clutch pedal pad, before clutch throwout bearing contacts the clutch fingers. In other words, the clutch pedal pad should move one inch before major resistance to movement is felt. This movement of the clutch pedal should be made by hand rather than the foot, as this feel is very sensitive.

CHECKING CLUTCH OPERATION

A clutch that has been slipping prior to free play adjustment may continue to slip right after the new adjustment, due to previous heat damage. Any slippage should then be evaluated as follows: Drive in high gear at 20-25 mph. Depress the clutch pedal to the floor and increase engine speed to 2500-3500 rpm. Engage the clutch quickly by removing foot from pedal, and press accelerator to full throttle. Engine speed should drop noticeably and accelerate with vehicle. If clutch is defective, the engine speed will increase. Be sure not to repeat more than once, or clutch will overheat.

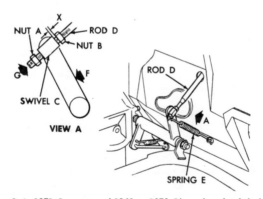

Fig. O-4. 1971 Corvette and 1962 to 1970 Chevrolet clutch linkage.

ADJUSTING 1962-1970 CHEVROLET CLUTCH

Disconnect spring E, Fig. O-4, between clutch push rod and cross-shaft lever. With the clutch pedal against stop, loosen jam nuts sufficiently to allow the adjusting rod to move against the clutch fork until the release bearing contacts the pressure plate fingers lightly. Rotate upper nut B, Fig. O-4, against swivel and back off 4-1/2 turns. Tighten lower nut A to lock swivel against nut B. Install return spring E and check clutch pedal free travel. Pedal free travel should be: Chevrolet 1 in. to 1-1/2 in.; Corvett Standard 1-1/4 in. to 2 in.; Corvett Heavy Duty 2 in. to 2-1/2 in.

1968-1970 CHEVELLE, CAMARO, NOVA AND CHEVY II ADJUSTMENT

Disconnect return spring at clutch fork, Fig. O-5. With clutch pedal against stop: Loosen lock nut C sufficiently to allow the adjusting rod to return out of swivel and against clutch fork, until the release bearing contacts pressure plate fingers lightly. Rotate push rod into swivel three turns and tighten lock nut.

Note: Chevy II and Camaro V-8 engine models use a two-piece push rod. Turn adjusting rod portion of push rod three turns into rod end, then tighten lock nut.

Reinstall return spring and check pedal free travel. Pedal travel should be: Chevelle 1-1/8 in. to 1-3/4 in.; Chevy II and Camaro 1 in. to 1-1/8 in.

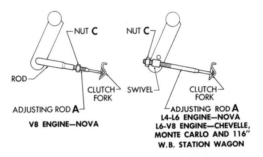

Fig. O-5. 1968–1970 Chevy II, Camaro, Monte Carlo and Chevelle clutch pedal free travel adjustment.

1962-1964 CHEVROLET CLUTCH ADJUSTMENT

Clutch adjustment, for all normal wear, is made at the swivel, Fig. O-6, on lower end of pedal push rod as follows: Remove clutch pedal return spring. Loosen nut B, Fig. O-6, and back off from swivel approximately 1/2 in. Hold clutch pedal push rod so pedal is against bumper stop and cross shaft lever is in the opposite direction so the throw-out bearing is against clutch fingers. Adjust nut B to obtain approximately 1/4 in. clearance between nut B and upper edge of swivel. Release push rod and cross shaft lever and tighten nut A to lock swivel against nut B. Free pedal play should be 7/8 in. to 1-1/8 in. Install pedal return spring.

1958-1961 CHEVROLET CLUTCH LINKAGE ADJUSTMENT

Remove clip B, retaining swivel to clutch lever and shaft assembly, Fig. O-7. Note: 348 cu. in. V-8 engine clutch lower push rod incorporates a long extension swivel as shown in insert, Fig. O-7.

Adjust by holding fork pushrod A rearward to remove all lash between release bearing and clutch diaphragm spring, then adjust swivel C to line

Clutch Service

up with a dimple located on the clutch lever and shaft assembly. The swivel has a conical point for a visual aid.

Reinstall swivel C at lower push rod A to clutch lever and shaft assembly with retainer clip.

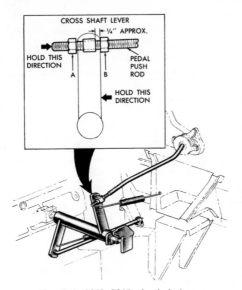

Fig. 0-6. 1962–1965 clutch linkage.

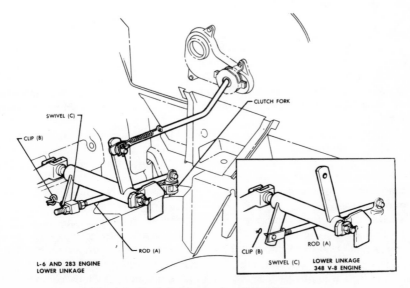

Fig. 0-7. Clutch linkage used on 1958–1961 cars.

ADJUSTING 1971-1972 CHEVROLET, CHEVELLE, CAMARO CLUTCH

Disconnect return spring at clutch fork. Rotate clutch lever and shaft assembly until clutch pedal is firmly against rubber bumper on dash brace. Push outer end of clutch fork rearward until throwout bearing lightly contacts pressure plate fingers. Loosen lock nut and adjust rod length so that swivel or rod slips freely in gauge hole and increases length until all lash is removed from the system. Remove swivel or rod from gauge hole and insert into lower hole in lever. Install retainer and tighten lock nut. Reinstall return spring. Pedal travel should be 1-1/8 to 1-3/4 in.

With the lower linkage adjusted as outlined, the pedal free travel will range from 1-1/4 in. to 1-5/8 in.

Do not use pedal free travel feel as a method of adjusting the linkage. This is important, because the over center spring feature which, due to its pedal assisting action, tends to give more free travel feel than actually exists.

REMOVING THE CLUTCH

1965-1971 models: Support the engine and remove the transmission as outlined in Chapter on Transmissions. Then disconnect clutch fork push rod and spring. Remove flywheel housing. Slide clutch fork from ball stud and remove fork from dust boot. Install pilot to support clutch assembly during the removal. Prick punch flywheel and clutch cover to permit reassembly in original position. Loosen clutch to flywheel attaching bolts evenly, turning one turn at a time until spring pressure is released. Then remove bolts and clutch assembly.

1954-1964 Chevrolet and 1958-1965 Corvette: Remove transmission. Remove clutch release spring bearing from fork. Remove clutch fork tension spring. Disconnect clutch fork push rod. Remove fork by pushing forward and to the center of the vehicle. Loosen clutch attaching screws one at a time until spring pressure is released. Then remove bolts and clutch.

Chevy II 1962-1964: Remove transmission as outlined in the Chapter on Transmissions. Disconnect clutch linkage return spring from clutch fork and let push rod hang free of fork. Remove throw-out bearing from fork. Remove clutch housing cover plate screws and clutch housing bolts, then remove housing. Note: The cover plate will now hang from starter gear housing.

Slide clutch fork from ball stud, and remove fork from dust boot. Note: The ball stud is threaded into clutch housing and is easily replaced, if necessary. Insert a pilot into clutch hub to support the clutch assembly during removal. Loosen the six clutch attaching bolts evenly a little at a time until clutch diaphragm spring tension is released. Then remove bolts, clutch assembly and pilot tool.

CLUTCH RELEASE BEARING

The clutch release bearing is permanently packed with lubricant and should not be soaked in cleaning solvent as this may dissolve the lubricant.

CLUTCH THROW-OUT BEARING

The clutch throw-out bearing, (release) Fig. O-8, should be packed with graphite grease when the clutch is dismantled.

TROUBLE SHOOTING

CLUTCH FAILS TO RELEASE

Improper adjustment, loose linkage. Weak retracting springs. Faulty pilot bearing. Faulty driven disc.

CLUTCH SLIPPING

Improper adjustment. Oil soaked facings. Worn splines on clutch gear. Warped pressure plate or flywheel. Weak diaphragm spring.

CLUTCH GRABBING

Oil or clutch facing. Burned or glazed facings. Worn splines on clutch gear. Loose engine mounts. Warped pressure plate or flywheel.

RATTLES

Weak retracting springs. Throw-out fork loose on ball stud or in bearing groove.

THROW-OUT BEARING SPINNING

When this occurs with the clutch fully engaged, the trouble may be caused by: Improper adjustment. Throw-out bearing binding on transmission. Insufficient tension between clutch fork spring and ball stud.

RAPID CLUTCH WEAR

Insufficient free play of clutch pedal.

NOISE

Worn throw-out bearing.

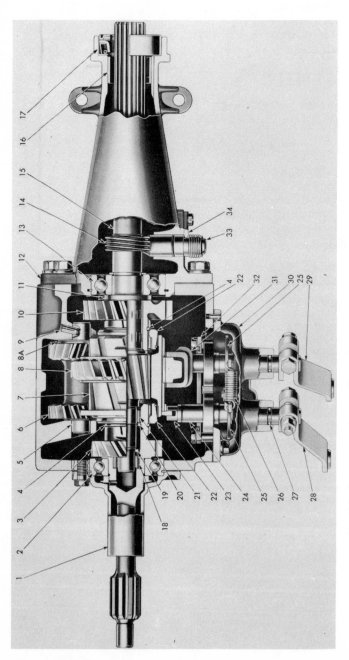

Fig. P-1. Cross section (top view) of transmission used on L-6 engine and Chevy II to 1965.

1-Clutch gear bearing retainer.
2-Clutch gear bearing.
3-Clutch gear.
4-Energizing spring.
5-Reverse idler shaft.
6-Reverse idler gear.
7-Second and third speed clutch.
8-First and reverse sliding gear.
8A-Thrust bearing and washer.

9-Reverse idler shaft pin.
10-Second speed gear.
11-Thrust washer.
12-Case extension.
13-Mainshaft rear bearing.
14-Speedometer drive gear.
15-Mainshaft.
16-Bushing.
17-Oil seal.

18-Front pilot bearing rollers.
19-Thrust washer.
20-Thrust washer.
21-Rear pilot bearing rollers.
22-Synchronizer ring.
23-Second and third shifter fork.
24-Second and third shifter shaft.
25-Detent cam.
26-Detent cam spring.

27-"O" ring oil seal.
28-Second an d third shifter lever.
29-First and reverse shifter lever.
30-Side cover.
31-First and reverse shifter fork.
32-Interlock retainer.
33-Speedometer shaft fitting.
34-Lock plate.

TRANSMISSION
SERVICE

MANUAL TRANSMISSION SERVICE

Several different types of three and four-speed manual shift transmissions have been used in Chevrolet built cars in recent years. The three-speed transmission shown in Figs. P-1 and P-2 was used from 1954 to 1965. A Warner model T-16 heavy-duty three-speed unit was also used for a time. From 1965 to date, the transmissions shown in Figs. P-3, P-4, P-5 and P-6 are being used. The particular transmission to be found in each vehicle is dependent primarily on the size of the engine installed.

REMOVING THE TRANSMISSION

While the procedure for removing the transmission of different cars varies slightly, the following procedure can be followed.

First, raise the car on a hoist or on jack stands. Disconnect speedometer cable at transmission and on floor shift models disconnect back-up lamp switch. Remove the propeller shaft assembly. On Camaro models, disconnect exhaust pipe at manifold. Remove cross member to frame attaching bolts.

On floor shift models, remove the cross member to control lever support attaching bolts. On Chevelle models also remove control lever brakes to cross member attaching bolt.

Remove bolts retaining transmission mount to cross member. Support engine and raise slightly until cross member may be slid rearward or removed. Remove shift levers at transmission side cover.

On floor shift models, remove stabilizer to control lever assembly retaining nut. Push bolt toward transmission until stabilizer rod can be disconnected.

Remove transmission to clutch housing upper retaining bolts, and install guide pins in holes then remove lower bolts. Slide transmission rearward and remove from vehicle.

On models earlier than 1958 it is not necessary to remove the transmission support (cross member). Transmission is replaced by reversing the above procedure.

DISASSEMBLING A THREE-SPEED TRANSMISSION

The following procedure pertains particularly to the 1966-1969 three-speed Saginaw transmission, but is also helpful in disassembling the case components of the other three-speed transmissions.

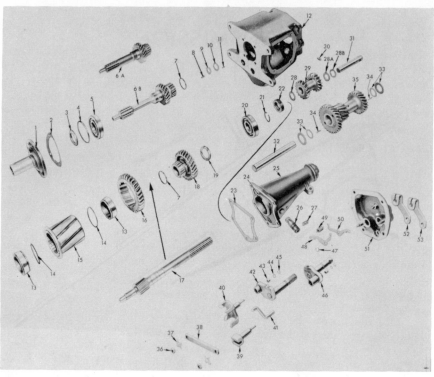

Fig. P-2. Layout of transmission shown in Fig. P-1.

1-Clutch gear bearing retainer.
2-Bearing retainer gasket.
3-Bearing nut and oil slinger.
4-Bearing snap ring.
5-Clutch gear bearing.
6-Clutch gear (a-V-8 and overdrive, b-L-6)
7-Energizing spring.
8-Front pilot bearing roller.
9-Thrust washer.
10-Thrust washer.
11-Rear pilot bearing rollers.
12-Transmission case.
13-Synchronizer ring.
14-Snap ring.
15-Second and third speed clutch.
16-First and reverse sliding gear.
17-Mainshaft.
18-Second speed gear.
19-Thrust washer.

20-Mainshaft rear bearing.
21-Snap ring.
22-Speedometer drive gear.
23-Case extension gasket.
24-Rear bearing snap ring.
25-Case extension.
26-Speedometer driven gear.
27-Lock plate.
28-Thrust washer.
28a-Thrust bearing.
28b-Thrust bearing washer.
29-Reverse idler gear.
30-Pin.
31-Reverse idler shaft.
32-Counter shaft.
33-Thrust washers.
34-Bearing roller.
35-Countergear.
36-Shifter interlock retainer nut.

37-Lock nut.
38-Shifter interlock retainer.
39-Second and third shifter fork.
40-First and reverse shifter fork.
41-Shifter interlock shaft.
42-First and reverse inner shifter lever.
43-Shifter fork spacer.
44-Washer.
45-Shifter fork retainer.
46-Second and third inner shifter lever.
47-Detent cam retainer.
48-First and reverse detent cam.
49-Detent cam spring.
50-Second and third detent cam.
51-Side cover.
52-First and reverse outer shifter lever.
53-Second and third outer shifter lever.

First remove side cover attaching screws and remove side cover assembly and shift forks. Remove clutch gear bearing retainer. Remove clutch gear bearing to gear stem snap ring, then remove clutch gear bearing by pulling outward on clutch gear until a screwdriver or other suitable tool can be inserted between bearing large snap ring and case to complete removal. The clutch gear bearing is a slip fit on the gear and into the case bore. (This provides clearance for removal of clutch gear and main shaft assembly.) Remove extension to case attaching bolts. Remove the reverse idler shaft snap ring. Remove clutch gear, main shaft and extension assembly together to the rear case opening. Using snap ring pliers, extend the snap ring in the extension which retains the mainshaft rear bearing, and remove the extension. Using a soft drift at the front of the counter-shaft, drive the shaft and its Woodruff key out of the rear of the case. Special tools are available for driving out the countershaft which will hold the roller bearings into position within the countergear bore. Then remove the gear and bearings.

Use a long drift or punch through the front bearing case bore, and drive the reverse idler shaft and Woodruff key through the rear of the case.

Fig. P-3. Exploded view of three-speed fully synchronized Saginaw transmission.

The mainshaft and other parts can then be disassembled. To disassemble the mainshaft, use snap ring pliers and remove the second and third speed sliding clutch hub snap ring from the mainshaft and remove the clutch assembly, second speed locker ring and second speed gear from the front of the mainshaft. Depress the speedometer gear retaining clip and slide gear from the mainshaft.

Remove rear bearing snap ring from the mainshaft groove. Support reverse gear with press plates and press on rear of mainshaft to remove re-

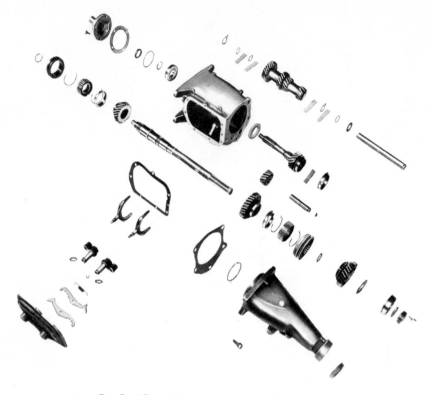

Fig. P-4. Exploded view of three-speed Muncie transmission.

verse gear, thrust washer, spring washer, rear bearing and snap ring from the rear of the mainshaft.

When pressing rear bearing be careful to center gear, washers, bearing and snap ring on the mainshaft.

Remove the first and reverse sliding clutch hub snap ring from the mainshaft and remove the clutch assembly, first speed blocker ring, and first speed gear from the rear of the mainshaft.

This completes the disassembly of the mainshaft.

Clean all parts carefully and examine for wear and other defects.

DISASSEMBLING THREE-SPEED SAGINAW

To disassemble the fully synchronized three-speed Saginaw transmission shown in Fig. P-3, first remove cover attaching screws and remove side cover and shift forks. Remove clutch gear bearing retainer. Remove clutch gear to gear stem snap ring. Then remove clutch gear bearing by pulling outward on clutch gear until a screwdriver can be inserted between bearing snap ring and case to complete the removal. The clutch gear bear-

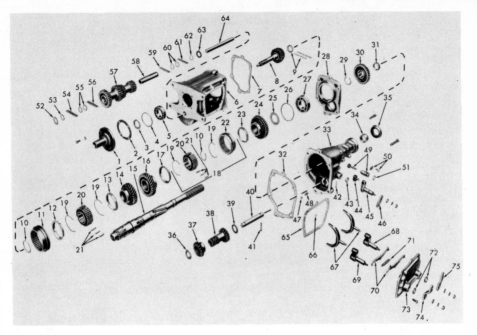

Fig. P-5. Typical four-speed Muncie transmission.

1. Bearing retainer.
2. Gasket.
3. Bearing retainer nut.
4. Bearing snap ring.
5. Main drive gear bearing.
6. Transmission case.
7. Rear bearing retainer gasket.
8. Main drive gear.
9. Bearing rollers and cage.
10. Snap ring.
11. Third and fourth speed clutch sliding sleeve.
12. Fourth speed gear synchronizing ring.
13. Third speed synchronizing ring.
14. Third speed gear.
15. Mainshaft.
16. Second speed gear.
17. Second speed gear synchronizing ring.
18. First and second speed clutch assembly.
19. Clutch key spring.
20. Clutch hub.
21. Clutch keys.
22. First and second speed clutch sliding sleeve.
23. First speed gear synchronizing ring.
24. First speed gear.
25. First speed gear thrust washer.
26. Rear bearing snap ring.
27. Rear bearing.
28. Rear bearing retainer.
29. Selective fit snap ring.
30. Reverse gear.
31. Speedometer drive gear.
32. Rear bearing retainer to case extension gasket.
33. Case extension.
34. Extension bushing.
35. Rear oil seal.
36. Reverse idler front thrust washer (tanged).
37. Reverse idler gear, front.
38. Reverse idler gear, rear.
39. Flat thrust washer.
40. Reverse idler shaft.
41. Reverse idler shaft roll pin.
42. Reverse shifter shaft lock pin.
43. Reverse shifter shaft lip seal.
44. Reverse shift fork.
45. Reverse shifter shaft and detent plate.
46. Reverse shifter lever.
47. Reverse shifter shaft detent ball.
48. Reverse shifter shaft ball detent spring.
49. Speedometer driven gear and fitting.
50. Retainer and bolt.
51. "O" ring seal.
52. Tanged washer.
53. Spacer .050 in.
54. Bearing rollers (20).
55. Spacers (2-.050 in.).
56. Bearing rollers (20)
57. Countergear.
58. Countergear roller spacer.
59. Bearing rollers (20).
60. Spacers (2-.050 in.).
61. Bearing rollers (20).
62. Spacer (.050 in.).
63. Tanged washer.
64. Countershaft.
65. Gasket.
66. Detent cams retainer ring.
67. Forward speed shift forks.
68. First and second speed gear shifter shaft and detent plate.
69. Third and fourth speed gear shifter shaft and detent plate.
70. Detent cams.
71. Detent cam spring.
72. Lip seals.
73. Transmission side cover.
74. Third and fourth speed shifter lever.
75. First and second speed shifter lever.

ing is a slip fit on the gear and into the case bore. This provides clearance for removal of clutch gear and mainshaft assembly. Remove extension to case attaching bolts. Remove reverse idler shaft snap ring. Remove clutch gear, mainshaft and extension assembly together through the rear case opening. Using snap ring pliers, expand snap ring in the extension which retains the mainshaft rear bearing and remove the extension. Use a drift at the front of the countershaft and drive the shaft and its Woodruff key out the rear of the case. There are special tools which will hold the roller bearings in position within the countergear bore. Remove the gear and bearings. Use a long drift through the front bearing case bore and drive the reverse idler shaft and Woodruff key through the rear of the case.

To disassemble the mainshaft, remove the 2nd and 3rd speed sliding clutch hub snap ring from the mainshaft and remove clutch assembly, second speed blocker ring and second speed gear from front of the mainshaft. Remove rear bearing snap ring from mainshaft groove. Support reverse gear with press plates and press on rear of mainshaft to remove reverse gear, thrust washer, spring washer, rear bearing and snap ring from rear of mainshaft.

When pressing rear bearing, be careful to center the gear, washers, bearings and snap ring on mainshaft.

Remove the first and reverse sliding clutch hub snap ring from the mainshaft and remove clutch assembly, first speed block ring and first speed gear from the rear of the mainshaft which completes the disassembly of the mainshaft.

FOUR-SPEED TRANSMISSION DISASSEMBLY

The disassembly procedure for the four-speed Muncie transmission shown in Fig. P-5 is as follows: Remove the transmission side cover and the four bolts, the two bolt lock strips from front bearing retainer, and remove retainer and gasket. Remove the maindrive gear retaining nut after locking up transmission by shifting into two gears. With the transmission gears in neutral, drive lock pin from reverse shifter lever boss and pull shifter shaft out about 1/8 in. This disengages the reverse shift fork from reverse gear.

Remove six bolts attaching the case extension to the case. Tap extension with soft hammer in a rearward direction to start. When the reverse idler shaft is out as far as it will go, move extension to left so reverse fork clears reverse gear and remove extension and gasket.

The reverse idler gear, flat thrust washer, shaft and roller spring pin may now be removed. Remove speedometer gear and reverse gear.

Slide three-four synchronizer clutch sleeve to fourth speed position (forward) before trying to remove mainshaft assembly from case. Carefully remove the rear bearing retainer and entire mainshaft assembly from the case by tapping the bearing retainer with a soft hammer. Unload 17 bearing rollers from main drive gear and remove fourth speed synchronizer blocker ring.

Lift the front half of reverse idler gear and its tanged thrust washer from case. Press main drive gear down from front bearing. From inside

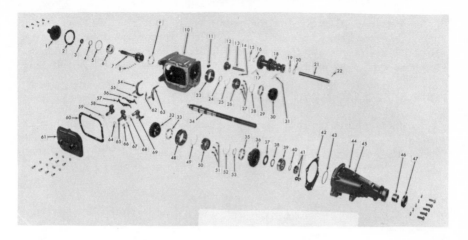

Fig. P-6. Four-speed Saginaw transmission.

1. Bearing retainer.
2. Gasket retainer to case.
3. Oil seal.
4. Snap ring.
5. Snap ring.
6. Clutch gear bearing.
7. Clutch gear.
8. Mainshaft pilot bearing.
9. Fourth speed blocker ring.
10. Case.
11. Filler plug.
12. Reverse idler gear.
13. Reverse idler shaft.
14. Woodruff key.
15. Thrust washer.
16. Needle retainer washer.
17. Needle bearings.
18. Countergear.
19. Needle retainer washer.
20. Thrust washer rear gear.
21. Countershaft.
22. Woodruff key.
23. Synchronizer sleeve.
24. Snap ring hub to shaft.
25. Key retainer.
26. 3-4 synchronizer hub.
27. Clutch keys.
28. Key retainer.
29. Third speed blocker ring.
30. Third speed gear.
31. Needle bearings.
32. Second speed gear.
33. Second speed blocker ring.
34. Mainshaft.
35. First speed blocker ring.

36. First speed gear.
37. Thrust washer.
38. Wave washer.
39. Rear bearing.
40. Snap ring bearing to shaft.
41. Speed drive gear and clip.
42. Gasket extension to case.
43. Snap ring extension.
44. Extension.
45. Vent.
46. Bushing.
47. Oil seal.
48. 1-2 syn. sleeve and rev. gear.
49. Key retainer.
50. 1-2 synchronizer hub.
51. Clutch keys.
52. Key retainer.
53. Snap ring hub to shaft.
54. 3-4 shift fork.
55. Detent spring.
56. 3-4 detent cam.
57. 1-2 detent cam.
58. 3-4 shifter fork.
59. "O" ring.
60. Gasket.
61. Cover.
62. Detent cam retainer.
63. 1—2 shift fork.
64. "O" ring.
65. 1-2 shifter fork.
66. Spring.
67. Ball.
68. "O" ring.
69. Rev. shifter shaft and fork.

case, tap out front bearing and snap ring. From the front of the case press out the countershaft, then remove the countergear and both tanged washers. Remove the 112 rollers, 6.070 in. spacers and roller spacers from countergear. Remove mainshaft front snap ring and slide third and fourth speed clutch assembly, third speed gear, and synchronizing spring from front of mainshaft. Spread rear bearing retainer snap ring and press mainshaft out of the retainer. Remove the mainshaft rear snap ring. Support second speed gear and press on rear of mainshaft to remove rear bearing, first speed gear and sleeve, first speed synchronizer ring, 1-2 synchronizer clutch assembly, second speed synchronizer ring and second speed gear.

FOUR-SPEED SAGINAW TRANSMISSION

To disassemble the four-speed Saginaw fully synchronized transmission, shown in Fig. P-6, first remove side cover attaching screws and remove side cover assembly and shift forks. Remove clutch gear bearing retainer. Remove clutch gear bearing to gear stem snap ring, then re-

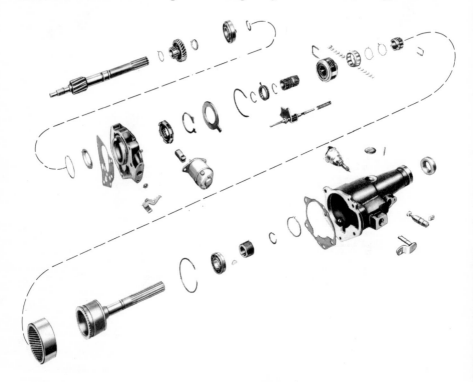

Fig. P-7. Exploded view of overdrive unit.

move clutch gear bearing by pulling outward on clutch gear until a screwdriver or other suitable tool can be inserted between bearing large snap ring and case to complete removal. The clutch gear bearing is a slip fit on the gear and into the case bore. This provides clearance for the removal of clutch gear and mainshaft assembly. Remove extension to case attaching bolts. Remove clutch gear, mainshaft and extension assembly together through the rear case opening. Using snap ring pliers, expand the snap ring in the extension which retains the mainshaft rear bearing and remove the extension. Drive the countershaft and its Woodruff key out the rear of the case. Remove the gear and the bearings.

Remove reverse idler gear stop ring. Using a long drift or punch to the front bearing case bore and drive the reverse idler shaft and Woodruff key to the rear of the case.

QUICK CHECKS ON OVERDRIVE TROUBLES

Details of a typical overdrive unit are shown in Fig. P-7, and the wiring diagram in Fig. P-8.

Troubles with the overdrive may be either mechanical or electrical. Mechanical difficulties will be discussed first.

If the unit does not drive unless locked up manually, the trouble may be caused by broken rollers in the roller clutch, sticking of the roller retainer upon the cam due to worn cam faces.

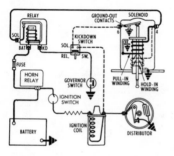

Fig. P-8. Overdrive electrical wiring diagram.

If it does not engage or lock up does not release, the dash control may be improperly connected or the transmission or overdrive improperly aligned. To test for misalignment, be sure that the transmission is not in reverse. Then disconnect the dash control wire from the lock up lever and feel the lever for free forward movement. If the lever can be moved forward more than 1/4 in. it indicates that misalignment probably exists.

If the kickdown switch is improperly adjusted, or the solenoid is improperly installed, or the blocker ring is improperly positioned, it will also result in the overdrive failing to engage or the lockup to release.

If the overdrive engages with a severe jolt or noise, the trouble may be caused by insufficient blocker ring friction.

If the unit free wheels at speeds above 30 mph, the cam roller retainer spring tension may be weak.

Failure of any of the electrical units, or defects in the electrical circuit may cause the system to fail to engage, fail to release or fail to kick down from overdrive.

1970 Chevrolet Caprice Coupe.

Transmission Service

If the system does not engage, first check the fuse and then the relay, Fig. P-8. Also make sure that the solenoid is operating. Check the kickdown switch and also the wiring between the relay and the kickdown switch. Also check the governor switch and the wiring between the kickdown and the governor switches.

If the system does not release, look for a grounded control circuit between the relay and the governor switch. Also check the relay.

If the system does not kick down from overdrive, check solenoid and make sure the wiring between the switch and coil are in good electrical condition. In addition check the kickdown switch and look for an open circuit in the wiring between the kickdown switch and the number six terminal of the solenoid, Fig. P-8.

AUTOMATIC TRANSMISSIONS

Several different types of automatic transmissions are found in Chevrolet built cars in the period covered by this book. These models include:

1955-61 Powerglide	1966-69 Turbo Hydra-Matic
1957-61 Turboglide	1969 Turbo Hydra-Matic 350
1962-68 Aluminum Powerglide	1969 Turbo Hydra-Matic 400

Because of the intricate design of the automatic transmission, major work should be left to the shop having the needed specialized equipment. However, such adjustments that are easily performed are included in this book and when necessary, the transmission can be removed from the vehicle and a factory rebuilt unit installed.

DRAIN AND REFILL INSTRUCTIONS

Starting with the 1968 models only fluid designated as Dexron automatic transmission fluid should be used. This same fluid can be used in older models, but the older type fluid Type A bearing the mark AQ-ATF followed by a number and a suffix "A" should not be used in 1968 and later models. Every 6000 miles check fluid level on dipstick with the engine idling, selector lever in neutral position, parking brakes set and the transmission at operating temperature. If the fluid level is below the full mark on the dipstick, add a small amount of automatic transmission fluid and then recheck the level. If necessary, again add a small amount of fluid as needed to bring the level to the full mark. Be careful not to overfill, as this will cause erratic action of the transmission.

Every 24,000 miles (more frequently depending upon the severity of service), if vehicle is used to pull trailers, carry heavy loads during high ambient temperatures, operate in mountainous terrain, or operate under other severe conditions, remove fluid from the transmission sump and add sufficient fluid to bring the level up to the full mark on the dipstick. Then start the engine and operate the transmission through all ranges and again check the fluid level as previously described.

Most automatic transmissions are provided with a drain plug. If none is provided, remove the lower pan to drain the fluid.

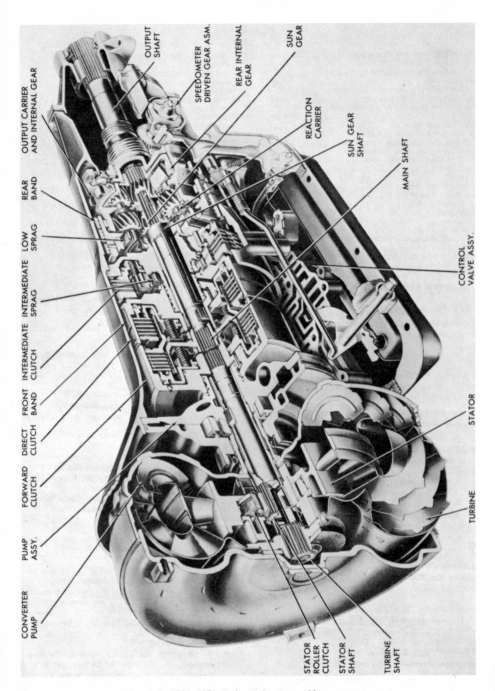

Fig. P-9. 1966–1971 Turbo Hydra-Matic 400 transmission.

Transmission Service

QUICK SERVICE ON 1966-1972 TURBO HYDRA-MATIC TRANSMISSION

The Turbo Hydra-Matic 400 transmission is a fully automatic unit consisting primarily of a three element hydraulic torque converter and a compound planetary gear set. Three multiple-disc clutches, one sprag unit, one roller clutch and two bands provide the friction elements to obtain the desired function of the planetary gear set. Fig. P-11 illustrates this transmission.

Check fluid level as indicated in other part of this chapter. Fluid level should be at the full mark with transmission at normal operating temperature. With cold fluid, the level should be approximately 1/4 in. below the "ADD" mark. Only Dexron fluid should be used.

Possible points for oil leakage are the same as those listed for the model 350 Turbo Hydra-Matic transmission.

To check vacuum diaphragm for leakage, insert a pipe cleaner into the vacuum connector pipe as far as possible and check for presence of transmission fluid. If fluid is found, the vacuum modulator should be replaced. If gasoline or water vapor is found in the modulator, the unit should not be changed. To check for atmospheric leakage, apply liquid soap to the crimped seams and the threaded screw seal. Using a short piece of rubber tubing apply air pressure to the vacuum pipe by blowing into the tube. If bubbles appear the modulator should be replaced.

External control connections to the transmission, Fig. P-9, are the manual linkage which selects the desired operating range; the engine vacuum which operates a vacuum modulator unit; and the 12V electrical signal to operate an electrical detent solenoid.

Before disconnecting any linkage, be sure that it is marked so that it can be reassembled in its original position. Also make sure that the engine vacuum line to the transmission is clear and without any leaks. Also be sure that all electrical connections are tight.

The neutral safety switch should be adjusted so that the engine will start in the park or neutral position of the transmission, but will not start in the other positions.

To replace the 1966-1970 Turbo Hydra-Matic transmission, remove the propeller shaft. Disconnect speedometer cable, electrical lead to case connector, vacuum line modulator, and oil cooler pipes.

Also, on Camaro models only, disconnect parking brake cables and remove underbody reinforcement plate on the convertible. Disconnect left exhaust pipe from manifold for clearance. On Corvette models remove both exhaust pipes.

On all models, disconnect shift control linkage. Support transmission with suitable transmission jack. Disconnect rear mount from frame cross member. Remove two bolts at each end of frame cross member (plus through bolt at inside of frame and parking brake pulley on Corvette models). Remove cross member. Remove oil cooler lines, vacuum modulator line, speedometer cable and detent solenoid connector wire at transmission.

215

Remove convertor underpan. Remove convertor to flywheel bolts. Loosen exhaust pipe to manifold bolts approximately one-quarter turn (Chevrolet and Chevelle). Lower transmission until jack is barely supporting it. Remove transmission to engine mounting bolts and remove oil filler tube at transmission. Raise transmission to its normal position, support engine with jack and slide transmission rearward from engine and lower it away from the vehicle.

The installation of the transmission is the reverse of the procedure.

Fluid leaks at the transmission oil pan may result from the attaching bolts not being correctly torqued. The pan gasket may be improperly installed or damaged, or the oil pan gasket mounting face may be uneven. Leaks at the rear extension may result from attaching bolts not being correctly torqued, the rear seal assembly may be damaged or improperly installed, the gasket seal (extension to case) may be damaged or improperly installed, or the casting may be porous.

Fluid leaks may result from a damaged "O" ring seal at the filler pipe, the modulator assembly "O" ring seal may be damaged, the governor cover gasket and bolts damaged or loose. The speedometer gear "O" ring may be damaged. The line pressure tap plug may be stripped or sealer compound missing. Parking pawl shaft cup plug may be damaged or improperly installed.

Fluid leaks at the front of the transmission may result from a damaged front seal, or the garter spring may be missing. Also pump attaching bolts and seals may be damaged, missing or loose.

If oil comes out the vent pipe, make sure the transmission has not been overfilled or there may be water in the fluid. In addition the pump to case gasket may be mispositioned or otherwise defective.

Transmission leaks caused by aluminum case porosity have been successfully repaired with the transmission in the vehicle by using the following procedure: First road test and bring the transmission to operating temperature. Raise the car, and with the engine running, locate the source of the oil leak. Check for leaks in all operating positions. The use of a mirror will be helpful in finding leaks. Shut off the engine and thoroughly clean area with a solvent and air dry. Following the instructions of the manufacturer, mix a sufficient amount of epoxy cement, which can be obtained from the Chevrolet dealer, to make the repair. While the transmission is still hot, apply the epoxy to the area, making certain that the area is fully covered. Allow the epoxy cement to dry for three hours and retest for leaks.

QUICK SERVICE ON TURBO HYDRA-MATIC 350

The Chevrolet three-speed automatic Turbo Hydra-Matic 350, Fig. P-10, is manufactured for use with engines up to 396 cu. in. displacement.

Four clutch packs and two roller clutches provide the driving force necessary for smooth operation. The direct and forward clutches have in-

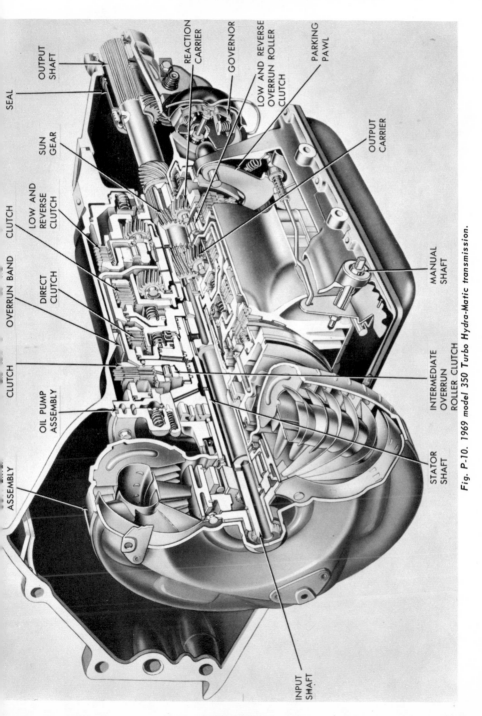

SEAL

OUTPUT SHAFT

REACTION CARRIER

GOVERNOR

LOW AND REVERSE OVERRUN ROLLER CLUTCH

PARKING PAWL

SUN GEAR

OUTPUT CARRIER

LOW AND REVERSE CLUTCH

OVERRUN BAND

DIRECT CLUTCH

CLUTCH

MANUAL SHAFT

OIL PUMP ASSEMBLY

INTERMEDIATE OVERRUN ROLLER CLUTCH

ASSEMBLY

STATOR SHAFT

INPUT SHAFT

Fig. P-10. 1969 model 350 Turbo Hydra-Matic transmission.

Fig. P-11. 1969–1972 model 400 Turbo Hydra-Matic transmission.

terchangeable parts, thereby keeping service parts to a minimum. Only one band, the intermediate overrun, is utilized with the band being internally adjusted at time of manufacture.

The output shaft contains a yoke seal to permit grease packing of the shaft lines, thereby reducing friction between the output shaft and yoke. Details of the model 350 Turbo Hydra-Matic are shown in Fig. P-10.

Possible points of oil leaks may occur at the following points: Transmission oil pan leaks resulting from attaching bolts not correctly torqued, damaged pan gasket, pan gasket mounting face not flat. Rear extension leak resulting from attaching bolts not properly torqued, rear seal assembly damaged, "O" ring in extension case damaged, porous casting. Case leak resulting from filler pipe "O" ring damaged, modulator "O" ring seal damaged, governor cover "O" ring seal damaged, speedometer gear "O" ring damaged, manual shift seal damaged. Line pressure tap plug leakage resulting from worn threads or lacking sealing compound. Detent cable "O" ring seal damaged. Front end leak resulting from damaged front seal, pump attaching bolts and seals damaged or loose, converter weld defective, pump "O" ring seal damaged. If oil comes out vent pipe, the trouble may be caused by too much fluid in transmission, water in the fluid, pump to case gasket mispositioned.

1962-1972 ALUMINUM POWERGLIDE

The aluminum Powerglide transmission, Fig. P-12, is a single case aluminum unit. When the manual control is placed in the drive position, the transmission automatically shifts to low gear for initial vehicle movement. As the car gains speed an automatic shift is made to high gear. A forced downshift feature provides a passing gear by returning the transmission to low gear.

The transmission neutral switch should be adjusted so the engine will start when the transmission is in park or neutral position, and will not start when the shift lever is in any other position.

The low band should be adjusted at 12,000 mile intervals, or sooner, if operating performance indicates low band slippage. To adjust the low band, raise the vehicle and place selector lever in neutral. Remove protective cap from transmission adjusting screw. Loosen adjusting locknut one-quarter turn, and hold in this position with a wrench. With a torque wrench, adjust band to 70 in. lb., Fig. P-13, and then back off four complete turns for a band that has been in operation for 6000 miles or more, or three turns for one in use less than 6000 miles. Be sure to hold adjusting screw lock nut at one-quarter turn loose with wrench during adjusting procedure.

Tighten the adjusting screw lock nut to 15 ft. lb. Method of making the adjustment is shown in Fig. P-13.

To remove the Powerglide transmission from the chassis, first place the car on hoist and move oil pan drain plug in order to drain oil. Discon-

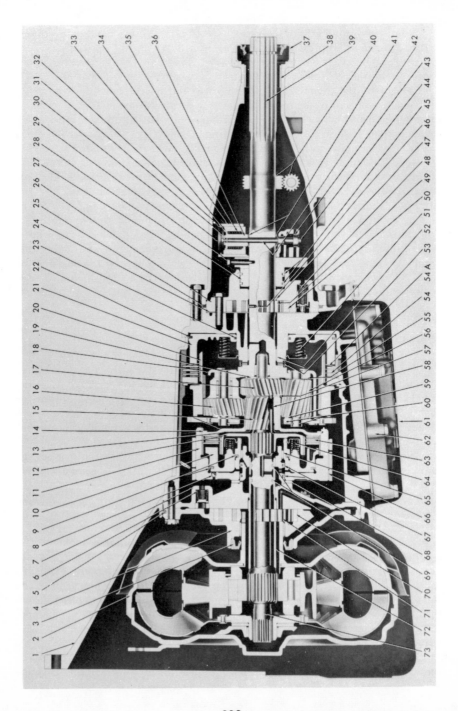

Transmission Service

Fig. P-12. 1962–1972 aluminum Powerglide transmission.

1-Transmission case.	26-Rear pump.	51-Reverse piston return springs.
2-Welded converter.	27-Extension.	52-Transmission rear case bushing.
3-Front oil pump seal assembly.	28-Governor hub.	53-Thrust bearing.
4-Front oil pump body.	29-Governor hub drive screw.	54-Reverse clutch pack.
5-Seal.	30-Governor body.	54a-Belleville spring.
6-Lube relief valve.	31-Retainer clip.	55-Thrust washer.
7-Oil pump cover.	32-Retainer ring.	56-Planet long pinion.
8-Clutch relief valve ball.	33-Retainer ring.	57-Thrust washer.
9-Seal.	34-Governor springweight.	58-Splined bushing.
10-Clutch piston.	35-Governor spring.	59-Thrust washer.
11-Clutch drum.	36-Governor weight.	60-Parking lock gear.
12-Clutch hub.	37-Oil seal.	61-Oil pan.
13-Thrust washer.	38-Extension rear bushing.	62-Valve body.
14-Clutch flange retaining ring.	39-Output shaft.	63-High clutch pack.
15-Low sun gear and clutch flange assembly.	40-Speedometer drive and driven gears.	64-Clutch piston return spring.
16-Planet short pinion.	41-Governor shaft Belleville springs.	65-Clutch drum bushing.
17-Planet input sun gear.	42-Governor shaft.	66-Low brake band.
18-Planet carrier.	43-Governor valve.	67-Seal rings.
19-Thrust washer.	44-Retaining clip.	68-Thrust washer.
20-Ring gear.	45-Seal rings.	69-Seal rings.
21-Reverse piston.	46-Drive pin.	70-Front pump driven gear.
22-Outer seal.	47-Rear pump bushing.	71-Front pump drive gear.
23-Inner seal.	48-Rear pump priming valve.	72-Stator shaft.
24-Extension seal ring.	49-Rear pump drive gear.	73-Input shaft.
25-Rear pump wear plate.	50-Rear pump driven gear.	

nect the oil cooler lines (external cooled models), vacuum modulator line and the speedometer drive fitting at the transmission. Tie the lines out of the way. Disconnect manual and throttle valve control lever rods from the transmission. Disconnect propeller shaft from transmission.

Install suitable transmission lift equipment or other lifting device and attach on transmission. Disconnect engine rear mount on transmission extension. Then disconnect the transmission support cross member and slide rearward. Remove cross member on Camaro models.

Remove convertor underpan, scribe flywheel convertor relationship for assembly, then remove the flywheel convertor attaching bolts.

Note the light side of the convertor is denoted by a blue stripe painted across the end of the convertor cover and housing. This marking should be aligned as closely as possible with a like stripe painted on the engine side of the flywheel outer rim (heavy side of engine) to maintain balance.

Support engine at the oil pan rail with a jack or other suitable brace capable of supporting the engine weight when the transmission is removed.

Fig. P-13. Adjusting low band on aluminum Powerglide transmission.

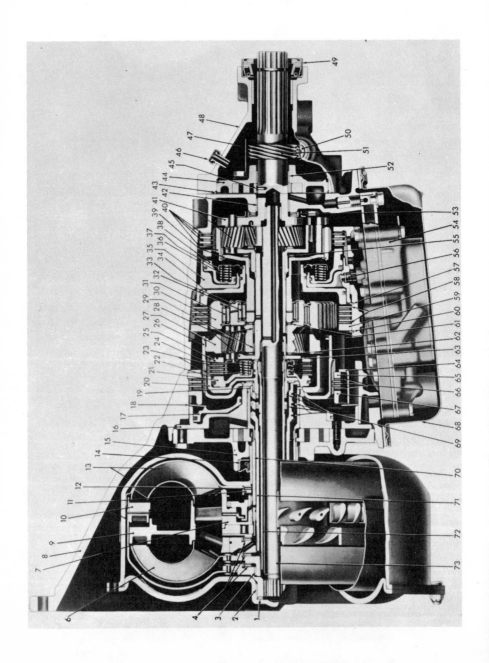

Transmission Service

Lower the rear of the transmission slightly so that the upper transmission housing to engine attaching bolts can be reached using a universal socket with long extension. Remove upper bolts.

On V-8 engines care must be taken not to lower rear of transmission too far as the distributor housing may be forced against the dash causing damage to the distributor. It is best you have an assistant observe clearance of upper engine components while the transmission rear end is being lowered.

Remove remainder of transmission housing to engine attaching bolts. Remove the transmission by moving it slightly to the rear and downward, then remove from underneath the car and transfer to workbench.

Note: Observe convertor when moving the transmission rearward. If it does not move with the transmission, pry it free of flywheel before proceeding.

1968-1969 TORQUE DRIVE TRANSMISSION

The Torque Drive transmission has been released for the Chevrolet II L4 and L6 engine, and the Camaro L6 engine. The Torque Drive transmission is a modified version of the Powerglide transmission with the automatic shifting provisions removed. Lubrication, maintenance and service information is the same as that listed for the aluminum Powerglide.

1957-1961 TURBOGLIDE TRANSMISSION

A cross section of the 1957-1961 Turboglide transmission is shown in Fig. P-14. The draining and refilling instructions for this transmission are the same as for the other automatic transmissions.

To adjust the neutral safety switch, place the gear shift lever in "N" position and loosen the screws securing the neutral safety switch retainer.

Fig. P-14. Details of 1957–1961 Turboglide transmission.

1-Bearing.
2-Converter hub bushing.
3-Bushing.
4-Caged needle bearings.
5-Converter cover.
6-Third turbine assembly.
7-Stator assembly.
8-Transmission case.
9-Second turbine assembly.
10-First turbine assembly.
11-Stator rear thrust pad.
12-Needle bearing.
13-Converter pump.
14-Oil seal.
15-Front pump assembly.
16-Front cover.
17-Reverse piston.
18-Spring.
19-Thrust washer.
20-Neutral clutch hub.
21-Neutral clutch piston.
22-Return spring.
23-Neutral clutch plates.
24-Return spring retainer.
25-Neutral clutch rear drive plate.

26-Front ring gear hub.
27-Front ring gear.
28-Front planet carrier assembly.
29-Bushings.
30-Forward clutch freewheel sprag race.
31-Outer sprag.
32-Inner sprag.
33-Front sun gear.
34-Forward piston.
35-Forward and brake piston support.
36-Return spring.
37-Spring seat.
38-Brake piston.
39-Rear ring gear.
40-Brake drive plates and reactor plates.
41-Rear planet carrier assembly.
42-Bushing.
43-Spacer.
44-Rear oil pump assembly.
45-Drive pin.
46-Vent assembly.
47-Oil deflector.
48-Extension.
49-Oil seal.
50-Speedometer driven gear.

51-Speedometer drive gear.
52-Bushing.
53-Thrust bearing.
54-Valve body assembly.
55-Needle bearing assembly.
56-Oil pressure tube.
57-Retainer ring.
58-Forward clutch drive plates and reaction plates.
59-Forward clutch pressure plate.
60-Retainer ring.
61-Needle bearing.
62-Needle bearing assembly.
63-Thrust washer.
64-Reverse clutch reaction insert.
65-Reverse rear pressure plate.
66-Reverse drive plates and reaction plates.
67-Reverse front pressure plate.
68-Oil pan.
69-Oil seal rings.
70-Stator support shaft.
71-Second turbine shaft.
72-Third turbine shaft.
73-First turbine shaft.

Then while holding the ignition switch in the start position, adjust position of switch until engine turns over. Hold switch in this position and tighten retainer screws. Engine should be cranked only when shift lever is in neutral or park positions. In case of oil leaks, the following points should be checked: Transmission oil pan gasket. Bypass valve and transmission case. Front of transmission case at flywheel. Transmission case extension and transmission case. Oil cooler pipe connections. Transmission case extension oil seal. Front pump attaching bolts.

If oil leakage shows at front of flywheel housing, remove underpan from bottom of transmission housing. Should an accumulation of oil be found in the housing, an oil leak is indicated and the following points should be checked: Seal ring between converter cover and pump assembly. Front pump seal ring. Front pump oil seal or front pump bolts.

To remove Turboglide transmission, raise car on hoist or jack stands. Remove drain plug of early production transmissions to drain oil. Remove transmission filler tube. This permits draining of oil on later transmissions without drain plugs in pan. Disconnect oil cooler lines and speedometer drive cable fitting at transmission. Tie the lines out of the way.

Remove crankcase ventilation tube clamp bracket bolt, washers and nuts from transmission. Remove vacuum modulator hose from vacuum modulator and from clamped attachment at side of transmission.

Disconnect manual and throttle valve control lever rods from transmission. Disconnect propeller shaft from transmission. Position a transmission jack under the transmission. Disconnect engine rear mount on transmission extension, then remove transmission support cross member. Note that cross member is attached to frame bracket at upper attaching holes. Use care to remove any shims which may be installed between extension mounting boss and cross member. It is vital that exactly the same number of shims be reinstalled in their respective positions as these affect the drive line angles. Remove transmission underpan, scribe flywheel converter relationship for assembly, then using a jumper to turn the engine, remove the flywheel to converter attaching bolts.

The "light" side of the converter is denoted by a blue stripe painted across the end of the converter cover and housing. This marking should be aligned as closely as possible with the white stripe painted on engine side of flywheel outer rim to maintain balance during assembly.

Lower the rear of transmission slightly, so that the three upper transmission housing-to-engine attaching bolts can be reached using a universal socket and long extension. Remove the upper bolts. Care must be taken not to lower rear of transmission too far as the distributor housing may be forced against the dash causing damage to distributor.

Support the engine at the oil pan rail with a jack capable of supporting the engine weight when the transmission is removed. Remove remainder of transmission housing to engine attaching bolts.

Remove transmission by moving it slightly to the rear and downward, then remove from beneath car and transfer to workbench. CAUTION: Keep front of transmission upward to prevent the converter from falling out.

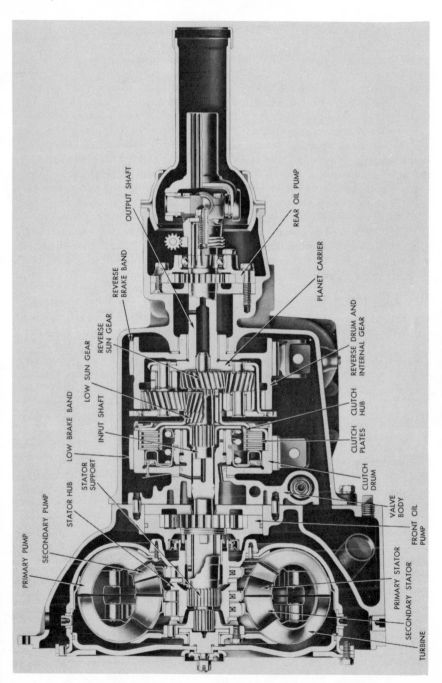

Fig. P-15. 1955–1961 Powerglide transmission.

1955-1961 POWERGLIDE TRANSMISSION

A sectional view of the 1955-1961 Powerglide transmission is shown in Fig. P-15.

The neutral safety switch is adjusted in the same manner as that described for the 1957-1961 Turboglide transmission.

In case of oil leakage, check the following points: Transmission housing side cover. Low drive valve body and transmission case. Servo cover and transmission case. Transmission housing and transmission case. Front of flywheel housing. Transmission case extension and transmission case. Oil cooler pipe connections. Transmission case extension oil seal. Make sure that the diaphragm in the vacuum modulator assembly has not ruptured, allowing manifold vacuum to pull transmission oil into the intake manifold. This will be evidenced by a very smoky exhaust. If oil leakage shows at front of the flywheel housing, remove plug from bottom of transmission housing. Should an accumulation of oil be found in the housing, an oil leak is indicated, and the following points should be checked: "O" ring seal between converter cover and pump assembly. Front pump "O" ring seal. Front pump oil seal. Oil drain in front pump plugged.

To remove the Powerglide transmission, raise the vehicle on jack stands and remove drain plug to drain oil. Remove transmission filler pipe. Disconnect the oil cooler lines, vacuum modulator hose, and speedometer drive cable fitting at the transmission. Tie the lines out of the way. Disconnect body ground strap. Disconnect manual and throttle valve control lever rods from the transmission. Disconnect propeller shaft from transmission. Install suitable transmission jack under the transmission. Disconnect engine rear mount on transmission extension then remove the transmission support cross member. Make careful note of the number and position of shims between the extension mounting boss and the cross member. It is vital that exactly the same number of shims be reinstalled. Remove flywheel cover, then using a jumper to turn the engine, remove the flywheel to converter attaching bolts. Lower the rear of the transmission slightly so that the three upper transmission housing to engine attaching bolts can be reached, using a universal socket and approximately a 39 in. extension. Remove the upper bolts.

Care should be taken not to lower the rear of the transmission too far as the distributor housing may be forced against the dash causing damage to the distributor. Support the engine at the oil pan rail with a suitable brace capable of supporting the engine weight when the transmission is removed. Remove remainder of transmission housing to engine attaching bolts.

Remove the transmission by moving slightly to the rear and downward, then remove transmission from beneath the vehicle and transfer to a work bench.

Be careful not to tip the front of the transmission downward as converter would fall out of transmission.

SYNCHROMESH TRANSMISSION TROUBLE SHOOTING

CAUSE	CORRECTION

SLIPS OUT OF HIGH GEAR

a. Transmission loose on clutch housing.
b. Dirt between transmission case and clutch housing.
c. Misalignment of transmission.

d. Clutch gear bearing retainer broken or loose.
e. Damaged mainshaft pilot bearing.
f. Shifter lock spring weak.
g. Clutch gear or second and third speed clutch improperly mated.

a. Tighten mounting bolts.
b. Clean mating surfaces.
c. Shim between transmission case and clutch housing.
d. Tighten or replace clutch gear bearing retainer.
e. Replace pilot bearing.
f. Replace spring.
g. Replace clutch gear and second and third speed clutch.

SLIPS OUT OF LOW AND/OR REVERSE

a. Worn first and reverse sliding gear.
b. Worn countergear bushings.
c. Worn reverse idler gear.
d. Shifter lock spring weak or broken.
e. Improperly adjusted linkage.

a. Replace worn gear.
b. Replace countergear.
c. Replace idler gear.
d. Replace spring.

e. Adjust linkage.

NOISY IN ALL GEARS

a. Insufficient lubricant.
b. Worn countergear bushings.
c. Worn or damaged clutch gear and countershaft drive gear.
d. Damaged clutch gear or mainshaft ball bearings.
e. Damaged speedometer gears.

a. Fill to correct level.
b. Replace countergear.
c. Replace worn or damaged gears.
d. Replace damaged bearings.
e. Replace damaged gears.

NOISY IN HIGH GEAR

a. Damaged clutch gear bearing.
b. Damaged mainshaft bearing.
c. Damaged speedometer gears.

a. Replace damaged bearing.
b. Replace damaged bearing.
c. Replace speedometer gears.

NOISY IN NEUTRAL WITH ENGINE RUNNING

a. Damaged clutch gear bearing.   a. Replace damaged bearing.
b. Damaged mainshaft pilot bearing.   b. Replace damaged bearing.

NOISY IN ALL REDUCTION GEARS

a. Insufficient lubricant.   a. Fill to correct level.
b. Worn or damaged clutch gear or counter drive gear.   b. Replace faulty or damaged gears.

TRANSMISSION SERVICING

TROUBLE	CORRECTION

NOISY IN SECOND ONLY

a. Damaged or worn second speed constant mesh gears.   a. Replace damaged gears.
b. Worn or shifted countergear rear bushing.   b. Replace countergear assembly.

NOISY IN LOW AND REVERSE ONLY

a. Worn or damaged first and reverse sliding gear.   a. Replace worn gear.
b. Damaged or worn low and reverse countergear.   b. Replace countergear assembly.

NOISY IN REVERSE ONLY

a. Worn or damaged reverse idler.   a. Replace reverse idler.
b. Worn reverse idler bushings.   b. Replace reverse idler.
c. Damaged or worn reverse countergear.   c. Replace countergear assembly.

EXCESSIVE BACKLASH IN SECOND ONLY

a. Second speed gear thrust-washer worn.   a. Replace thrustwasher.
b. Mainshaft rear bearing not properly installed in case.   b. Replace bearing, lock or case as necessary.
c. Universal joint retaining bolt loose.   c. Tighten bolt.
d. Worn countergear rear bushing.   d. Replace countergear assembly.

EXCESSIVE BACKLASH IN ALL REDUCTION GEARS

a. Worn countergear bushings.
b. Excessive end play in counter-gear.

a. Replace countergear.
b. Replace countergear thrustwashers.

LEAKS LUBRICANT

a. Excessive amount of lubricant in transmission.
b. Loose or broken clutch gear bearing retainer.
c. Clutch gear bearing retainer gasket damaged.
d. Cover loose or gasket damaged.
e. Operating shaft seal leaks.

f. Idler shaft expansion plugs loose.
g. Countershaft loose in case.

a. Drain to correct level.

b. Tighten or replace retainer.

c. Replace gasket.

d. Tighten cover or replace gasket.
e. Replace operating shaft seal.
f. Replace expansion plugs.

g. Replace case.

POWERGLIDE TROUBLE SHOOTING

OIL BEING FORCED OUT OF FILLER TUBE

a. Oil level too high, aeration and foaming caused by planet carrier running in oil.

b. Split in suction pipe permitting aeration of oil.

c. Damaged suction pipe seal permitting aeration of oil.

d. Ears on suction pipe retainer bent, thereby preventing proper compression of the suction pipe seal, permitting aeration of oil.

e. Bore for suction pipe in housing too deep, thereby preventing proper compression of suction pipe seal, permitting aeration of oil.

f. Sand hole in suction bore in transmission housing or case, permitting aeration of oil.
g. Sand hole in suction cavity in valve body permitting aeration of oil.

POWERGLIDE TROUBLE SHOOTING

Difficulty in shifting from drive to low, and from low to high can be caused by an improperly drilled high clutch feed orifice in the valve body.

This causes slow application of the clutch. Condition can be diagnosed by connecting pressure gauges to low servo apply, and the release side of low servo.

Slipping and chatter in the low range can be caused by a poor ring fit on the low servo piston. Condition can be checked by connecting pressure gauges to the low servo apply, and the release side of low servo test points. With the selector lever in low range and the brakes set, accelerate the engine to stall speed and if everything is normal, low servo apply gauge should register 160 to 200 lb. and the high clutch gauge should register zero.

In case of high clutch failures, the transmission should be checked carefully, both before and after disassembly. With pressure gauges connected to low servo apply, high clutch and reverse servo test points check the following: 1. With selector in drive, check for slow build up of pressure on high clutch gauge. Slow pressure build up would indicate restriction in high clutch apply orifice. 2. With selector lever in low, check pressure on high clutch gauge. If any pressure is indicated, leakage past the low servo piston ring is indicated. 3. With selector lever in reverse, check pressure on high clutch gauge. If any pressure is indicated, there is probably leakage between the converter out and low servo release channels in the valve body, or a damaged housing-to-valve body gasket. The valve body should be carefully checked for porosity, or sand holes, or a damaged gasket between the transmission housing and the valve body.

If the transmission cannot be shifted into reverse with the engine running, but can be shifted into reverse with the engine stopped, the probable cause is that the accumulator snap ring is out of place.

TURBOGLIDE TROUBLE SHOOTING

TROUBLE	CAUSE
a. No drive in any selector position.	a. Front pump assembled backward.
b. Drive in Grade Retard only.	b. Both overrun clutches assembled backward.
c. Drive in Grade Retard and Reverse only.	c. Outer overrun clutch assembled backward. Leakage in forward clutch hydraulic circuit.
d. No reverse. Poor low speed, Grade Retard normal.	d. Inner overrun clutch assembled backward.
e. Creeps in neutral.	e. Neutral clutch not released.
f. Normal neutral and drive, no reverse.	f. Forward clutch not released.
g. Unable to push start.	g. Rear oil pump drive pin broken.

h. Clutch slippage on fast starts.

h. Low oil pressure due to leakage. Mechanical interference preventing application of forward or neutral piston. Check clutch facings.

i. No Grade Retard. No Drive. Reverse normal.

i. Reverse clutch not disengaged.

j. Shifts from standstill fast and harsh.

j. Accumulator control valve spring too strong or valve stuck open.

k. Grade Retard brakes violently.

k. Vacuum hose disconnected. Pressure in Grade Retard position should be 55-65 psi at 18 - 26 in. vacuum.

l. Grade Retard slow to apply.

l. Control linkage out of adjustment. Leakage to Grade Retard clutch. Mechanical interference of Grade Retard piston. Glazed retard plates.

1969 line of Chevrolet cars, from top: Camaro RS Convertible, Chevelle SS 396 Sport Coupe, Chevy Nova Coupe, and Impala Custom Coupe.

PROPELLER SHAFT, UNIVERSAL JOINTS

Propeller shaft and universal joint design on Chevrolet cars has been changed several times during the past few years. From 1955 to 1957 a single propeller shaft with two universal joints was used. From 1958 to 1964 a two-piece propeller shaft with three universal joints was standard, and from 1965 to date, a single shaft with two universal joints was used on all models. The two joints used currently are lubricated for life.

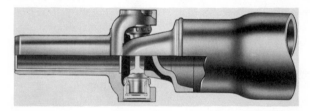

Fig. Q-1. Typical Chevrolet propeller shaft and universal joint.

1965-1972 UNIVERSAL JOINTS AND SHAFT

Fig. Q-1 is typical of the universal joints used in this period. To remove the propeller shaft (Dana) first raise the vehicle and mark relationship of shaft to companion flange and disconnect the rear universal joint by removing the trunnion bearing U-bolts, Fig. Q-2. Tape bearing cups to trunnion to prevent dropping or loss or roller bearings. On Corvette models, remove trunnion U-bolts at transmission yoke also.

Withdraw propeller shaft front yoke from transmission by moving shaft rearward, passing it under the axle housing. Watch for oil leakage from transmission output shaft housing. When reassembling these joints, repack the bearings and lubricate reservoir at end of trunnions with high melting point wheel bearing lubricant and replace the dust seals.

Remove bearing lock rings from the trunnion yoke. Support trunnion yoke on a piece of 1-1/4 in. pipe on an arbor bed. Due to the length of the propeller shaft, it may be more convenient to use a bench vise, for removal and installation, instead of an arbor press. In this case, proceed with disassembly and assembly procedure as with an arbor press.

Using a suitable socket or rod, press trunnion down far enough to drive

233

bearing cup from yoke, Fig. Q-3. Remove dust seals from trunnion, clean and inspect bearing rollers and trunnion. Relubricate bearings with a lithium base chassis lubricant. Make sure reservoir at end of each trunnion is completely filled with lubricant.

Place new dust seals on trunnions and press seal into position. Installation of seal is critical to proper sealing. Special tools are available for installation which prevents seal distortion and assures proper seating of seal.

Partly install one bearing cup into yoke. Place trunnion in yoke and into bearing cup. Install other bearing cup and press both bearing cups into yoke, being careful to keep trunnion aligned in bearing cups. Press bearing cups far enough to install lock rings and install lock rings.

When installing the propeller shaft, make sure it is aligned with companion flange, using reference marks established before the shaft was removed.

To remove the Saginaw propeller shaft, first raise the vehicle sufficiently to permit access to propeller shaft and mark relationship of rear yoke to companion flange. Remove trunnion bearing retaining strap attaching screws from both bearings, Fig. Q-2. Lower rear of propeller shaft, being careful not to dislodge bearing caps from trunnion, and tape bearing caps to trunnion. Withdraw propeller shaft front yoke from transmission by moving shaft rearward, passing it under the axle housing. Watch for oil leakage from transmission output shaft housing.

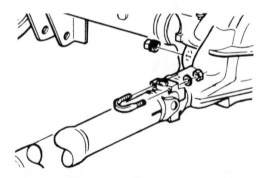

Fig. Q-2. Removing propeller shaft strap and U-bolt.

Because of the elastic properties of the nylon retainers, trunnions must be pressed from the yokes. Pressing the trunnions from the yokes will shear retainers which render the bearing caps unsuitable for reuse. A service kit which employs a snap ring to retain the trunnion must be used when reassembling the propeller shaft.

Remove trunnion at differential end of propeller shaft, using the following procedure: Support trunnion on a press bed so that the propeller shaft yoke can be moved downward. Support front of propeller shaft so that the shaft is in a horizontal position.

Propeller Shaft, Universal Joints

Using a piece of pipe, with an inside diameter slightly larger than 1-1/8 in., press bearing from yoke. Apply force on yoke around bearing until nylon retainer breaks. Continue to apply force until the downward movement of the yoke forces the bearing as far as possible from the yoke.

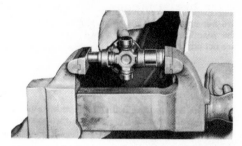

Fig. Q-3. Using bench vise and socket to disassemble a universal joint.

Complete removal of bearing by tapping around the circumference of exposed portion with a small hammer. Rotate propeller shaft so that the opposite bearing may be removed in the same manner. Then remove trunnion from yoke.

1958 TO 1964 UNIVERSAL JOINTS AND SHAFT

To remove the 1958 to 1964 Chevrolet propeller shaft and universal joints, first remove the two bolts attaching center bearing support to frame X-member. Then split the rear universal joint by removing trunnion bearing U-clamps. Tape bearings to keep them from becoming damaged. Remove the propeller shaft and bearing assembly by moving it rearward and to the left passing under the axle housing.

On these models with three universal joints, the angles of the respective shafts are critical and must be checked when any part, such as rear

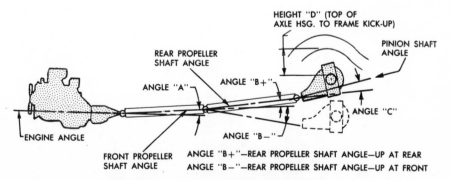

Fig. Q-4. Illustrating propeller shaft angularity.

axle, engine, springs or control arms are removed. Removal of such parts could alter the angle of the propeller shaft and cause severe vibration. These drive line angles are illustrated in Fig. Q-4, and are measured in relation to horizontal or level plane by means of a protractor with a bubble-type spirit level. A positive or negative angle is determined when the imaginary center line of the propeller shaft is above or below the center line of the following section. Angle A is normally positive, that is the engine-transmission center line is down at the rear with relation to the front propeller shaft center line. Angle B is normally negative and angle C is normally positive. The specifications for these angles are as follows:

	Angle A	Angle B	Angle C	Height D
1965 - 1959	2 3/4 deg.	-1 1/4 deg.	3 deg.	6 1/4 in.
1958	2 3/4 deg.	-1 1/4 deg.	2 3/4.deg.	6 3/4 in.

To avoid a lot of work, check the effective angles before removing parts of the engine, rear axle, control arms, rear springs, universal joints driveshaft center bearing and engine mounts. Then, on reassembly, be sure to reinstall the part in exactly the same as its original position.

TROUBLE SHOOTING

EXCESSIVE VIBRATION

Incorrect drive line angles. Worn universal joints. Bent propeller shaft. Universal joint yoke bearings worn. Run-out of pinion flange. Out-of-balance propeller shaft.

EXCESSIVE BACKLASH

Worn universal joints. Worn drive shaft or joint spline. Also check adjustment of rear axle pinion and ring gear.

Shortcuts on
REAR AXLE SERVICE

Details of the rear axle assemblies used in the Chevrolet, Chevelle, Chevy II, Camaro and Corvette cars are shown in Fig. R-1, Fig. R-2, Fig. R-3 and Fig. R-4. Without specialized equipment it is not advisable to overhaul a rear axle as a high degree of precision is required. However, details of replacing a rear axle shaft and removal of the complete rear axle assembly are provided.

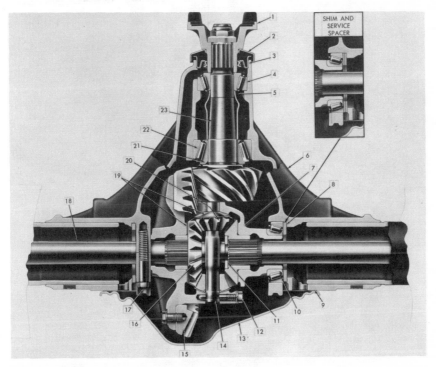

Fig. R-1. Details of rear axle used on 1965 to 1972 Chevrolet, Chevy II, Camaro, Monte Carlo, Nova and Vega. On late model Chevrolet and Camaro axles a longer pinion bearing spacer is used.

1-Companion flange.	7-Differential case.	13-Cover.	19-Thrust washer.
2-Deflector.	8-Shim.	14-Pinion shaft	20-Differential pinion.
3-Pinion oil seal.	9-Gasket.	15-Ring gear.	21-Shim.
4-Pinion front bearing.	10-Differential bearing.	16-Side gear.	22-Pinion rear bearing.
5-Pinion bearing spacer.	11-"C" lock.	17-Bearing cap.	23-Drive pinion.
6-Differential carrier.	12-Pinion shaft lock bolt.	18-Axle shaft.	

REPLACING THE AXLE SHAFT

Removing rear axle shaft on the 1965 to 1971 Chevrolet, Chevelle, Chevy II, Nova, and Camaro cars, and the 1964 Chevelle and Chevy II is not difficult, and the procedure is as follows:

Raise the vehicle to desired working height and remove wheel and tire assembly and brake drum. Clean all dirt from area of carrier cover. Drain lubricant from carrier by removing cover. Remove the differential pinion shaft lock screw, Fig. R-1, and the differential pinion shaft. Push end of axle shaft toward center of vehicle and remove the "C" lock, Fig.

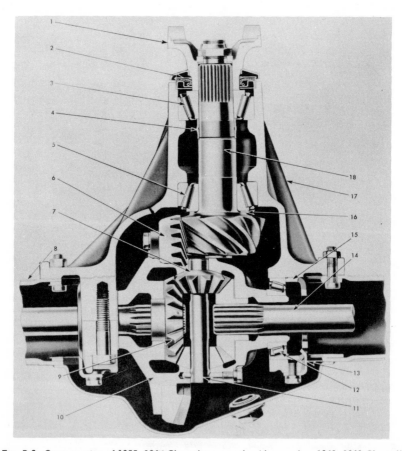

Fig. R-2. Cross section of 1955–1964 Chevrolet rear axle. Also used on 1962–1963 Chevy II.

1-Pinion drive flange.	7-Differential pinion.	13-Differential side bearing.
2-Oil seal.	8-Axle housing.	14-Adjusting sleeve lock.
3-Front pinion bearing.	9-Differential side gear.	15-Axle shaft.
4-Pinion bearing spacer.	10-Differential side gear thrust washer.	16-Adjusting sleeve.
5-Pinion rear bearing.	11-Differential case.	17-Pinion shim.
6-Ring gear.	12-Differential pinion shaft.	18-Carrier.

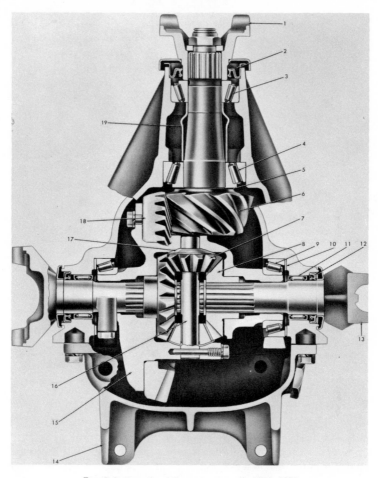

Fig. R-3. Details of Corvette rear axle 1966–1972.

1-Companion flange.
2-Pinion seal.
3-Front pinion bearing.
4-Rear pinion bearing.
5-Pinion shim.
6-Pinion.
7-Differential pinion.

8-Differential side gear.
9-Differential bearing.
10-Differential bearing shim.
11-Yoke bearing.
12-Yoke bearing seal.
13-Side gear yoke.
14-Carrier cover.

15-Differential case.
16-Differential pinion shaft.
17-Thrust washer.
18-Ring gear.
19-Pinion bearing spacer.

R-1, from the button end of the shaft. The axle shaft can now be pulled from the housing. However, be careful not to damage the oil seal.

To remove the rear axle shaft from the 1955-1964 Chevrolet, 1962-1963 Chevy II, 1959-1962 Corvette, Fig. R-2, the procedure is as follows: After removing the brake drum, remove the four nuts and lock washers from bearing retaining bolts on inside of axle flange. Attach a slide type puller to the axle flange, Fig. R-5, and remove the axle shaft and bearing

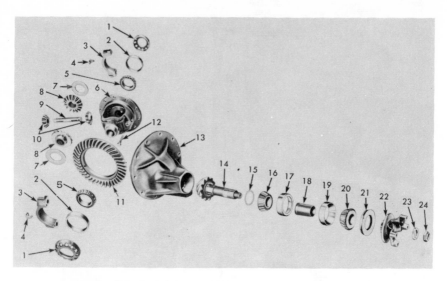

Fig. R-4. Exploded view of 1964 and earlier Chevrolet rear axle.

1-Differential bearing adjusting nut.
2-Differential bearing outer race.
3-Differential bearing caps.
4-Adjusting lock nut.
5-Differential bearing cone and roller assembly.
6-Differential case.
7-Thrust washer.
8-Differential side gear.
9-Pinion gear shaft.
10-Differential pinion gear.
11-Ring gear.
12-Pinion gear shaft lock.

13-Differential carrier.
14-Drive pinion gear.
15-Pinion depth adjusting shim.
16-Pinion rear bearing cone and roller assembly.
17-Pinion rear bearing outer race.
18-Pinion bearing spacer.
19-Pinion front bearing outer race.
20-Pinion front bearing cone and roller assembly.
21-Companion flange oil seal.
22-Companion flange.
23-Special washer.
24-Self locking nut.

assembly. If bearing retainer and parking brake interfere, raise strut slightly with a screwdriver to obtain clearance. Install bolt and nut to hold brake back in position on axle housing. Always install new oil seals after the rear axle shaft has been removed or when the oil leaks from the axle shaft onto the brakes.

Corvette 1966-1969, Fig. R-3: Disconnect inboard drive shaft trunnion from side of yoke. Bend bolt lock tabs down and remove the four bolts fastening shaft flange to spindle drive flange. Pry drive shaft out of outboard drive flange pinion and remove by withdrawing outboard end first.

OIL SEAL AND/OR BEARING REPLACEMENT

The oil seal as installed in the axle shown in Fig. R-1 can be removed by using the button end of the axle shaft. Insert the button end of the shaft into the steel case of the oil seal, then pry seal out of the bore, being careful not to damage the housing. The bearing can be removed by means of a slide hammer. When installing a bearing, first lubricate it thoroughly with wheel bearing lubricant, and press it into position until it bottoms against the shoulder in the axle housing. Pack cavity between the seal lips with a high melting point wheel bearing lubricant and tape the seal into place so that it bottoms against the bearing. Use a round piece of tubing of suitable diameter to tap seal into position.

In the case of the axle shown in Fig. R-2, the bearings are pressed on the shaft and a suitable press is required to remove the bearings from the shaft.

REMOVING REAR AXLE ASSEMBLY

On 1964-1970 models, raise the vehicle to a height that will permit axle assembly to hang freely and position supports under side rails. Disconnect brake lines at backing plates. Remove the brake hose and line from carrier cover. Loosen parking brake equalizer and remove brake cable. Disconnect rear universal joint and wire propeller shaft to side rail. Support axle

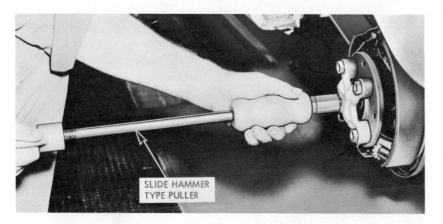

SLIDE HAMMER
TYPE PULLER

Fig. R-5. Removing rear axle shaft using a slide or impact type puller.

assembly with a jack. On Chevrolet and Chevelle models, loosen upper and lower control arm attaching bolts at axle housing. On Chevrolet, disconnect the tie rod and axle. Disconnect shock absorbers. On Chevrolet and Chevelle, lower axle assembly until suspension reaches end of travel. Then disconnect spring retainer, Chevrolet only, and withdraw springs from vehicle. On Chevy II and Camaro, remove four nuts securing lower spring seat to axle housing, then remove spring eye attaching bracket and swing spring to rear. On Chevrolet and Chevelle, disconnect control arm at axle housing and lower axle assembly.

To remove rear axle assembly on earlier models, raise vehicle and support with jack stands under the frame side rails. Remove the rear wheels. Remove the two trunnion bearing U-bolts from the rear yoke, Fig. Q-2, and split rear universal joint. Tape the bearings to the trunnion. Dis-

1968 line of Chevrolet cars. Reading from top to bottom: Chevrolet Impala 4-door Sedan; Chevrolet Caprice Coupe; Chevelle SS 396 Sport Coupe; Camaro Rally Sport Coupe; Chevy II Nova Coupe; Corvette Sport Coupe.

connect brake cable. Disconnect hydraulic brake lines at rear axle housing. Disconnect shock absorbers. Support rear axle assembly with hydraulic jacks on Chevrolet cars from 1958 to 1963. Remove rear suspension upper and lower control arms and tie rod. On 1957 and earlier Chevrolet cars, remove spring U-bolts.

On Chevy II, remove four nuts fastening lower spring seat to axle housing. Remove spring front eyebolts. Lower spring and swing back. The axle assembly can then be lowered to the floor.

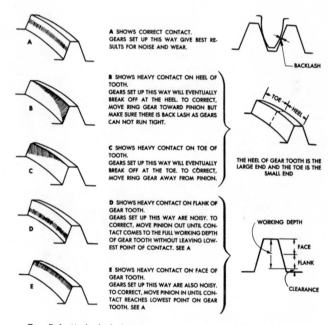

A SHOWS CORRECT CONTACT. GEARS SET UP THIS WAY GIVE BEST RESULTS FOR NOISE AND WEAR.

B SHOWS HEAVY CONTACT ON HEEL OF TOOTH. GEARS SET UP THIS WAY WILL EVENTUALLY BREAK OFF AT THE HEEL. TO CORRECT, MOVE RING GEAR TOWARD PINION BUT MAKE SURE THERE IS BACK LASH AS GEARS CAN NOT RUN TIGHT.

C SHOWS HEAVY CONTACT ON TOE OF TOOTH. GEARS SET UP THIS WAY WILL EVENTUALLY BREAK OFF AT THE TOE. TO CORRECT, MOVE RING GEAR AWAY FROM PINION.

D SHOWS HEAVY CONTACT ON FLANK OF GEAR TOOTH. GEARS SET UP THIS WAY ARE NOISY. TO CORRECT, MOVE PINION OUT UNTIL CONTACT COMES TO THE FULL WORKING DEPTH OF GEAR TOOTH WITHOUT LEAVING LOWEST POINT OF CONTACT. SEE A

E SHOWS HEAVY CONTACT ON FACE OF GEAR TOOTH. GEARS SET UP THIS WAY ARE ALSO NOISY. TO CORRECT, MOVE PINION IN UNTIL CONTACT REACHES LOWEST POINT ON GEAR TOOTH. SEE A

BACKLASH

TOE — HEEL

THE HEEL OF GEAR TOOTH IS THE LARGE END AND THE TOE IS THE SMALL END

WORKING DEPTH

FACE

FLANK

CLEARANCE

Fig. R-6. Method of obtaining correct mesh of pinion and ring gear.

OVERHAULING REAR AXLE ASSEMBLY

Special gauges and tools should be used to overhaul the differential assembly and rear axle assembly properly. Unless such equipment is available, a noisy rear axle will likely result. Without such equipment it becomes necessary to adjust the mesh of pinion and ring gear by noting the tooth contact, Fig. R-6.

Without specialized equipment an approximation of the correct pinion and ring gear mesh is obtained as follows:

First raise the rear of the car on jacks. Drain and thoroughly clean the lubricant from the gears. After the pinion and ring gears have been wiped clean, paint the ring gear teeth lightly and evenly with red lead or Prussian blue. With the parking brake applied, run the engine slowly with the transmission in first gear and then in reverse. Stop the engine and observe the marks on the gear teeth and compare them, as shown in Fig. R-6. Readjust as indicated and repeat the check with red lead until the desired tooth contact is obtained.

In case of oil leakage at the companion flange nut, pack cavity between high point pinion shaft, pinion flange and pinion washer with sealant. Rear axle oil level should be checked periodically and maintained at the level of the filler plug.

Fig. R-7. Details of Positraction rear axle (Eaton).

1-Ring gear-to-case bolt.	6-Shims.	11-Spring retainer.
2-Differential case.	7-Clutch pack guide.	12-Pinion thrust washer.
3-Side bearing.	8-Clutch disc.	13-Pinion gear.
4-Pinion lock screw.	9-Clutch plates.	14-Pinion shaft.
5-Ring gear.	10-Side gear.	15-Preload spring.

POSITRACTION DIFFERENTIAL

There are two types of Positraction differentials used on Chevrolet built cars, one manufactured by Eaton and the other by Dana.

The purpose of this unit is to divide torque equally between both driving wheels under all road surface conditions, thereby eliminating a major amount of one-wheel slip and affording better traction.

The optionally available Positraction differential unit is installed in the conventional carrier to replace the standard differential unit.

Rear Axle Service

Overhaul procedures for the Positraction equipped axle are for the most part the same as on a conventional axle.

Differential chatter on this device usually results from the use of incorrect lubricant. In some cases the slightest bit of incorrect lubricant is enough to cause considerable chatter. Chevrolet emphasizes the importance of using only lubricants which are specified for the Positraction unit.

Under some operating conditions, where one wheel is on excessively slippery surface, it may be necessary to apply the parking brake slightly to produce enough resistance to the spinning wheel to cause axle lockup.

As a safety precaution, always have both rear wheels jacked up if the engine is to be operated. If only one wheel is jacked up the car will move when the engine is operating and the transmission is engaged.

TROUBLE SHOOTING

EXCESSIVE BACKLASH

Loose wheel bolts. Worn universal joint. Loose propeller shaft to pinion splines. Incorrect ring gear and pinion adjustment. Worn differential gears or case. Worn axle shaft with differential gear splines.

CLUNKING NOISE ON TURNS

Excessive end play in axle shafts.

AXLE NOISE ON DRIVE

Ring gear and pinion adjustment too tight. Pinion bearings rough.

AXLE NOISE ON COAST

Ring gear and pinion adjustment too loose. Pinion bearings rough.

AXLE NOISE ON BOTH DRIVE AND COAST

Pinion bearings rough. Loose or defective differential side bearings. Damaged axle shaft bearing. Worn universal joint. Badly worn pinion and ring gear teeth. Pinion too deep in ring gear. Loose or worn wheel bearings.

AXLE LUBRICANT LEAKS

Axle shaft bearing seals leaking. Pinion shaft oil seal leaking. Differential carrier to housing gasket leaking.

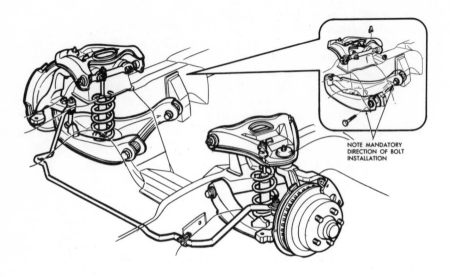

NOTE MANDATORY
DIRECTION OF BOLT
INSTALLATION

*Details of 1971 Chevrolet front suspension. 1972 is similar
except for construction changes in control arm bushings.*

SHOCK ABSORBERS AND
SPRING SERVICE

In order to maintain a comfortable ride, shock absorbers must be re-placed as soon as they no longer control spring rebound. In addition, worn shock absorbers will result in more rapid tire wear, as the wheels will spin when the rebound is not controlled. Of even greater importance is the fact that worn shock absorbers are dangerous, as it is extremely difficult to control a car that is bouncing up and down. Shock absorbers are not re-

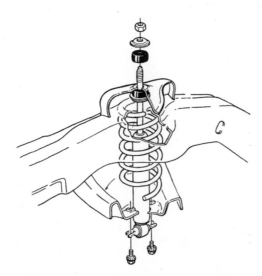

Fig. S-1. Typical front shock absorber installation, all cars except 1962–1967 Chevy II.

paired when they no longer control rebound of the car, instead the com-plete unit is replaced. So that rebound control is the same on both sides of the car, shock absorbers should always be replaced in pairs.

To determine whether shock absorber replacement is necessary, grasp the bumper of the vehicle and jounce it up and down. If the car continues to jounce up and down after releasing the bumper, the shock absorbers should be replaced.

CHEVROLET, CHEVELLE, CAMARO, NOVA, CORVETTE AND 1968 to 1971 CHEVY II

To remove the front shock absorbers, Fig. S-1, hold the upper stem from turning with a 1/4 in. wrench. Remove upper stem retaining nut and lock washer. Next remove two bolts holding shock absorber lower pivot to lower control arm and pull shock absorber assembly and mounting out from the bottom. To install the shock absorbers on the Chevrolet, Chevelle, Camaro, Nova, Corvette and Chevy II, place the retainer and rubber grommet in place over the upper stem. Install the shock absorber fully extended up to the lower control arm and spring so that the upper stem passes through the mounting hole in the upper support arm. Install the rubber grommet, retainer and attaching nut over the shock absorber upper stem. With an open-end wrench, hold the upper stem from turning and tighten the retaining nut. Install the two bolts attaching the shock absorber lower pivot to the lower control arm and tighten.

To remove the rear shock absorber on the Chevrolet and Chevelle, raise the rear of the vehicle and support the rear axle assembly. If equipped with superlift shock absorber, disconnect air line from shock absorber. Disconnect shock absorber at upper mounting bracket by removing the two retaining bolts, Fig. S-2. Disconnect shock absorber at lower attaching bracket and remove the shock absorber.

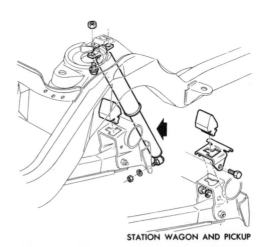

STATION WAGON AND PICKUP

Fig. S-2. Shock absorber mounting. (Typical)

To remove the rear shock absorbers from Camaro and Nova cars, raise the vehicle and support axle housing with adjustable jack. Then disconnect the shock absorber at the lower end and then disconnect it at the upper end and withdraw the shock absorber.

CHEVY II 1962-1967

To remove the front shock absorbers on the 1962-1967 Chevy II, Fig. S-3, first place a block between upper control arm and frame side rail. Then raise the vehicle and remove tire and wheel assembly. Disconnect lower shock absorber mounting from lower spring seat. Remove shock absorber and upper mounting bracket bolts, Fig. S-3. Lift shock absorber assembly from the vehicle.

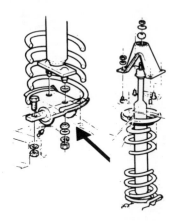

Fig. S-3. Front shock absorber mounting on 1962–1967 Chevy II.

To install the front shock absorber, assemble upper washer and rubber bushing to shock absorber rod, Fig. S-3. Assemble upper mounting bushing washer and nut to rod. Install rubber washers to shock absorber lower seat studs and insert shock absorber and upper bracket assembly to shock

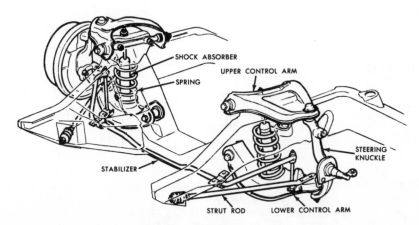

Fig. S-4. Chevrolet and 1970 Monte Carlo front suspension.

249

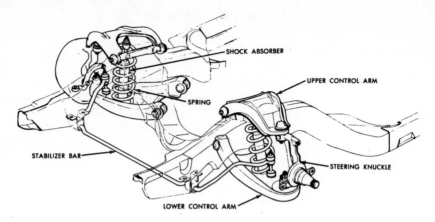

Fig. S-5. Front suspension on 1968–1972 Chevy II, 1964–1972 Chevelle, 1962–1964 Chevrolet.

absorber access hole and position to the lower spring seat. Install washers and nuts.

To remove the rear shock absorbers from a Chevy II 1962-1967, raise the vehicle and support the axle housing with adjustable jack stand. Loosen and remove shock absorber lower mounting bolt from shock absorber eye. Remove shock absorber upper mounting bracket bolts and withdraw shock absorber and brackets. Replacement is accomplished by reversing the procedure.

SPRING SERVICE

Several different types of front suspension systems are used on Chevrolet built cars. These are illustrated in Figs. S-4, S-5, S-6, and S-7.

The rear suspension system of the Chevrolet 1958-1969 is shown in Fig. S-8. The Chevelle also uses coil springs at the rear, but has a different type of control arm, Fig. S-11. Fig. S-9 shows a typical installation of leaf type springs as used on the Nova, Camaro and Chevy II.

Details of the Corvette independent suspension are illustrated in Fig. S-10.

REMOVING FRONT COIL SPRINGS

The following procedure applies particularly to the Chevrolet and the Chevelle. Remove the shock absorber, the front wheel, stabilizer to lower control arm link, strut rod to lower control arm and the tie rod end, Figs. S-4 and S-5, after supporting the car by the frame so that the control arms hang free. Scribe the position of the inner pivot camber cam bolt and then remove the nut, lock washer and outer cam. Install a notched steel bar, Fig. S-5A, through the shock absorber mounting hole in the lower control arm so that the notch in the bar seats over the bottom spring coil and the bar extends inboard and under inner bushing. Fit a 5 in. wood block between the bar and the lower arm inner support bushing. With a floor jack, raise the outer end of the steel bar enough to remove the tension from the inner pivot cam bolt. The bolt can then be removed. Carefully lower the inner end of the control arm. Tension of the spring must be removed before the spring can be taken from the car.

REMOVING REAR COIL SPRINGS

The following procedure applies particularly to the Chevrolet rear springs, Fig. S-8, but is in general, typical of the other installations.

The procedure is as follows: Raise the rear of the vehicle and place jack stands under the frame. Use a jack to support vehicle weight at the

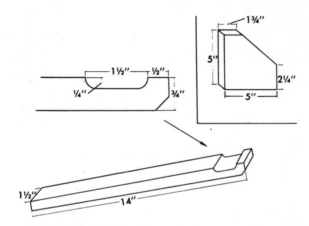

Fig. S-5A. Details of steel bar used when removing front spring.

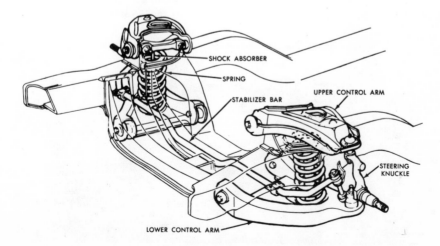

Fig. S-6. Front suspension system on 1967–1971 Camaro and 1970–1972 Nova.

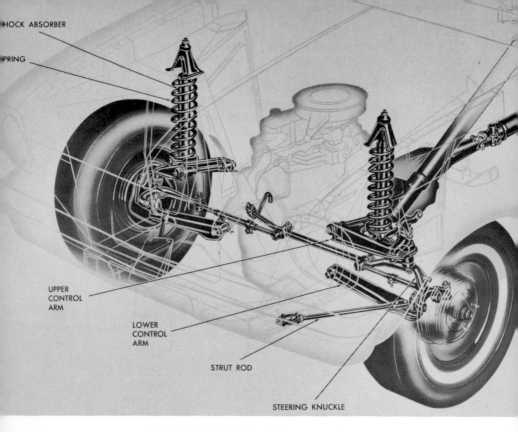

SHOCK ABSORBER

SPRING

UPPER
CONTROL
ARM

LOWER
CONTROL
ARM

STRUT ROD

STEERING KNUCKLE

Fig. S-7. 1962–1967 Chevy II front suspension system.

rear. Remove both rear wheels. With the car supported so the rear springs
are compressed by the weight of the vehicle, proceed as follows: Disconnect both rear shock absorbers from the anchor pin lower attachment.
Loosen the upper control arms rear pivot bolt but do not remove the nut.

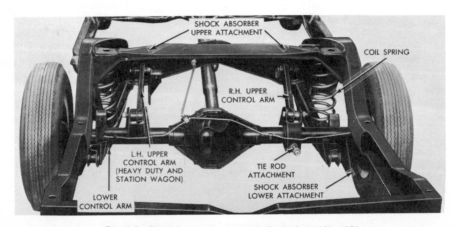

SHOCK ABSORBER
UPPER ATTACHMENT

COIL SPRING

R.H. UPPER
CONTROL ARM

L.H. UPPER
CONTROL ARM
(HEAVY DUTY AND
STATION WAGON)

TIE ROD
ATTACHMENT

SHOCK ABSORBER
LOWER ATTACHMENT

LOWER
CONTROL ARM

Fig. S-8. Chevrolet rear suspension. Typical of 1958–1970.

Loosen both the left and right lower control arm rear attachments, but do not disconnect from axle brackets. Remove the rear suspension tie rod from the studs on the axle tube. Lift the lower seat of both rear coil springs, slightly loosen the nut on the bolt that retains the spring and seat to the control arm. When the nut has been backed off the maximum amount permissible, all threads on the nut should still be engaged on the bolt.

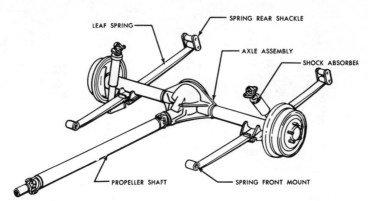

Fig. S-9. Camaro and Nova rear suspension system. Chevy II is similar.

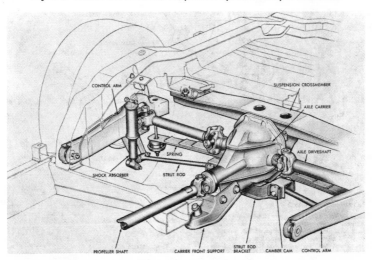

Fig. S-10. Corvette rear suspension and drive line components.

CAUTION: Under no condition should the nut at this time be removed from the bolt in the seat of either spring.

Slowly lower the support jack that has been in place under the rear axle, thereby allowing the axle to swing down, carrying the springs out of their upper seat and providing access for spring removal. Remove the

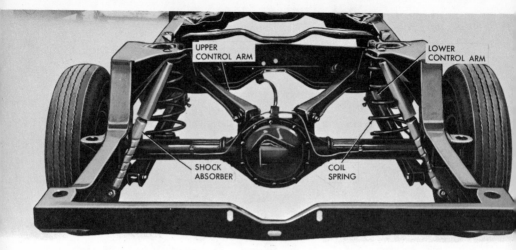

Fig. S-11. Rear suspension system of Chevelle, Monte Carlo and 1971–1972 Chevrolet.

lower spring attaching rods from each spring, then remove the springs and insulators from the vehicle.

On the Chevelle, Fig. S-11, raise the vehicle to a height that will allow axle assembly to hang freely and position supports under both frame side rails. Support axle assembly with an adjustable jack and disconnect shock absorber at axle bracket. Lower axle assembly until suspension reaches the end of travel. Then pry lower pigtail over vertical retainer on axle bracket and remove spring and insulator from vehicle.

LEAF SPRING REMOVAL

To remove the leaf springs on Camaro, Nova and 1962-1967 Chevy II vehicles, Fig. S-4, raise rear of vehicle sufficiently to allow axle assembly to hang freely, then support weight of the vehicle at both side rails and near front eye of spring. Raise axle assembly so that all tension is removed from the spring. Loosen and remove shock absorber lower attaching bolt. Loosen the spring eye-to-bracket retaining bolt. Remove the screw securing the spring retainer bracket to the under body. Lower axle sufficiently to permit access to spring retainer bracket and remove bracket from spring.

The spring eye bushing can be replaced without completely removing the spring from the vehicle if necessary.

Shortcuts on
WHEEL ALIGNMENT, STEERING

To do an accurate job of aligning the front wheels requires specialized equipment, and accuracy is a must if tire wear is to be kept to a minimum. In an emergency, however, approximate adjustment can be made without such equipment.

Before altering the alignment of the front wheels it is important to make sure what is causing the tire wear or other steering difficulties. In many cases the difficulty results from some easily remedied cause. Therefore, it is recommended that the following factors be checked and corrected if necessary prior to adjusting front wheel alignment.

1. Loose or improper adjusted steering gear.
2. Steering gear housing loose at frame.
3. Play or excessive wear in spherical joints or steering shaft coupling.
4. Loose tie rod or steering connections.
5. Improper front spring heights.
6. Underinflated tires.
7. Unbalanced wheel and tire assembly.
8. Wheel bearings improperly adjusted.
9. Shock absorbers not operating properly.

Many authorities recommend that tire pressure be maintained 2 lb. higher than the specified value. This increases tire life and makes the car steer easier, but at a slight sacrifice to riding comfort. Further in regard to tries, make sure the valve cap is in place as it is the cap which seals the valve and prevents leakage of air.

CHECKING THE BALL JOINTS

With the front of the car jacked up, shake each front wheel, grasping it at the top and bottom. Any looseness indicates front wheel bearings need adjusting. To check the ball joints for wear proceed as follows: The upper ball joint, Fig. T-1 and Fig. U-7, is checked for wear by checking the torque required to rotate the ball stud in the assembly. To make such a check, the stud must be removed from the steering knuckle. Install a nut on the ball stud and measure the torque required to turn the stud in the assembly. The specified torque for a new ball joint is 3 to 10 ft. lb. If the readings are too high or too low, replace the ball stud.

Excessive wear of the lower ball joint is indicated when difficulty is experienced when lubricating the joint. If the liner has worn to a degree where the lubrication grooves in the liner have been worn away, then greater than normal pressure is required to force lubricant through the joint. When that occurs both lower joints should be replaced.

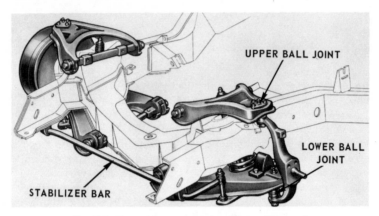

Fig. T-1. Typical front suspension system, (Corvette).

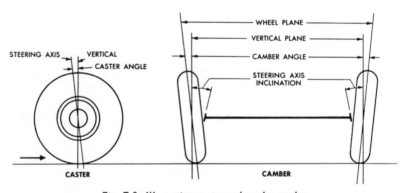

Fig. T-2. Illustrating caster and camber angles.

CASTER, CAMBER AND TOE-IN

The conditions that are included in wheel alignment are caster, camber and toe-in, together with ball joint inclination.

Camber is the amount in degrees the front wheels are tilted outward at the top from the vertical, Fig. T-2.

Toe-in is the amount in fractions of an inch that the wheels are closer together at the extreme front of the car than at the rear.

Caster is the angle of inclination, between the steering axis and the vertical, Fig. T-2. It is considered positive when the steering axis is inclined to the rear.

Toe-in is probably the most important factor affecting tire wear and can be measured to a fair degree of accuracy without specialized equipment.

Before attempting to align the front wheels, the car should always be rolled forward several feet to place the wheels in normal straight ahead running position.

An approximation of the camber angle can be made by placing the car on a level floor and then placing a large carpenter's square against the hub and tire rim. Measure the distance from the square to the rim at the top and also at the bottom. The difference in the distance between these measurements is the camber in inches. There are no factory specifications available for camber measurements of this type. However, the difference in the measurements should be no less than 1/32 in. nor more than 1/16 in. It must be emphasized that checking camber by this method is an emergency method only.

A quite accurate method of measuring toe-in without the use of special equipment is as follows: With the car on a level floor, jack up the front wheels, and with the wheels spinning hold a piece of chalk against the center of the tire tread. Then with the wheels still spinning, hold a pointed tool such as an ice pick, against the chalk mark to scribe a fine line. Do this to both front wheels. Lower the car from the jacks, and roll the car forward several feet. Then suspend a plumb bob from the scribed line at the rear of the tire and make a mark on the floor where it is contacted by the point of the plumb bob. Repeat this operation at the front of the wheel and also on both wheels. Then measure the distance between the two marks at the front of the tires and also at the back of the tires. The difference between these two measurements will be the toe-in, and obviously these

Fig. T-3. Method of adjusting caster and camber on 1955–1964 Chevrolet, 1964–1972 Chevelle, 1968–1972 Chevy II, 1963–1972 Corvette, 1967–1972 Camaro, 1969–1972 Nova, 1970–1972 Monte Carlo.

measurements should be made with a high degree of accuracy. Toe-ins for the various models are given in the Specification Pages.

Caster can only be measured with specialized equipment.

1955-1964 CHEVROLET, 1964-1972 CHEVELLE, 1968-1972 CHEVY II, 1963-1972 CORVETTE, 1967-1972 CAMARO, 1969-1972 NOVA, 1970-1972 MONTE CARLO WHEEL ALIGNMENT

The caster and camber adjustments on these cars are made by means of shims between the upper control arm inner support shaft and the support bracket attached to the frame side rail, Fig. T-3.

The addition of shims at the front bolt, or removal of shims at the rear bolt, will decrease positive caster. One shim (1/32 in.) transferred from the rear attaching bolt to the front attaching bolt will change caster approximately one-half degree.

Adding an equal number of shims at both front and rear of the support shaft will decrease positive camber. One shim (1/32 in.) at each location will move camber approximately 1/5th degree on the Chevelle, Camaro and Nova cars; and 1/6th degree on the Corvette.

To adjust for caster and camber, loosen the upper support shaft to cross member nuts, add or subtract shims as required and retighten nuts.

Caster and camber can be adjusted in one operation.

Fig. T-4. Caster adjustment on 1965–1970 Chevrolet and 1962–1967 Chevy II.

CHEVROLET 1965-1972, CHEVY II 1962-1967

The caster angle' on these cars is adjusted by turning the two nuts at the front of the lower control arm strut rod, Fig. T-4. Shortening this rod will increase caster. Lengthening the rod will decrease caster.

Camber angle is adjusted by loosening the lower control arm pivot bolt and rotating the cam located on this pivot, Fig. T-5. This eccentric cam action will move lower control arm in or out, thereby varying camber.

Wheel Alignment, Steering

STEERING AXIS INCLINATION ADJUSTMENT

Camber is the outward tilt of the wheel and steering axis inclination is the inward tilt of the steering knuckle. Camber cannot be changed without changing steering axis inclination. Correct specifications are given at the back of this book. If, with the camber correctly adjusted, steering axis inclination does not fall within the specified limits, the knuckle is bent and should be replaced.

If a new knuckle is installed, caster, camber and toe-in should be re-adjusted.

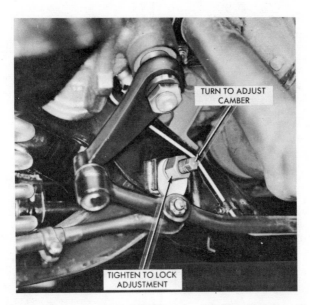

Fig. T-5. Camber adjustment on 1965–1972 Chevrolet. The 1962–1967 Chevy II is similar.

TOE-IN ADJUSTMENT

Toe-in is checked with the wheels in a straight ahead position. It is a difference of the distance measured between the extreme front and the distance measured between the extreme rear of both front wheels. Toe-in must be adjusted after caster and camber adjustment.

To adjust the toe-in, set the front wheels in a straight ahead position. Loosen the clamp bolts on one tie rod and adjust for the proper toe-in, as given in the specifications. Then loosen the clamp bolts on the other tie rod and turn both tie rods the same amount, and in the same direction, to place the steering gear on its high point, and position the steering wheel in its straight ahead position.

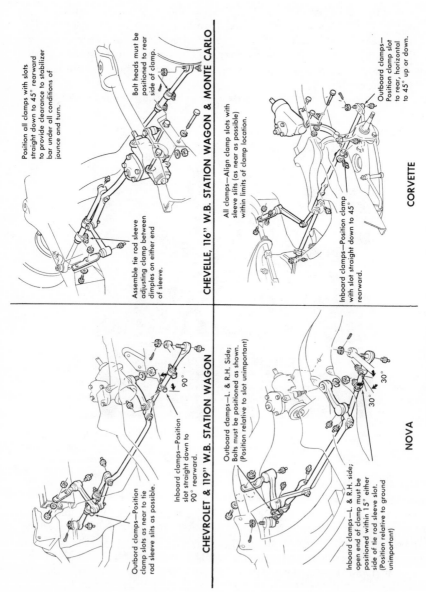

Position all clamps with slots straight down to 45° rearward to provide clearance to stabilizer bar under all conditions of jounce and turn.

Bolt heads must be positioned to rear side of clamp.

Assemble tie rod sleeve adjusting clamp between dimples on either end of sleeve.

CHEVELLE, 116" W.B. STATION WAGON & MONTE CARLO

Outboard clamps— Position clamp slot to rear, horizontal to 45° up or down.

All clamps—Align clamp slots with sleeve slits (as near as possible) within limits of clamp location.

Inboard clamps—Position clamp with slot straight down to 45° rearward.

CORVETTE

Outboard clamps—Position clamp slots as near to tie rod sleeve slits as possible.

Inboard clamps—Position slot straight down to 90° rearward.

CHEVROLET & 119" W.B. STATION WAGON

Outboard clamps—L. & R.H. Side; Bolts must be positioned as shown. (Position relative to slot unimportant)

Inboard clamps—L. & R.H. side; open end of clamp must be positioned within 15° either side of tie rod sleeve slot. (Position relative to ground unimportant)

NOVA

Fig. T-6. Steering linkage. Typical of recent models.

After adjusting toe-in, care must be exercised to avoid stabilizer link bolt interference.

On the Chevrolet, position the inboard tie rod clamp slot straight down to 90 deg. rearward to avoid stabilizer link bolt interference. Position outboard tie rod clamp slots as near to tie rod sleeve slots as possible.

On the Chevelle, position all the tie rod clamps with slots straight down to 45 deg. rearward to avoid interference. Bolt heads must be positioned to rear side of clamp.

On the Nova and Camaro, position the inboard tie rod clamps with open end of clamp and slot in line. Clamp open end must be within 15 deg. either side of tie rod sleeve slot. Position relative to ground is unimportant. Position outer clamps open end upward, with bolt top facing the rear and the bolt position 30 deg. either side of horizontal. Position relative to slot is unimportant.

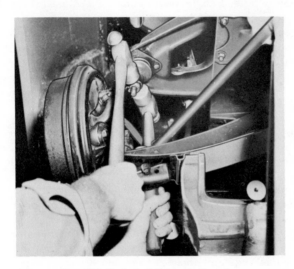

Fig. T-7. Method of freeing ball stud.

SERVICING STEERING LINKAGE

A typical steering linkage is shown in Fig. T-6. It will be noted that each tie rod is of three-piece construction, consisting of the tie rod and two tie rod end assemblies. The ends are threaded into the rod and locked with clamps. Right and left-hand threads are provided to facilitate toe-in adjustment and steering gear centering. Replacement of the tie rod ends should be made when excessive up-and-down motion is evident, or if any lost motion or end play at ball end of stud exists.

To remove tie rod ends, first remove cotter pins from ball studs and remove castellated nuts. To remove outer ball stud, tap on steering arm on tie rod end with a hammer while using a heavy hammer or similar tool as a backing, Fig. T-7. If necessary pull downward on tie rod to remove from steering arm.

Remove inner ball stud from relay rod using same procedure.

To remove tie rod ends from tie rods loosen clamp bolts and unscrew end assemblies.

Installation of the tie rod ends is accomplished by first lubricating the tie rod threads with EP chassis lubricant, and install ends on the tie rod making sure both ends are threaded at equal distance from the tie rod. Make sure that threads on ball stud and in ball stud nuts are perfectly clean and smooth. Install neoprene seals on ball studs.

If threads are not clean and smooth, ball studs may turn in tie rod ends when attempting to tighten nut.

Install ball studs in steering arms and relay rod. Install ball stud nut, and install cotter pins. Lubricate tie rod ends. Adjust toe-in as described previously.

Before locking clamp bolts on the rods, make sure that the tie rod ends are in alignment with their ball studs (each ball joint is in the center of its travel). If the tie rod is not in alignment with the studs, binding will result.

REPLACING THE STABILIZER BAR

Place the vehicle on a hoist and support both front wheels. Disconnect the stabilizer bar, Fig. T-1, from the lower control arm. Remove the stabilizer bar brackets from the frame and remove the stabilizer. Remove the stabilizer link bolts, spacers and rubber bushings from the lower control arms. Inspect the rubber stabilizer link bushings and stabilizer insulator bushings for aging and wear. Replace these bushings if necessary.

If new insulators are necessary, coat stabilizer with recommended rubber lubricant and slide frame bushings into position. Insert stabilizer brackets over bushings and connect to frame. Connect stabilizer rings to link bolts on lower control arms. Then torque bracket bolts and link nuts to 15 ft. lb.

HOW TO BALANCE WHEELS

If specialized wheel balancing equipment is not available, an emergency job which is fairly satisfactory can be done by mounting the wheel to be balanced on the front wheel spindle. The procedure is to first back off on the brake adjustment until the wheel rotates freely. If the wheel bearing adjustment is tight it may be necessary to loosen that adjustment also. With the wheel in position on the spindle, allow it to rotate until it comes to a stop. The heavy area of the wheel will be at the bottom. Temporarily attach a wheel balance weight to the rim at the top. Again allow the wheel to rotate. If the weighted area of the wheel now stops at the bottom, the

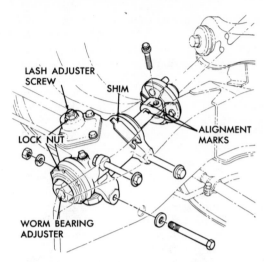

LASH ADJUSTER
SCREW

SHIM

ALIGNMENT
MARKS

LOCK NUT

WORM BEARING
ADJUSTER

Fig. T-8. Location of steering gear adjustments.

weight is too heavy. Change the weight until the wheel always stops in a different position.

If, for example, it takes three ounces to balance the wheel, take a 1-1/2 oz. weight and place it on the inside of the rim, and another 1-1/2 oz. weight and place it on the outside of the rim.

ADJUSTING THE STEERING GEAR

Before any adjustments are made on the steering gear, make a careful check of the front end alignment, wear of the steering linkage, shock absorbers, wheel balance, and tire pressure. After these have been corrected, adjust the steering gear as follows:

Remove the pitman arm nut and mark the relation of the pitman arm position to the sector shaft. Remove the pitman arm.

Loosen the pitman shaft lash adjuster screw lock nut and turn the adjuster screw a few turns in the counterclockwise direction, Fig. T-8. This removes the load imposed on the worm bearings by the close meshing of rack and sector teeth. Turn steering wheel gently in one direction until stopped by gear, then back away about one turn.

Do not turn steering wheel hard against stops when steering relay rod is disconnected as damage to the ball guides may result.

Disconnect wiring harness at column connector. On vehicles with regular steering, check preload by removing horn button or shroud and applying a torque wrench with a 3/4 in. socket on the steering wheel nut. Total steering gear preload should be 14 in. lbs.

On vehicles with tilt steering columns, it will be necessary to disconnect the steering coupling to obtain a torque reading of the steering column. This reading should then be subtracted from any reading taken on the gear. On vehicles with telescopic steering columns, check preload by removing the horn button and applying torque wrench with a Phillips head adaptor socket on the star-headed screw in the center of the steering wheel.

To adjust worm bearings, loosen worm bearing adjuster lock nut and turn worm bearing adjuster, Fig. T-8, until there is no perceptible end play in the worm. Check pull at steering wheel, readjusting if necessary to obtain proper pull. Tighten lock nut and recheck pull. If the gear feels "lumpy" after adjustment of worm bearings, the bearings are probably damaged.

After proper adjustment of the worm is obtained, and ball mounting bolts securely tightened, adjust lash adjuster screw, Fig. T-8. First, turn the steering wheel gently from one stop all the way to the other, carefully counting the total number of turns. Then turn wheel back exactly half way to center position. Turn lash adjuster screw clockwise to take out all lash in gear teeth and tighten lock nut.

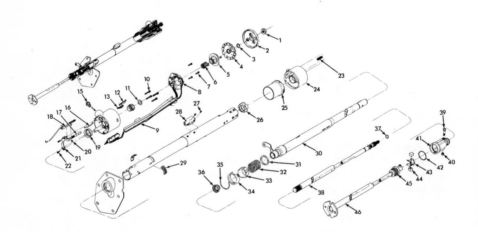

Fig. T-9. 1971 Energy absorbing steering column. (Except tilt and tilt-telescope.)
Previous models similar.

1—Shaft nut.	17—Shaft lock bolt.	33—Lower bearing adapter.
2—Cover.	18—Switch rod and rack assembly.	34—Lower bearing reinforcement.
3—Lock plate retaining ring.	19—Thrust cap.	35—Retainer.
4—Lock plate.	20—Shaft lock bolt washer.	36—Lower bearing.
5—Cancelling cam.	21—Shaft lever detent plate.	37—Shaft stop ring.
6—Bearing preload spring.	22—Detent plate screws.	38—Steering shaft.
7—Turn signal screws.	23—Shift lever spring.	39—Pot joint bolt.
8—Turn signal switch.	24—Gearshift lever housing.	40—Nut.
9—Protector cover.	25—Shift shroud.	41—Pot joint cover.
10—Turn signal housing screws.	26—Gearshift housing bearing.	42—Seal retaining ring.
11—Bearing thrust washer.	27—Ignition switch screws.	43—Bearing spring.
12—Key warning switch.	28—Ignition switch.	44—Bearing blocks.
13—Switch clip.	29—Neutral safety or back-up switch retainers.	45—Pot joint seal.
14—Turn signal housing.	30—Shift tube.	46—Intermediate shaft.
15—Ignition switch selector.	31—Thrust spring washer.	
16—Switch rack preload spring.	32—Shift tube thrust washer.	

STEERING WHEEL REMOVAL

To remove the regular production steering wheel, first disconnect battery ground cable. Pull out horn button cap or center ornament and retainer. Remove three screws from receiving cup. Remove the receiving cup, Belleville spring, bushing and pivot ring. Remove the steering wheel nut and washer. Using a special tool which will engage the threaded holes provided in the steering wheel, the wheel can then be pulled.

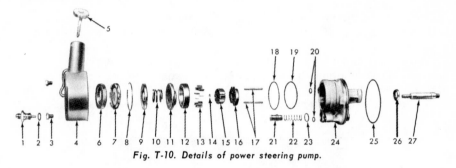

Fig. T-10. Details of power steering pump.

On deluxe type steering wheels, first disconnect the battery ground cable and remove the four attaching screws on underside of steering wheel. Lift steering wheel shroud from wheel and then pull horn wires from cancelling cam tower. Remove steering wheel nut and washer and the wheel can then be pulled with a special tool with anchor screws which can be threaded into the holes provided in the steering wheel.

ENERGY ABSORBING STEERING COLUMN

The energy absorbing steering column in Fig. T-9 is designed to absorb forces resulting from collision. The mast jacket shift tube and steering shaft are designed to collapse under various front impact conditions.

Several different types are used, depending on the type of transmission used. The 1968 model was of the collapsible steel mesh design, while in the 1969 design, Fig. T-9, the jacket features a ball bearing energy absorbing device. Ball bearings imbedded in plastic are pressed between the upper and lower jackets. The steering shaft and shift tube collapse under predetermined loads by sheering injected plastic pins. The 1969 columns also include the ignition lock, ignition switch and antitheft system. The ignition key cannot be removed unless the transmission is in "park" on automatic, or "reverse" on manual shift transmission.

When servicing the energy absorbing steering column, several precautions are necessary.

The outer mast jacket shift tube, steering shaft and instrument panel mounting bracket are designed as energy absorbing units. Because of the design of these components, it is necessary to handle the column with

Fix Your Chevrolet

care when performing any serious operation. Avoid hammering, jarring, dropping or leaning on any portion of the column.

When reassembling the column components, use only the specified screws, nuts and bolts and tighten to specified torque. Care should be exercised in using over-length screws or bolts, as they may prevent a portion of the column from compressing under impact.

POWER STEERING SERVICE

Details of the power steering pump are shown in Fig. T-10. While replacement parts are available, most mechanics prefer to replace the entire unit.

It is most important that the correct belt tension be maintained. The belt is correctly adjusted when a 15 lb. force applied to the center of the belt will produce a deflection of 1/2 to 3/4 in., Fig. T-11. To bleed the hydraulic steering system, proceed as follows: Fill oil reservoir to proper

Fig. T-11. Method of adjusting tension of steering pump belt.

level and let oil remain undisturbed for at least two minutes. Start the engine and run only for about two seconds. Add oil if necessary. Repeat above procedure until oil level remains constant during running of engine.

Next raise front end of vehicle so that the wheels are off the ground. Increase the engine speed to approximately 1500 rpm. Turn the wheels right and left, slightly contacting the wheel stops. Add oil to the hydraulic system, if necessary. Lower the car and turn wheels right and left on the ground. Again check the oil level and refill as required. If oil is extremely foamy, allow the vehicle to stand a few minutes with engine off, and repeat the above procedure.

TROUBLE SHOOTING

HARD STEERING

Low air pressure in tires. Lack of lubrication. Improper wheel alignment. Sagging chassis springs. Bent wheel or spindle. Broken wheel bearings. Tight spherical joints. Incorrect steering gear adjustment. Tie rod ends out of alignment.

FRONT WHEEL SHIMMY

Under-inflated tires. Broken or loose wheel bearings. Worn spherical joints. Unbalanced wheels. Steering gear loose. Tie rod ball loose. Loose wheel lugs. Bent wheel. Incorrect wheel alignment.

EXCESSIVE TIRE WEAR

Wheels out of balance. High speed cornering. Incorrect air pressure in tires. Defective shock absorbers. Failure to rotate tires. Grabbing brakes. Excessive acceleration. Incorrect wheel alignment. Violent brake applications.

HARD RIDING

Excessive tire pressure. Seized shock absorber.

ROAD WANDER

Under-inflated tires. Lack of lubrication. Tight steering gear. Incorrect toe-in. Incorrect caster or camber. Worn tire rod ends. Loose relay rod. Worn or incorrectly adjusted steering gear. Loose steering gear housing.

NOISE IN FRONT WHEELS

Loose wheel lugs. Loose or broken brake shoe return spring. Defective front wheel bearings. Scored brake shoes. Lack of lubrication. Blister or bump on tire.

WHEEL TRAMP

Wheel assembly out of balance. Blister or bumps on tire. Defective shock absorbers.

POWER STEERING

HARD STEERING

Power drive belt loose. Low oil level in reservoir.

LOW OIL PRESSURE

Generator drive belt loose. Low oil level in reservoir. Pump defective. Pressure loss in steering control valve. Pressure loss in power cylinder. External or internal oil leaks.

POOR CENTERING OR RECOVERY ON TURNS

Valve spool sticking in valve housing. Incorrect worm thrust bearing adjustment. Sticky cylinder assembly.

OIL PUMP NOISY

Incorrect oil level. Air in system. Reservoir air vent plugged. Dirt in pump. Worn pump parts.

OIL LEAKS

Loose line connections. Faulty "O" ring seals. Hose leaks. Leaking housing. Cylinder seal leaking.

Quick Service on
BRAKES

From 1951 to 1962, Chevrolet cars were equipped with Bendix Duo Servo type brakes, Fig. U-1. In 1963, the Bendix self-adjusting brake, Fig. U-2, was adopted. Similarly, the Chevy II used the Bendix Duo Servo brake up to and including 1962, and then together with the Chevelle,

Fig. U-1. Details of brake used on Chevrolet 1951 to 1962 and Chevy II up to 1962.

1-Backing plate.	5-Pull back spring.	9-Hold down pin.
2-Anchor pin.	6-Primary brake shoe.	10-Adjusting screw.
3-Guide plate.	7-Pull back spring.	11-Adjusting screw spring.
4-Secondary brake shoe.	8-Hold down spring.	

Camaro and Nova cars, was equipped with the Bendix self-adjusting brakes, Fig. U-2.

Four wheel disc brakes of the dual piston type, Fig. U-3, are standard equipment on the Corvette, 1967-1970, and optional equipment on the Camaro. This same type dual piston disc brake was available as optional equipment for front wheel installation of the Chevrolet, Chevelle, Camaro,

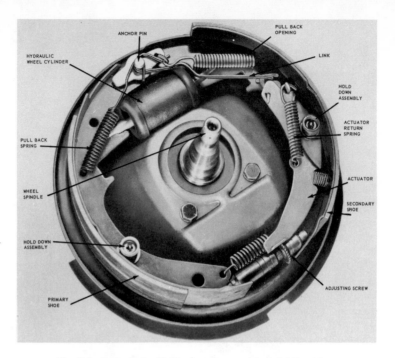

Fig. U-2. Typical of self-adjusting drum type brake 1963–1971.

Chevy II and Nova models. However, on the 1969 Chevrolet, Chevelle, Camaro and Nova models, a new single piston sliding caliper brake, Fig. U-4, was available as optional equipment. In 1972 front disc brakes and rear drum brakes became standard equipment on all models.

SERVICING THE 1951-1962 BRAKES

Service brakes should be adjusted when the brake pedal goes to within one inch of the floor board on brake application. Adjusting these brakes is easily accomplished and the procedure is as follows: Jack up all wheels to clear the floor. Make sure the hand brake is in the release position and

Fig. U-3. Details of four piston, fixed caliper disc brake: 1—Caliper bolts. 2—Bleeder valve. 3—Caliper half. 4—Piston spring. 5—Seal. 6—Assembly. 7—Piston boot. 8—Brake shoes. 9—"O" rings. 10—Caliper half. 11—Retaining pin. 12—Cotter pin.

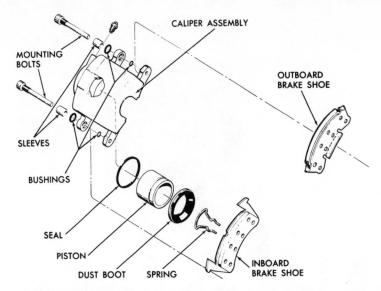

Fig. U-4. Single piston, sliding caliper disc brake available as optional equipment as front brakes 1969–1971 and as standard equipment on some models.

loosen the check nut at the brake cable equalizer to remove tension from the brake cable, Fig. U-5.

Remove the adjusting hole cover from the brake backing plate. Expand the brake shoes by turning the adjusting screw, Fig. U-1, with a brake tool or screwdriver, as shown in Fig. U-6, until a light uniform drag is felt as the drum is rotated. Moving the handle of the tool upward will expand the shoes against the drums.

On Chevy II and Chevrolet brakes, back off 12 notches on both front and rear brakes to insure running clearance. Some mechanics when adjusting these brakes, will not count the number of notches backed off, but will back off on the adjustment until the wheel rotates freely.

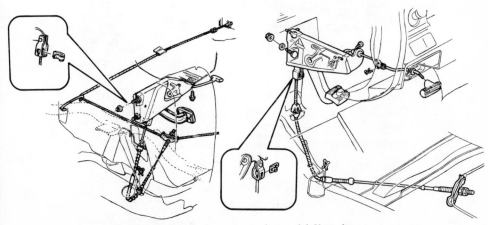

Fig. U-5. Parking brake system on late model Chevrolet cars.

Fig. U-6. Method of adjusting brake shoe clearance on 1951–1962 type brake.

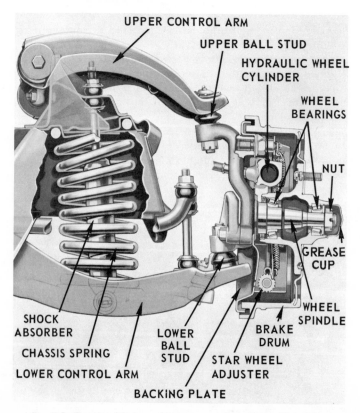

UPPER CONTROL ARM

UPPER BALL STUD

HYDRAULIC WHEEL CYLINDER

WHEEL BEARINGS

NUT

GREASE CUP

WHEEL SPINDLE

BRAKE DRUM

STAR WHEEL ADJUSTER

BACKING PLATE

LOWER BALL STUD

LOWER CONTROL ARM

CHASSIS SPRING

SHOCK ABSORBER

Fig. U-7. Details of brake and front suspension system. (Camaro)

ADJUSTING SELF-ADJUSTING BRAKES

These brakes are so designed that the adjusters operate only when the brakes are applied, as the car is moving backward. Although the brakes are self-adjusting, a preliminary or initial adjustment may be necessary after the brakes have been relined or replaced, or whenever the length of the adjusting screw has been changed.

Such an initial adjustment can be made by inserting an ice pick or some similar pointed tool into the slot in the backing plate, to push the adjusting lever out of the way so that it is not engaged with the adjusting screw. A brake tool or screwdriver can then be used to turn the adjustment wheel until the brakes are correctly adjusted. Such an adjustment may also be necessary when the brakes are dragging as the result of making a great many stops with the car in reverse.

On some installations a "knock-out" area is provided in the web of the brake drum for servicing purposes in the event retracting of the brake shoes becomes necessary.

REMOVING FRONT BRAKE DRUMS

To remove the front brake drums on Chevrolet, Chevelle, Chevy II, Camaro and Nova cars, first, jack up the front wheels and remove the wheel cover or hub cap. Then remove the grease cup from the hub, Fig. U-7. Remove the cotter pin and nut from the end of the wheel spindle, and the brake drum can then be pulled from the wheel spindle. In some cases it will be necessary to back off on the adjustment of the brakes to provide additional clearance so the drum can be easily removed.

REMOVING REAR BRAKE DRUMS

To remove the rear brake drums on Chevrolet, Chevelle, Chevy II, Nova, and Camaro cars, first remove the wheel covers and wheels. Remove the spring clips from the wheel studs, or in some cases the small bolt holding the drum to the axle shaft flange. The drum can then be removed from the axle flange. In some cases it will be necessary to back off on the brake adjustment to supply the additional clearance between the brake shoes and the brake drum.

SHOULD BRAKE DRUMS BE RECONDITIONED

It is not always necessary to have brake drums reconditioned. If the drums have been severely scored, Fig. U-8, they should be reconditioned. Light scratches will not affect the operation of the brake. In addition to examining the friction surface of the brake, the drums should be checked for out-of-round, Fig. U-9. Some authorities recommend drum reconditioning if the out-of-round condition exceeds .007 in. Other authorities set the limit at .010 in. Automotive machine shops have the necessary equipment for reconditioning the brake drums. It must be remembered that when drums are .060 in. oversize they should be replaced. Thin brake drums will distort and expand excessively on brake application with the result that brake action will "fade."

It must also be remembered that when drums are .015 in. oversize, standard thickness brake lining should not be installed. Oversized lining should be used.

Fig. U-8. Badly scored brake drum. Such drums should be reconditioned or replaced.

WHEN TO RELINE BRAKES

Brakes should be relined when the lining is worn to 1/32 in. of the rivet heads which attach the lining to the brake shoes. In the case of cemented lining, new shoes should be installed when the lining is worn to 1/16 in. of the shoe platform. Another reason for relining brake shoes is when they become deeply scored as shown in Fig. U-10.

RELINING DRUM BRAKES

To reline brakes it is first necessary to remove the brake drums as previously explained. Then remove the brake shoes. The procedure for removing brake shoes is as follows: To remove the brake shoes on the Bendix Duo Servo brake, Fig. U-1 and Fig. U-11, first remove the brake drums and then be sure the hand brake is in the fully released position. Unhook the brake shoe pull back springs from the anchor pin, using a special tool as shown in Fig. U-11. If a special tool is not available, use a heavy long-handled screwdriver to lever the spring from the anchor pin.

Fig. U-9. Measuring diameter of brake drum. Drums more than .060 in. oversize should be replaced.

Fig. U-10. When brake lining becomes deeply scored it should be replaced.

Fig. U-11. Removing pull-back spring on drum type brake.

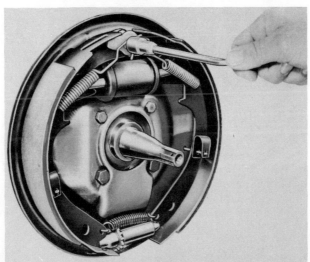

When removing these springs, be sure to identify each of the springs so that they can be replaced in their original position. These springs have different tensions. The secondary spring has a tension of 50 lb. and is painted gray, while the primary shoe spring has a tension of 40 lb. and is painted black.

Fig. U-12. Using pliers to remove hold-down spring. Special tools are also available.

Next, remove the brake shoe hold-down springs, Fig. U-12. To do this, press down on the spring cap and give it a half turn. As pin passes through the backing plate, it is necessary to hold the head of the pin while applying pressure on the cap.

The shoes can now be removed by spreading them apart at the top, Fig. U-13.

Relined brake shoes can be obtained from any Chevrolet dealer, or automotive parts jobber.

Replacing the shoes is done by reversing the above procedure. The pullback springs can be installed by levering them onto the anchor pin by means of a heavy long-handled screwdriver, Fig. U-14.

SERVICING SELF-ADJUSTING DRUM BRAKES

Servicing procedure for the self-adjusting brake, Fig. U-2, is very similar to that of the conventional brake (Bendix Duo Servo).

To remove the brake shoes on the self-adjusting brakes, shown in Fig. U-2, first, raise the car on a hoist and loosen check nuts of parking brake equalizer sufficiently to remove all tension from the brake cable. Then remove the brake drums. Unhook the brake shoe pull back spring from anchor pin, using a special tool or a heavy screwdriver. Remove the actuator return spring and link. Remove hold-down pin and springs. Them remove the actuator assembly.

Brake Service

The actuator, pivot and override spring are an assembly. It is not recommended that they be disassembled for service purposes unless they are broken. It is much easier to assemble and disassemble the brakes by leaving them intact.

Separate the brake shoes by removing adjusting screw and spring. On the rear brakes, remove the parking brake lever from the secondary brake shoe. Be sure to keep the hands clean while handling brake shoes. Do not permit oil or grease to come in contact with lines. When working on rear brakes, lubricate parking brake cable. On rear brakes only, lubricate fulcrum end of parking brake lever, and the bolt with brake lubricant, then attach lever to secondary shoe with bolt, spring washer, lock washer and nut. Make sure that lever moves freely.

Fig. U-13. Removing brake shoes from backing plate. Installation is similar.

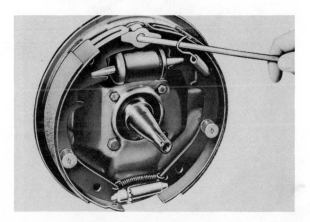

Fig. U-14. Installing pull-back spring.

Put a light coat of Lubriplate on backing plate contact surfaces and threads of the adjusting screw.

Before installation, make certain the adjusting screw is clean and lubricated properly.

Fig. U-15. Checking operation of actuating lever on self-adjusting drum brake.

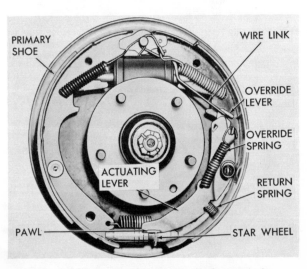

Fig. U-15A. Details of late type self-adjusting brake.

Connect brake shoes together with adjusting screw spring, then place adjusting screw, socket and nut in position.

Make sure the proper adjusting screw is used ("L" for left side of vehicle, "R" for right side of vehicle). The star wheel should only be installed with the star wheel nearest to the secondary shoe and the adjusting screw spring inserted to prevent interference with the star wheel.

On rear wheels, connect parking brake cable to lever. Secure the primary brake shoe (short lining faces forward) first with the hold-down pin and spring, using a pair of pliers. Engage shoes with the wheel cylinder connecting links. Install and secure the actuator assembly and secondary brake shoe with the hold-down pin and spring using a pair of needle-nose pliers. On rear wheels, position parking brake strut and strut spring. Install guide plate over anchor pin. Install the wire link. Do not hook the wire link over the anchor pin stud with the regular spring hook tool. This may damage the cylinder boot seal. Fasten the wire link to the actuator assembly first, then place over the anchor pin stud by hand while holding the adjuster assembly in the pull down position.

Install actuator spring. Do not pry actuator lever to install return spring. Keep it in place using the end of a screwdriver.

If old brake pull-back springs are nicked, distorted, or if strength is doubtful, install new springs. Hook springs in shoes by installing the primary spring from the shoe over the anchor pin and then the spring from secondary shoe over the wire link end.

After completing installation, make certain the actuator lever functions easily by hand operating the self-adjusting feature, Figs. U-15, and U-15a. Follow the above procedure on all wheels. Adjust brakes as previously described. When installing drums align drum tang with wheel hub.

SERVICING DISC BRAKES

Chevrolet uses two different types of disc brakes. The dual piston type disc brake, Fig. U-3, is used as standard equipment on all four wheels of the Corvette and some Camaro models. It is also used as optional equipment on the front wheels of 1966-1968 Chevrolet, Chevelle, Chevy II and Nova cars. In 1969-1971, a single piston, sliding caliper brake, Figs. U-4 and U-18, was available for front brakes on these same cars. In 1972 the single disc brake was standard equipment on the complete line, except the Vega which has a disc brake of a slightly different type.

DUAL PISTON DISC BRAKE

The dual piston disc brake, Fig. U-3, consists of a fixed caliper, splash shield, mounting bracket, and rotating disc. The caliper assembly contains four pistons and two shoe and lining assemblies. A seal and dust boot are installed in each piston, with a piston spring in the caliper cylinder bore beneath each piston, Fig. U-3. A retaining pin extends through each caliper half and both shoes to hold the shoes and lining in position in the caliper. ·

The disc, which has a series of air vent louvers to provide cooling, is mounted on the front wheel hub.

The Corvette heavy-duty option includes a pressure regulator valve, Fig. U-16, mounted in the rear brake line just below the main cylinder. The valve regulates the hydraulic pressure to the rear brakes resulting in simultaneous braking balance between the front and rear brake systems. This valve guards against premature lock-up of rear wheels when brakes are applied.

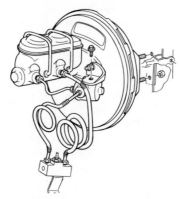

Fig. U-16. Pressure regulating valve on disc brake system.

Shoes with bonded linings should be replaced when the lining is worn to approximately 1/16 in. of thickness. Shoes with linings retained by rivets should be replaced when the lining is worn to approximately 1/32 in. thickness over the rivet heads. To replace the brake shoes on this fixed type caliper disc brake, first siphon two-thirds of the brake fluid from the main cylinder reservoir. If fluid is not removed, insertion of the new full thickness lining will force the pistons back into the housings, displacing fluid into the master cylinder. This will cause the main cylinder to overflow. Do not drain the reservoirs completely or air will be pumped into the system.

Raise the car and remove the wheels. Remove and discard the cotter pin from the inboard end of the shoe retaining pin and slide out the retaining pin. On Corvette heavy-duty disc brakes, two retaining pins must be removed, one on each end of the caliper assembly. Remove the inboard shoe by pulling up.

Insert the new shoe with lining in position. Use a putty knife to push each piston back as the shoe is inserted, as shown in Fig. U-17. Replace the outboard shoe as described above. When both caliper shoes have been replaced, install the shoe retaining pin throughout outboard caliper half, outboard shoe, inboard shoe and inboard caliper half. Insert a new 3/32 x 5/8 plated cotter pin through the retaining pin and bend back ends of cotter pin.

Brake Service

Repeat above procedure on each wheel where shoes are to be replaced. Refill master cylinder to fluid level and if necessary bleed brake system.

To remove the brake caliper, place car on hoist and remove wheels and disconnect hydraulic brake lining, taping the open tube to prevent entrance of foreign material.

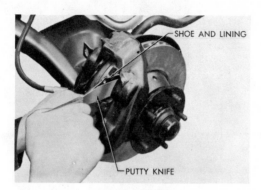

SHOE AND LINING

PUTTY KNIFE

Fig. U-17. Installing brake shoes on fixed caliper disc brake.

Remove pin and shoe assembly from caliper. Identify inboard and outboard shoe if they are to be reused. Remove the end of the brake hose at bracket by removing U-shape retainer from the hose fitting and withdraw the hose from bracket. The caliper assembly can then be removed by removing the two hex-head bolts.

SINGLE PISTON, SLIDING CALIPER, FRONT DISC BRAKE

Starting with the 1969 models, a new single piston, front disc brake, Fig. U-4 and Fig. U-18, is available either as standard or optional equipment on the different models. This system includes a pressure metering valve which meters the hydraulic pressure to the front brakes, obtaining simultaneous application of both front and rear brakes.

The 1971 design also has a combination valve below the main cylinder which houses a brake failure warning switch, metering valve and proportioning valve in one assembly.

The single piston sliding caliper assembly utilizes a one-piece housing design with the inboard side bored for a single piston, Fig. U-18. A seal within the cylinder bore provides a hydraulic seal between the piston and the cylinder wall. When the brake pedal is depressed, hydraulic pressure forces the piston against the inner surface of the disc. This force causes the caliper to slide inboard, on four bushings, forcing the outer brake shoe and lining assembly against the outer surface of the disc.

Brake shoes should be replaced when the lining is worn to approximately .030 in. thickness over the rivet heads. Before removing the shoes, syphon fluid from the master cylinder to bring the level to 1/3 full. Raise

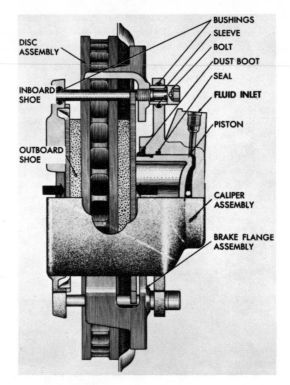

Fig. U-18. Details of sliding caliper disc brake.

Fig. U-19. Pushing piston back into its bore with a C-clamp when removing caliper and shoes from sliding anchor type disc brake.

the vehicle and remove the front wheels and push the piston back into its bore. This can be accomplished by using a C-clamp, Fig. U-19.

Remove the two mounting bolts which attach the caliper to the support and lift the caliper off the disc, Fig. U-20.

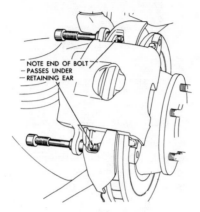

Fig. U-20. Removing sliding caliper from disc brake.

Remove the inboard shoe. Dislodge the outboard shoe and position the caliper on the front suspension arm so that the brake hose will not support the weight of the caliper.

Remove the shoe support spring from the piston. Remove the two sleeves, Fig. U-4, from the inboard ears of the caliper. Remove the four rubber bushings from the grooves in each of the caliper ears.

If the inside of the caliper shows evidence of fluid leakage, the caliper should be overhauled. Do not use compressed air to clean the inside of the caliper, as this would cause the dust boot to become unseated.

When reassembling the sliding caliper disc brake, first, lubricate new sleeves, new rubber bushings, the bushing grooves and the end of the mounting bolts, using Delco Moraine silicone lubricant, or its equivalent. Install the new rubber bushings in the caliper ears. Install the new sleeves to the inboard ears of the caliper. Position the sleeves so that the ends are toward the shoe and lining assembly is flush with the machine surface of the ear.

Install the shoe support spring in the center of the piston cavity. Position inboard shoe in the caliper so that the spring ends centrally contact the shoe edge. Initially this will place the shoe on an angle with the upper edge up. Push upper edge down until the shoe lays flat against the caliper, Fig. U-21. When properly sealed, the ends of the spring will not extend more than .110 in. beyond the metal part of the brake shoe.

Position the outboard shoe in the caliper with the ears at the top of the shoe over the caliper ears and the tab at the bottom of the shoe engaged in the caliper cutout.

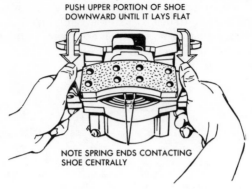

PUSH UPPER PORTION OF SHOE
DOWNWARD UNTIL IT LAYS FLAT

NOTE SPRING ENDS CONTACTING
SHOE CENTRALLY

Fig. U-21. Installing shoe to caliper.

With both shoes installed, lift up the caliper and rest the bottom edge of the outboard lining on the outer edge of the brake disc to make sure there is no clearance between the tab at the bottom of the outboard shoe and the caliper abutment.

Using a 1/4 x 1 x 2-1/2 in. metal bar to bridge the caliper cutout, clamp the outboard shoe to the caliper using a C-clamp, Fig. U-22.

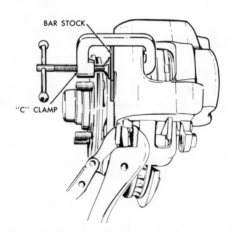

BAR STOCK

"C" CLAMP

Fig. U-22. Fitting shoe to caliper on single piston disc brake.

Using vice-grip pliers, Fig. U-22, bolt upper ears of the outboard shoe over the caliper until the clearance between the shoe ear and the caliper (measured at both the edge and side of the caliper) is .005 in. or less. Remove the C-clamp and position the caliper over the brake disc, lining up the hole in the caliper ears with the holes in the mounting bracket.

Make sure that the brake hose is not twisted or kinked. Start the cali-

1967 line of Chevrolet cars. Reading from top to bottom: Corvette Sting Ray Sport Coupe, Corvair Monza Sport Sedan, Chevy II Nova Super Sport Sedan, Chevelle Malibu Sport Sedan, Chevrolet Impala Sport Coupe.

per to mounting bracket bolts through the sleeves in the inboard caliper ears and the mounting bracket, making sure that the ends of the bolts pass under the retaining ears on the inboard shoe, Fig. U-20.

Push the outboard bolts through to engage the holes in the outboard ears. Then thread the mounting bolts into the mounting bracket. Torque the mounting bolt to 30-40 ft. lb.

Reinstall front wheel and lower vehicle. Add brake fluid to master cylinder reservoir to bring fluid level up to within 1/4 in. of the top.

Before moving the vehicle, pump the brake pedal several times to make sure that it is firm. Do not move vehicle until a firm pedal is obtained.

RECONDITIONING BRAKE DISCS

Servicing of the brake disc is extremely critical due to tolerances required in machining of the disc to insure proper brake operation.

Manufacturing tolerance for flatness and parallelism of the brake disc is held to .0005 in. while lateral run-out of the brake disc surfaces cannot exceed .002 in. total indicator reading.

Excessive lateral run-out of the brake disc will cause a knocking back of the pistons, which will create increased pedal travel and vibration when the brakes are applied. The finish of the frictional surfaces must be maintained at 30-50 micro inches.

It has been found that once a wear pattern has been established, disc brakes are less susceptible to scoring problems than are drum brakes. Disc surface scoring imperfections less than .015 in. in depth have negligible effect on disc brake operation.

The minimum thickness allowable after refinishing is .965 in. for the 1 in. thick disc and 1.215 in. for the 1 1/4 in. thick disc. Refinishing the disc surfaces can be performed if precision equipment is available and the minimum specifications can be maintained.

ADJUSTING PARKING BRAKES

To adjust the parking brake on the fixed caliper type brake, Fig. U-3, proceed as follows:

Place car on hoist and remove the rear wheels. Loosen brake cables at the equalizer until the parking brake levers move freely to the off position with slack in the cables. Turn the disc until the adjusting screw can be seen through the hole in the disc. Insert an adjusting tool or screwdriver through the hole in the disc and tighten the adjusting screw by moving the handle of the tool away from the floor on both right and left sides, Fig. U-23. Tighten until the disc will not move, then back off six to eight notches.

Apply the parking brake two notches from inside the car. Tighten the brake cables at the equalizer to produce a light drag with the wheels mounted. Fully release the parking brake and rotate rear wheels. No drag should be evident with the parking brake released.

Fig. U-23. Adjusting parking brake shoe on fixed caliper disc brake.

BLEEDING THE HYDRAULIC BRAKE SYSTEM

"Bleeding the brakes" is a process whereby any air in the hydraulic system is removed. It is very important that there be no air in the hydraulic system as such air would be compressed instead of transmitting the motion of the fluid. When there is air in the system, the brake pedal will have a spongy feel, instead of the normal solid feel when the brakes are applied. The spongy feel results from the air being compressed.

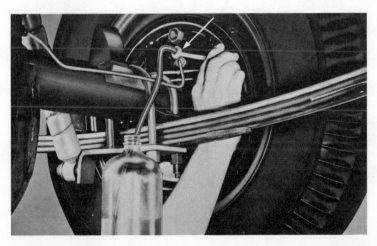

Fig. U-24. Method of bleeding hydraulic brakes. Note location of bleeder valve.

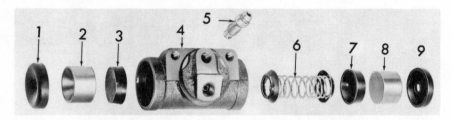

Fig. U-25. Details of typical hydraulic wheel cylinder.

1-Push rod boot.	4-Housing.	7-Piston cup.
2-Piston.	5-Fluid inlet.	8-Piston.
3-Piston cup.	6-Spring.	9-Push rod boot.

To bleed the hydraulic brake system, a small valve is provided at each of the wheel cylinders, Fig. U-25 and Fig. U-26. The valve is operated from the back side of the backing plate.

Brakes should be bled whenever any part of the hydraulic system has been disconnected, or when, on brake application, the pedal has a spongy feel. When bleeding brakes, the master cylinder must always be kept full of new, clean fluid during the entire bleeding process. The left rear wheel cylinder should be bled first, then the right rear, right front and finally the left front, in that order.

Fig. U-26. Left: Method of filling master cylinder while bleeding brakes. A simpler method is to pour the brake fluid direct from container as needed. Right: A special bleeder is installed on the dual type master cylinder as an aid when bleeding.

The procedure on conventional drum type brakes is to attach a rubber hose to the end of the bleeder screw at the wheel cylinder, Fig. U-24. The tube should fit snugly around the screw so that no air can enter. The free end of the tube is immersed in a jar or container partly filled with clean brake fluid. Then loosen the bleeder screw with a 3/8 in. open-end wrench. Have a helper slowly depress the brake pedal. Just as the brake pedal reaches the end of its travel, close the bleeder valve and allow brake pedal to return slowly to the fully released position. Repeat this procedure until the expelled brake fluid flows in a solid stream in the bleeder hose and no bubbles or contamination are present. Then close the bleeder valve tightly. During the bleeding operation, the level of the fluid in the master cylinder must not be permitted to reach the bottom of the reservoir as that would permit air to enter the system. Note that in systems with dual type master cylinders, the front reservoir is connected to the front brakes and the rear reservoir to the rear brakes.

After bleeding one wheel cylinder, proceed to the next one in order, always making sure that the master cylinder, which is mounted on the dash panel is filled to within one-quarter inch of the top of the reservoir.

Pressure type bleeders which permit one man to bleed the brakes are available, but are relatively expensive. Equipment for maintaining fluid level in the master cylinder during the bleeding operation is shown in Fig. U-26.

When bleeding brakes equipped with power brake units, do not use the vacuum assist. The engine should not be running and the vacuum reserve should be reduced to zero by applying the brakes several times with the engine off before starting the bleeding operation.

The operation of bleeding the four piston type disc brake is the same as described for the conventional Duo Servo system, which was just discussed. The front calipers contain one bleeder valve. The rear calipers on Corvettes contain two bleeder valves, one inboard and one outboard, which necessitates the removal of the rear wheels for bleeding.

Tapping the caliper with a rawhide mallet as the fluid is flowing out may assist in obtaining a good bleeder job.

In regard to the sliding caliper single piston type disc brake, this system includes a pressure metering valve, Fig. U-16, in the front brake system. This valve meters the hydraulic pressure to the front brakes to obtain simultaneous application of the front and rear brakes. The operation of bleeding the front disc brake hydraulic system is the same as the four piston type, except that the spring-loaded end of the pressure metering valve, Fig. U-16, must be depressed while bleeding. This can be done by depressing and holding in the plunger in the end of the valve either by hand or by clamping.

FLUSHING THE BRAKE SYSTEM

The hydraulic system should be flushed annually, or every 10,000 miles, and the procedure is the same as bleeding. However, sufficient fluid should be bled from each line until the fluid is clear and the same as new fluid. When flushing a brake system, it is generally advisable to draw approximately one pint of fluid from the first cylinder bled. This will insure that all fluid from the master cylinder has been drained. On subsequent cylinders, it is then necessary to drain the line until clear fluid is obtained.

QUICK SERVICE ON WHEEL CYLINDERS

The life of wheel cylinders, Fig. U-25, can be prolonged by more frequent flushing of the hydraulic system, and by use of high quality brake fluid. It is necessary to service wheel cylinders when they start to leak fluid. This becomes apparent when the brake pedal gradually goes to the floor when the brakes are applied and pumping the pedal becomes necessary in order to stop the car.

The condition of the wheel cylinders can be checked by removing the brake drums and pulling back the boots from the ends of the wheel cylinder, Fig. U-27. If the inside of the boot is wet with fluid, there is leakage present and it will be necessary to recondition or replace the wheel cylinder.

Kits of the necessary parts are readily available, and the installation of the parts is not difficult.

The procedure, after removing the brake drum and brake shoes, is to pull off the boots from each end of the cylinder. After that, the pistons, cups and springs, Fig. U-25, can be pushed out either end.

It is necessary to carefully examine the interior of the wheel cylinder to make sure it is not scored, pitted or covered with gummy fluid. Before inspecting the wheel cylinder the interior should be carefully cleaned with

Fig. U-27. Pulling back boot on wheel cylinder to see if there is evidence of fluid leakage.

a cloth moistened with clean brake fluid. If any scoring is present, the old cylinder can be honed, or many mechanics prefer to install a completely new wheel cylinder assembly. Each wheel cylinder is attached to the backing plate by means of two cap screws, which can be removed by means of a 1/2 in. wrench. Before removing the cap screws, disconnect the brake line from the wheel cylinder.

If it is decided to install a new kit of parts, all the parts should be first immersed in new brake fluid.

MASTER CYLINDER TIPS

The master or main cylinder, as it is also called, is mounted under the hood on the dash panel. On power brake systems it forms part of the power brake unit. Prior to 1967 a single type master cylinder, Fig. U-28, was used, but starting with the 1967 models, a Duo (split) type master

Fig. U-28. Details of single reservoir master cylinder. (Typical)

1-Seal.	6-Spring.	11-Seal.
2-Lock ring.	7-Valve assembly.	12-Body.
3-Secondary cup.	8-Valve seat.	13-Bleeder valve.
4-Piston.	9-Bail wire.	
5-Primary cup.	10-Reservoir cover.	

cylinder, Fig. U-29, was standard equipment. In this design, separate hydraulic systems are provided for the front and rear brakes. If a wheel or brake line should fail at either front or rear of the system, the other part of the system would continue to function. In the split system, there are two entirely separate reservoirs and outlets in a common body, Fig. U-30. The front outlet is connected to the front wheel brakes, and the rear outlet to the rear brakes.

Two types of split master cylinders are used on Chevrolet built cars, Delco-Moraine and Bendix. The capacity of these units varies with different vehicles so it is essential that the make and model of the master cylinder be correctly identified before ordering replacements. Note that the Bendix unit can be identified by a secondary stop piston on the bottom of the casting, Fig. U-30, whereas the stop bolt on the Delco-Moraine is on the inside.

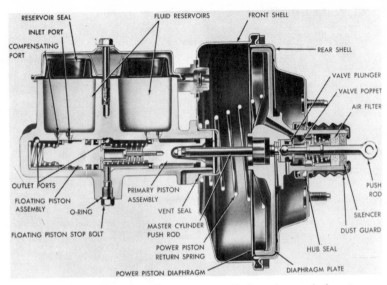

Fig. U-29. Details of Bendix dual master cylinder with power brake unit.

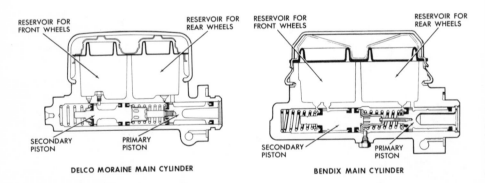

DELCO MORAINE MAIN CYLINDER

BENDIX MAIN CYLINDER

Fig. U-30. Two types of master or main cylinders. The Delco-Moraine is on the left and the Bendix on the right.

In general, master cylinders require servicing when one of the following conditions occurs:

1. All brakes drag.
2. Pedal goes to the floor on brake application.
3. Brakes do not apply.
4. Fluid is found in the boot on the cylinder.

While it is not difficult to overhaul a master cylinder, most mechanics prefer to install a new or rebuilt unit rather than take the time to do the work themselves. However, if it is decided to overhaul the unit, complete instructions are provided with the kit of replacement parts.

Brake Service

When overhauling a master cylinder, care must be taken to keep all parts clean and away from grease and oil. The master cylinder housing must be carefully cleaned using clean brake fluid. Also, all new parts must be dipped in clean fluid before installation.

POWER BRAKE SERVICE

Several different types of power brake units have been used on recent models of Chevrolet built cars, including both single diaphragm type and double diaphragm type.

The single diaphragm Bendix master cylinder is shown in Fig. U-29, and the Delco-Moraine power brake cylinder is shown in Fig. U-31. The Bendix dual diaphragm power brake cylinder is shown in Fig. U-32.

In general these units give very little trouble. When major servicing is required, most mechanics prefer to have the rebuilding done by a specialist or to install a rebuilt unit.

Power brake units are equipped with an air cleaner, Fig. U-32.

A power brake unit is built integral with the master cylinder and is mounted on the dash panel. Fig. U-33 shows a typical installation.

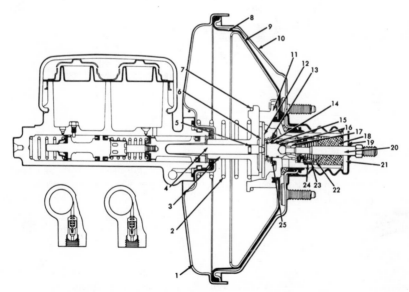

Fig. U-31. Typical Delco-Moraine vacuum power cylinder.

1-Front shell.	10-Rear shell.	19-Boot.
2-Piston return spring.	11-Power piston.	20-Push rod.
3-Reaction retainer.	12-Reaction levers.	21-Silencer.
4-Master cylinder piston rod.	13-Air valve spring.	22-Limiter washer.
5-"O" ring.	14-Reaction bumper.	23-Floating control valve assembly.
6-Reaction plate.	15-Snap ring.	24-Floating control valve retainer.
7-Lock ring.	16-"O" ring.	25-Air valve spring retainer.
8-Diaphragm.	17-Air valve.	
9-Support plate.	18-Air filters.	

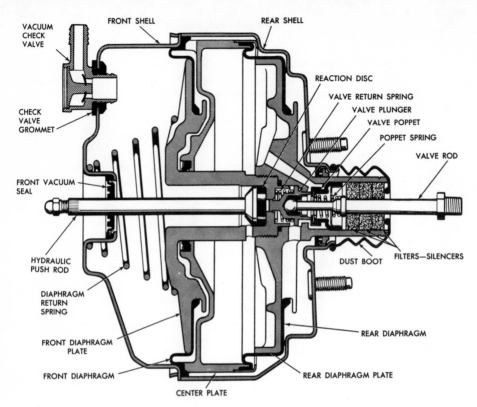

Fig. U-32. Sectional view of Bendix double diaphragm power brake.

POWER BRAKE SERVICE

As previously pointed out, power brake units give very little difficulty. However, a quick check to determine whether the power brake is operating can be made as follows: With the engine not running, apply the brakes ten or twenty times to exhaust the vacuum. Then, while keeping the brake pedal depressed, start the engine. If the power brakes are operating, the brake pedal will move a slight amount so as to further apply the brakes. If the power brake is not operating, no movement of the brake pedal will be noticed when the engine starts. The following checks and inspections can be made:

Check vacuum line and vacuum line connections as well as vacuum check valve in front shell of power unit for possible vacuum loss.

Inspect all hydraulic lines and connections at the wheel cylinders and main cylinder for possible hydraulic leaks.

Check brake assemblies for scored drums, grease or brake fluid on linings, worn or blazed linings, and make necessary adjustments.

Check brake fluid level in hydraulic reservoirs. The reservoirs should be filled to within 1/4 in. of the top. Check for loose mounting bolts at main cylinder and power section.

Check air cleaner filter in power piston extension and replace filter if necessary.

Check brake pedal for binding and misalignment between pedal and push rod.

Note that the push rod, whereby the power brake unit operates the master cylinder, is adjustable. Gauges such as shown in Fig. U-34 can be used for adjusting the push rod. On recent model Delco-Moraine brakes, the dimensions are as indicated. In the case of the Bendix brake, the depth should be 1.220 to 1.225 in.

Fig. U-33. Power brake unit with dual type master cylinder mounted on dash.

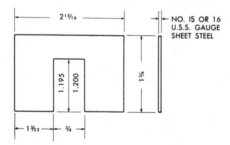

Fig. U-34. Typical gauge for measuring extension of push rod.

CHECKING THE VACUUM

To make sure that full vacuum is reaching the power brake unit, disconnect the vacuum line at the power brake unit and attach a vacuum gauge to the line. Then, with the engine operating at idle speed, note the reading of the gauge. This should be the same as when the vacuum is checked at the intake manifold. Normally this is about 18 in.

TROUBLE-SHOOTING
STANDARD DRUM BRAKE SYSTEM

SYMPTOM AND PROBABLE CAUSE	PROBABLE REMEDY

PEDAL SPONGY

a. Air in brake lines.

a. Bleed brakes.

ALL BRAKES DRAG

a. Improper pedal to push rod clearance blocking compensator port.

a. Adjust clearance.

b. Compensating port in main cylinder restricted.

b. Overhaul main cylinder.

c. Mineral oil in system.

c. Flush entire brake system and replace all rubber parts.

ONE BRAKE DRAGS

a. Loose or damaged wheel bearings.

a. Adjust or replace wheel bearings.

b. Weak, broken or unhooked brake retractor spring.

b. Replace retractor spring.

c. Brake shoes adjusted too close to brake drum.

c. Correctly adjust brakes.

d. Parking brake adjustment too tight.

d. Readjust parking brake.

EXCESSIVE PEDAL TRAVEL

a. Normal lining wear or improper shoe adjustment.

a. Adjust brakes.

b. Fluid low in main cylinder.

b. Fill main cylinder and bleed brakes.

BRAKE PEDAL APPLIES BRAKES BUT PEDAL GRADUALLY GOES TO FLOOR BOARD

a. External leaks.

a. Check main cylinder, lines and wheel cylinder for leaks and make necessary repairs.

b. Main cylinder leaks past primary cup.

b. Overhaul main cylinder.

BRAKES UNEVEN

a. Grease on linings.

a. Clean brake mechanism; re-place lining and correct cause of grease getting on lining.

b. Tires improperly inflated.

b. Inflate tires to correct pres-sure.

EXCESSIVE PEDAL PRESSURE REQUIRED, POOR BRAKES

a. Grease, mud or water on linings.
b. Full area of linings not contacting drums.
c. Scored brake drums.

a. Remove drums-clean and dry linings or replace.
b. Free up shoe linkage, sand linings or replace shoes.
c. Turn drums and install new linings.

The same types of brake troubles are encountered with power brakes as with conventional or standard brakes. Before checking the power sys-tem for source of trouble, be sure to check the braking system as de-scribed for a standard brake system.

TROUBLE SHOOTING
POWER BRAKES

SYSTEM TESTS

1. Road test brakes by making a brake application at about 20 mph to de-termine if vehicle stops evenly and quickly. If pedal has a spongy feel when applying the brakes, air may be present in the hydraulic system. Bleed system as described in this section.
2. With engine stopped and transmission in Neutral, apply brakes sever-al times to deplete all vacuum reserve in the system. Depress brake pedal, hold light foot pressure on pedal and start engine. If the vacuum system is operating pedal will tend to fall away under foot pressure, and less pressure will be required to hold pedal in applied position. If no action is felt, vacuum system is not functioning.
3. Stop engine and again deplete all vacuum reserve in system. Depress brake pedal and hold foot pressure on pedal. If pedal gradually falls away under foot pressure, the hydraulic system is leaking.
4. If the brake pedal travels to within 1 in. of the toeboard, brakes re-quire adjustment or brake shoes require relining.
5. Start engine. With brakes off, run to medium speed and turn off igni-tion, immediately closing throttle. This builds up vacuum. Wait no less than 90 seconds, then try brake action. If not vacuum assisted for three or more applications, vacuum check valve is faulty.

HARD PEDAL-
VACUUM FAILURE DUE TO:

1. Faulty vacuum check valve.
2. Collapsed vacuum hose.
3. Plugged or loose vacuum fittings, hose or pipes.
4. Leak between vacuum power cylinder and hydraulic master cylinder.
5. Leak in vacuum reservoir tank.

BOUND UP PEDAL MECHANISM
POWER BRAKE UNIT TROUBLE

1. Internal vacuum hose loose or restricted.
2. Jammed sliding air valve.
3. Vacuum leaks in unit caused by loose piston plate screws, loose piston packing, leaks between hydraulic master cylinder and vacuum power cylinder, or by faulty master cylinder piston, or vacuum seal.
4. Defective diaphragm.
5. Restricted air cleaner.

GRABBY BRAKES (APPARENT OFF-AND-ON CONDITION)

Power Brake unit valve trouble.
   a. Sticking air valve.
   b. Master cylinder piston binding in power piston guide.
   c. Improper number of shims on air valve.
   d. Dented or distorted power cylinder housing.

PEDAL GOES TO FLOOR (OR ALMOST TO FLOOR)

1. Brake adjustment.
2. Fluid reservoir needs replenishing.
3. Power brake hydraulic leakage.
   a. Defective primary or secondary cup.
   b. Defective head nut or head nut gasket.
   c. Cracked master cylinder casting.
   d. Leaks at wheel cylinder in pipes, or in connections.
   e. Defective annular ring on cylinder plug.
4. Faulty master cylinder check valve that has permitted air to enter system causing spongy pedal.

BRAKES FAIL TO RELEASE

1. Faulty check valve at head nut.
2. Excessive friction at seal of master cylinder piston.
3. Excessive friction at power piston cup.

4. Blocked air passage in power piston.
5. Air cleaner blocked or choked.
6. Air valve sticking shut.
7. Broken piston return spring.
8. Broken air valve spring.

TROUBLE SHOOTING
DISC BRAKE

ROUGHNESS OR CHATTER

1. Rotor faces not parallel.
2. Excessive runout of disc.

SQUEAL ON APPLICATION

1. Disc too thin.
2. Wrong type of shoe (lining).

EXCESSIVE PEDAL TRAVEL

1. Piston, shoe and lining assembly not correctly seated.
2. Loose wheel bearing adjustment.
3. Air leak or insufficient fluid in system.
4. Damaged caliper piston seal.
5. Incorrect push rod adjustment.
6. Shoe out of flat more than .005 in.

UNEVEN OR GRABBING BRAKES

1. Seized pistons.
2. Grease or fluid on lining surface.
3. Caliper out of alignment.
4. Incorrect front wheel alignment.
5. Loose caliper.
6. Lining extending beyond end of shoe.

BRAKE RATTLE

1. Excessive clearance between shoe and caliper.
2. Shoe hold-down clips missing.

BRAKE DRAG

1. Seized pistons.
2. Linkage interference causing incomplete pedal return.
3. Defective booster check valve holding pressure in system.
4. Residual pressure in front system.

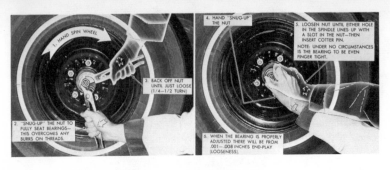

Wheel bearing adjustment procedure.

CALIPER FLUID LEAK

1. Worn piston seal.
2. Scored cylinder bore.
3. Metal clip in seal groove.

NO BRAKES

1. Piston and shoe assembly not correctly seated.
2. Air in system.
3. Insufficient fluid in system.
4. Defective caliper piston seal.
5. Bleeder screw open.

HOW TO ADJUST FRONT WHEEL BEARINGS

In order to get proper steering, good braking and maximum tire life it is essential that the front wheel bearings be correctly adjusted.

To adjust ball type bearings used on older models proceed as follows:

With the wheel raised, remove hub cap and dust cap and then remove the cotter pin from the end of the spindle. While rotating the wheel, tighten spindle nut to 15 ft. lb. of torque. Back off adjusting nut one flat and insert cotter pin. If slot and pin hole do not line up, back off the adjusting nut an additional 1/2 flat or less as required to insert cotter pin. Spin the wheel to check that it rolls freely, then spread end of cotter pin. Bearings should have zero preload and .000 in. to .007 in. end movement when correctly adjusted. Replace dust and hub caps and install wheel.

To adjust the taper roller bearings used on the front wheels of recent model Chevrolet vehicles proceed as follows: These bearings have a slightly loose feel when properly adjusted. They must never be preloaded. Raise the front of the car and spin the wheel to check for unusual noise. If noisy, bearings should be cleaned and inspected prior to adjustment. To check for loose bearing, grasp the wheel at top and bottom and move the assembly in and out. Movement should be less than .008 in.

Remove hub cap or wheel disc from spindle. Remove dust cap from hub. Remove cotter pin from spindle and spindle nut. Adjust bearings as shown in illustration. Insert cotter pin and bend ends against the nut. Cut off extra length to insure ends will not interfere with dust cap. Reassemble dust cap or wheel disc. Lower car to ground.

Hints on
LUBRICATION AND TIRES

The selection of the proper lubricant and its correct application at regular intervals does much to increase the life of all moving parts and greatly reduce the cost of operation.

ENGINE OIL TO USE

The latest recommendations covering type of engine oil to use on Chevrolet, Chevelle, Chevy II, Nova, Camaro and Corvette engines are as follows:

For temperatures ranging from 20 deg. F. above zero to 100 deg. F. above zero, any of the following oils are satisfactory: 20W, 10W-30, 10W-40, 20W-40. For temperatures ranging from zero to 60 deg. F., any of the following oils can be used: 10W, 5W-30, 10W-30, 10W-40.

For temperatures ranging from -30 deg. F. to 20 deg. F. above zero, any of the following oils are satisfactory: 5W, 5W-20, 5W-30.

SAE 5W, and 5W-20 oils are not recommended for sustained high speed driving. SAE 30 oils may be used at temperatures above 60 deg. F.

Naturally, the oil used must not only conform to the above viscosities, but should also be of good quality and should be certified by the supplier as meeting or exceeding the maximum severity requirements of General Motors Standard 6041-N.

CRANKCASE CAPACITIES

153 cu. in. four	4 qt.	307 cu. in.	4 qt.	402 cu. in.	4 qt.
194 cu. in. six	4 qt.	327 cu. in. V-8	4 qt.	409 cu. in. V-8	5 qt.
230 cu. in. six	4 qt.	348 cu. in. V-8	5 qt.	427 cu. in. Chev.	4 qt.
235 cu. in. six	5 qt.	350 cu. in.	4 qt.	427 cu. in. Corv.	5 qt.
250 cu. in.	4 qt.	396 cu. in.	4 qt.	454 cu. in.	4 qt.
283 cu. in. V-8	4 qt.	400 cu. in.	4 qt.		

WHEN TO CHANGE ENGINE OIL

To insure continuation of best performance, low maintenance cost and long engine life, it is necessary to change the crankcase oil whenever it becomes contaminated with harmful foreign materials. Under normal driving conditions, refilling the crankcase with fresh oil every 4 months or every 6000 miles whichever occurs first, is recommended. In certain types of service including trailer hauling, extensive idling, short trip operation in freezing weather (engine not thoroughly warmed up), or in commercial use, such as taxicab or limousine service, the oil change interval should not exceed 2 months or 3000 miles.

It is always advisable to drain the crankcase only after the engine has become thoroughly warmed up or reaches normal operating temperature. The benefit of draining is to a large extent lost if the crankcase is drained when the engine is cold as some of the suspended matter will cling to the sides of the oil pan and will not drain out with the cold oil.

For vehicles in heavy-duty operation involving continuous start, stop or prolonged idling, engine oil should be changed every 2500-3000 miles of operation. The filter should be changed after 5000-6000 miles of operation.

Under normal operating conditions, change the engine oil filter every second oil change.

SERVICING THE AIR CLEANER

Every 12,000 miles, the element of the polyurethane type air cleaner should be cleaned in solvent and after squeezing dry it should be soaked in engine oil, after which the excess oil is squeezed out.

Every 12,000 miles the oil-wetted paper type air cleaner should be inspected for dust leaks, holes or other damage. Replace if necessary. If satisfactory, rotate element 180 deg. from original installed position. Replace at 24,000 miles. Element must not be washed, oiled, tapped or cleaned with an air hose.

If so equipped, replace the bow-tie filter every 24,000 miles.

FUEL FILTER

On systems equipped with the replaceable type filter element, located in the carburetor inlet, replace the element every 12,000 miles or twelve months, whichever occurs first.

CRANKCASE VENTILATION VALVE

Every 24,000 miles or 24 months, the crankcase ventilation valve, Fig. V-1, should be replaced. Connecting hoses, fittings and flame arrester should be cleaned. At every oil change, the system should be tested for proper function and serviced, if necessary.

AIR INJECTOR REACTOR SYSTEM

The air injection reactor system should have A.I.R. pump filter serviced and the drive belt inspected for wear and tension every 12,000 miles, or 12 months, whichever occurs first. In addition, complete effectiveness

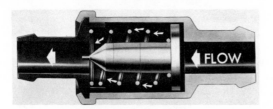

Fig. V-1. Crankcase ventilating valve.

of the system, as well as full power and performance, depends on idle speed, ignition timing, and idle fuel mixture being set according to specifications. A quality tune-up which includes these adjustments should be performed periodically to assure normal engine efficiency, operation and performance.

DISTRIBUTOR LUBRICATION

On the four and six cylinder engine, remove the distributor cap and rotate lubricator one-half turn at 12,000 mile intervals. Replace at 24,000 mile intervals.

On the eight cylinder engine, change cam lubricator end-for-end at 12,000 miles intervals. Replace at 24,000 mile intervals.

AUTOMATIC TRANSMISSION LUBRICATION

On the Powerglide, Torque Drive, and Turbo Hydra-Matic 350 automatic transmissions, check the fluid level on the dip stick every 6,000 miles with the engine idling, selector lever in neutral position, parking brake set, and the transmission at operating temperature. Be careful not to overfill the transmission.

General Motors Dextron-automatic transmission fluid, has been especially formulated and tested for use in these transmissions. Other automatic transmission fluid identified by the mark Dextron can also be used. This fluid is a must in 1968-1969 transmissions. It may also be used in older models. However the type A fluid bearing the mark AQ-ATF followed by a number and suffix A can still be used in the older transmissions.

Every 24,000 miles (more frequently depending upon the severity of service, if vehicle is used to pull trailers, carry heavy loads during high ambient temperatures, operate in mountainous terrain, or operate under other severe conditions), remove fluid from the transmission sump and add sufficient fluid to bring the level to the full mark on the dipstick. Then operate transmission through all stages and recheck level.

Lubrication for the Turbo Hydra-Matic 400 will, except for fluid capacity and filter change, follow the recommendations above. After checking transmission fluid level, it is important that dipstick be pushed all the way into the fill tube. Every 24,000 miles, after removing fluid from the transmission sump, approximately 7-1/2 pints will be required to return level to proper mark on dipstick. Every 24,000 miles, the transmission sump strainer should be replaced. On Turbo Hydra-Matic 400 transmissions provided in heavy-duty service options, drain the converter and sump every 24,000 miles and add approximately 9 quarts of fresh fluid for Chevrolet and Chevelle, and 7-1/2 quarts for the Nova transmission.

REAR AXLE LUBRICATION

In standard rear axles (hypoid) use SAE 80 or SAE 90 GL-5 gear lubricant. Straight mineral oil gear lubricants must not be used in these axles.

On Positraction rear axles, use special Positraction lubricant.

STEERING GEAR LUBRICATION

Check the lubricant level in the manual type steering gear every 36,000 miles. If required, add EP chassis lubricant which meets General Motors specifications GM 6031M.

On models equipped with power steering gear, check fluid at operating temperature in pump reservoir. Add GM power steering fluid, or if this is not available use Dextron Automatic Transmission fluid to bring level to full mark on dipstick.

UNIVERSAL JOINT LUBRICATION

Starting with the 1964 models, the Cardan-type universal joints were used which require no periodic maintenance. Prior to that time, it is recommended that the universal joint be disassembled every 25,000 miles, cleaned and lubricated with a high-melting point wheel bearing type lubricant.

GENERATOR AND STARTER LUBRICATION

Alternators which were adopted with the 1963 models require no lubrication.

Direct current generators used prior to that time are provided with an oil cup at each end of the unit which should be filled with engine oil every 1000 miles.

No lubrication of the starter is required as it is equipped with oilless type bearings.

FRONT WHEEL BEARING LUBRICATION

To lubricate the front wheel bearings it is necessary to remove the front wheels, hub and brake drums, as described in the Chapter on Brakes.

Front wheel bearings of the tapered roller type which have been used on Chevrolet built cars since 1961 should be packed, according to latest recommendations, every 24,000 miles with a high-melting point water resistant front wheel bearing lubricant whenever wheel and hub are removed.

Long fibre or viscose type lubricant should not be used.

Also, different kinds of lubricants should not be used as all lubricants are not compatible. It is therefore necessary to first clean the old lubricant from the bearing, using clean solvent, before repacking the bearings with the new lubricant.

Ball bearings used in front wheels should be packed with high melting point front wheel bearing grease.

TIRE SERVICE

Tire life can be greatly increased by careful and conservative driving habits, by maintaining the specified inflation, and not overloading the vehicle.

High speeds, sudden stops and fast acceleration greatly shorten tire life.

With only 25 percent overloading, tire life will be only 64 percent of normal. Fig. V-2 shows the effect of tire pressure on tire life. Note that if the tire is inflated to only 80 percent of normal, (corresponding to about 20 lb. pressure on Chevrolet size tires), tire life is only about 85 percent of what it should be.

Similarly over-inflation will also reduce tire life.

Some authorities advise inflating tires approximately 2 lb. over the recommended pressure to insure better than normal tire life. However, under such conditions there will be some sacrifice of riding comfort.

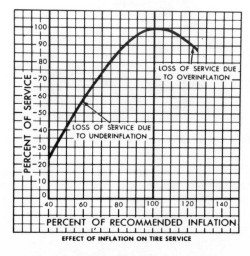

Fig. V-2. Tire pressure must be maintained in order to get maximum mileage from tires.

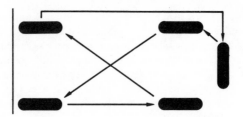

Fig. V-3. Method of rotating tires to obtain increased tire mileage.

As the result of crowned roads, distribution and weight in the vehicle and other factors, tires wear at different rates. Therefore, it is advisable to rotate the tires on a vehicle as shown in Fig. V-3. If tires are rotated, as shown in the diagram, every 4000 miles, approximately 20 percent increase in tire life will be obtained.

CHANGING AND REPAIRING TIRES

The main difficulty in removing a tire from the wheel is breaking the tire bead from the wheel rim. That operation can be made much easier by laying the tire and wheel assembly on the ground under the front bumper of the car. The jack is then placed between the tire and the bumper. As the jack is raised, it will force the tire bead from the wheel rim, Fig. V-4.

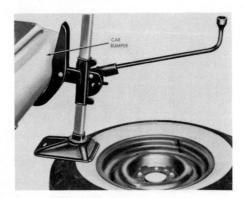

Fig. V-4. Method of loosening tire from wheel rim by using bumper jack.

It is difficult to inflate the modern tubeless tire with a hand pump. An air compressor is needed. Before attempting to inflate the tire, it is usually necessary to spread the tire into the rim. This can be done by using a length of rope and a tire iron, or other tool as shown in Fig. V-5. Turning the tool in the tourniquet will spread the tire into the rim and the tire can then be inflated without any difficulty.

There are many different methods of repairing tubeless tires and the manufacturer's instructions should be followed in each case. The Rubber Manufacturers Association has issued a warning against repairing tires with rubber plugs inserted from outside the tire, or using other temporary methods, except in an emergency. A combination vulcanized plug and patch repair applied from inside the tire is the recommended method for permanent repair of punctures, nail holes and cuts up to 1/4 in. confined to the tread only. Section repairs must be made for larger holes in the tread area.

The only way to detect internal damage to a tire is through off-the-wheel inspection. Two out of three tires run even a short distance at turnpike speed are damaged beyond repair.

Fig. V-5. How to spread tubeless tire into wheel rim, prior to inflation.

The Rubber Manufacturers Association says that tires should never be repaired if they are worn below 1/16 in. tread depth in major grooves, or where inspection shows ply separation; chafer fabric injuries in tubeless tires; broken or damaged bead wires; loose cords on band ply or evidence of having been run flat; tread separation; cracks which extend into the tire fabric; any open liner splice which shows exposed fabric; any tire with a liner showing evidence of having been run under-inflated or excessive overload.

Strict limits have been set by the industry on the use of all temporary repairs, including blow-out patches and areosol sealants as well as plugs. Should such methods be used, the motorist is cautioned not to exceed 50 mph nor drive more than 100 miles before having a permanent vulcanized repair made.

1972 Vega Sedan.

EMERGENCY
TROUBLE SHOOTING

When the car engine suddenly stops, the brakes fail, the horn continues to sound, or some similar trouble occurs, the situation may range from extreme danger to one of annoyance. What to do in such emergencies is described in the following pages. It is hardly possible to describe all possible emergencies that may occur, but the usual ones are listed here, together with suggestions on ways and means of overcoming them. For more details on diagnosing troubles and making permanent repairs, the car owner is referred to other chapters in this volume. In presenting the material in this chapter, it is assumed that the owner has become familiar with automotive terms by studying the other chapters in this book.

ENGINE STOPS SUDDENLY

This condition, often described as the engine "conking out," usually is caused by running out of fuel, and the first check to be made is to note the fuel indicator gauge or light. Another reason is failure of the fuel pump, and still another reason is known as vapor lock. This latter is caused by the fuel vaporizing in the fuel lines, fuel pump, or float chamber of the carburetor. The remedy is to wait until the engine has cooled and then it will start easily.

To check for the failure of a fuel pump takes a bit longer. It is necessary to disconnect the fuel line from the carburetor, and with the end of the fuel line directed into a container, crank the engine for several revolutions. If the fuel pump is working, fuel will spurt from the end of the fuel line in a strong stream.

A loose connection in the primary circuit of the ignition system will also cause the engine to conk out suddenly. A defective switch or a burned resistor are possible causes of this trouble. Wiring around the switch will permit the engine to start in case the switch is defective. If the resistor, or resistor wiring, is burned out, running a wire from the switch connection to the "+" terminal on the coil will permit the engine to start. This should never be done except in the case of extreme emergency, as this will place full battery voltage on the coil, and operation for more than a short time will ruin the coil and ignition breaker points.

EMERGENCY TROUBLE SHOOTING

ENGINE WON'T CRANK

The most common cause of the trouble is a defective starting battery or corroded battery connection.

Another cause is a defective starter solenoid.

ENGINE CRANKS BUT WON'T START

No fuel in the fuel tank. Defective fuel pump. Check by disconnecting fuel line at carburetor, directing line into a container and cranking the engine. A pump in good condition will deliver a strong stream of fuel.

Details of 1971 307 cu. in. engine.
Typical V-8 design.

Remove air cleaner and looking into the throat of the carburetor, note if choke plate is closed or open. If the engine is cold the choke plate should be closed. If the engine is hot, the choke plate should be open. Also work the throttle by hand and note if fuel spurts from the accelerating pump nozzle. If no fuel is seen, it indicates that no fuel is reaching the carburetor. Check supply tank and fuel pump. If fuel is seen spurting from the accelerating pump nozzles, the fuel system is apparently in good condition and the trouble is probably in the ignition or starting system.

Excessive moisture on the ignition wiring and/or in distributor. Mop up excess moisture with cloth and then spray with carbon tetrachloride to hasten drying.

Loose or defective connections in primary ignition system. The remedy is to tighten connections.

Burned out primary resistor or resistor wire. Cut unit or wire out of circuit as an emergency measure only. Prolonged operation will ruin coil and breaker points.

Worn or badly adjusted breaker points. Points should be smoothed and cleaned. Correct gap on V-8 engines is .015 in. and on a Six is .025 in. If points are severly pitted, the condition can be improved by filing. A nail file can be used in an emergency.

Dirty or incorrectly adjusted spark plugs will also prevent engine from starting. Correct gap is .035 in.

A flooded carburetor will prevent engines from starting. In most cases a strong odor of fuel will be noted. The best procedure is to wait for about 10 minutes and try again. Or, depress accelerator to floor and hold it there while engine is started in usual manner. In some cases it may be necessary to remove air cleaner and note position of choke plate in the carburetor. If it is in closed position, work carburetor linkage to make sure choke valve will open.

If engine is cranked at lower than normal speed, most likely cause is partly discharged battery, loose, or corroded battery connections.

SUDDEN BRAKE FAILURE

If brakes fail suddenly while car is in motion, shut off ignition, apply hand brake, and leave transmission in gear or in drive position, as the case may be. Sudden and complete failure of brakes is caused by a break in the hydraulic line or leakage of fluid at some other point. The only remedy is replacement of defective parts.

SPONGY BRAKE PEDAL

If, when pressing on the brake pedal it has a spongy feel, there is air in the hydraulic line, and it is necessary to bleed the system to remove the air.

Complete instructions for bleeding the brake system are given in the Chapter on Brakes.

BRAKE PEDAL SINKS TO THE FLOOR

If the brake pedal sinks to the floor when the brakes are applied, the trouble is caused by a defective master cylinder or a leak in the system. The remedy is replacement of parts.

BRAKES WILL NOT HOLD

If this condition occurs suddenly and the brakes have been operating satisfactorily before that time, the condition may result from having driven through puddles of water. Condition can be minimized by driving with the brakes lightly applied for a short distance.

BRAKES GRAB

When brakes tend to grab for several applications after the car has been parked for several hours, the trouble is probably caused by moisture absorbed by the brake lining and is a characteristic of many different makes of lining. There are many other causes of grabbing brakes, which are discussed in the Chapter on Brakes.

ALTERNATOR AND GENERATOR FAILURE

When the generator fails as indicated by the warning light on the instrument panel, the first point to check is the belt which drives the fan and generator or alternator. If this belt is loose or broken, the generator or alternator will not be driven at sufficient speed to generate current. As a result, the battery will quickly become discharged, and if the same belt is driving the water pump the engine will overheat with probable damage to the engine bearings, pistons and cylinder walls. The remedy is to tighten the belt by means of the adjuster, or install a new belt as needed.

RADIATOR BOILS OVER

This condition is usually caused by insufficient water in cooling system and is indicated by the temperature gauge, or the temperature warning light, on the instrument panel. Trouble can be caused by leaking radiator, water pump, hose connections, defective core plugs in engine water jacket, or loose or broken belt driving the water pump and fan. The best procedure is to shut off engine and let it cool. While it is cooling, look for leaks in the system. Tighten hose connections if necessary, then place cloth over radiator cap and remove the cap. Cap must be removed slowly to avoid burst of steam in high pressure system. Start and idle engine and add water slowly, until system is full. If leaks have been noted in radiator core or core plugs, special radiator sealing compounds can be used to stop the leak.

HIGH PITCHED SQUEAL

A high pitched squeal when engine is first started and apparently coming from front of engine is often caused by a worn or glazed fan belt, or a water pump seal that needs lubrication. The fan belt can be silenced by applying belt dressing or in an emergency soap can be used. For a complete cure the belt should be replaced. In the case of the water pump seal, it can be lubricated by adding a water pump lubricant and rust inhibitor to the coolant in the radiator.

HARSH RATTLE

A harsh rattling noise at the front of the engine can be caused by a dry or defective fan belt. To check, stop the engine and press together belt on both sides of pulley. A harsh rasp or creaking noise will be made if the belt is dry. Laundry soap can be used as a lubricant on the belt in an emergency.

THROBBING ROAR

A throbbing roar coming from under the car is caused by muffler and pipes that have rusted through, permitting the escape of poisonous gases. Defective parts should be replaced immediately, as the escaping exhaust gases are highly toxic and lethal. Noise is usually accompanied by odor of exhaust gases in the car.

NO LIGHTS

When lights in one circuit, such as headlights, will not light, the trouble is usually caused by a burned fuse or defective circuit breaker. On late models the fuses are located on left-hand air duct, and circuit breaker is built into headlight switch. On older models, headlight switch assembly includes fuses and circuit breaker.

OTHER TROUBLES

The foregoing has covered many of the annoying situations that may occur. For other troubles, together with their solution, the reader is referred to the major trouble shooting sections of this book and also the specific chapters dealing with the different units.

MAKE YOUR OWN SAFETY CHECK

There are many conditions contributing to the safety of the car that can be checked by the average driver and which should then be corrected, either by the driver, or by the mechanic.

Before starting on a drive, adjust the rear view mirror or mirrors for comfortable viewing. For safety the car should be equipped with two side view mirrors and the usual mirror centrally located above the windshield.

If your inside mirror vibrates as the car is driven on a smooth road, it is an indication of an unbalanced condition of some rotating part. Check the wheels for roundness and a bent condition. Wheels should not be more than 1/16 in. out-of-round, or 1/16 in. laterally. Also check tires for out-of-round, and make sure they are accurately balanced. For slow speed driving, static balance is usually satisfactory. For higher speeds dynamic balancing is advised. Be sure tires are inflated to the factory's specified value.

Also check the steering wheel, making sure there is not excessive play. Do not take a chance on the condition of the brakes. With self-adjusting brakes the height of the brake pedal is not a gauge as to the condition of the brakes. The only sure way of determining the condition of the brakes is to remove a drum and look at the thickness of the lining and the condition of the drums. If, when applying the brakes the pedal has a spongy feel, it indicates there is air in the system and servicing is indicated.

Make sure the engine is in good condition and has ample power for emergency passing. The passing capacity of an untuned engine is reduced considerably. In addition, economy is seriously affected. It pays to have the engine tuned every 10,000 miles. If you are pulling a trailer, remember that the added weight will reduce your available power for acceleration and also stopping. Also the added weight of a trailer will tend to tilt the headlights upward and will blind approaching drivers. The lights should be readjusted to take care of that condition.

For safety's sake, the level of your eyes should be several inches above the rim of the steering wheel. So adjust your seat accordingly, or use a cushion.

Tips on
BODY SERVICE

The outside finish of the car body should be washed frequently. Never wipe the painted surfaces with a dry cloth as that will tend to scratch the surface and quickly remove its high luster. To keep the finish bright and attractive, and eliminate the necessity of using polish, wash the car whenever it has accumulated a moderate amount of dirt. Chevrolet cars are finished with acrylic lacquer which maintains a very high luster.

If the car is being operated in areas where salt is used on the road to melt ice, the vehicle should be washed as often as possible so that all salt is removed from the car. Pay particular attention to the underside of the fenders.

The bright metal parts of the car ordinarily require no special care. Periodic cleaning should preserve the beauty and life of these finishes. Wash with clear water, and if the parts are very dirty, use a mild soap, or special cleaning preparation designed for automotive bodies. Do not scour chrome finished parts with steel wool or polish them with a polish containing abrasives.

CLEANING THE INTERIOR

Use a broom or vacuum cleaner to remove dirt and dust from the upholstery and floor covering. Vinyl and woven plastic trim that is dusty can usually be cleaned with a damp cloth.

Dirty or stained upholstery can be cleaned with special cleaner designed for that purpose. Special cleaners are available which can be used on leather, plastic, vinyl, imitation leather, fabric upholstery, rubber mats and carpeting. If such special cleaner is not available to remove grease stains, a volatile type of cleaner such as carbon tetrachloride, or benzine can be used.

When cleaning the interior trim (upholstery) with volatile cleaners, care should be taken not to use too much solvent and to apply it only with a clean cloth. It is the solvent that does the work, so only a minimum of pressure should be applied.

First, brush away all loose particles of dirt and soil. Then dampen a clean cloth (cheesecloth may be used) with a volatile cleaner. Open the cloth and allow a portion of the cleaner to evaporate so that the cloth is just slightly damp.

Using very light pressure and a circular lifting motion, rub the stained area, starting at the outer edge and working toward the center until the entire area has been covered. Change to a clean portion of the cloth every few strokes.

Use a clean white blotter and blot the stained area to remove any excess cleaner. Change to a new portion of the blotter each time stained area is blotted. The blotting action should be repeated until no stain is transferred to the blotter surface.

Before proceeding, wait several minutes to allow most of the volatile cleaner to evaporate. Be careful not to saturate the stained area. This will avoid the danger of the cleaner penetrating to the padding under the upholstery. Certain cleaners will deteriorate sponge rubber which is often used in padding.

It may be necessary to repeat the above procedure several times before the stain has been satisfactorily removed.

If a ring should form on the fabric when removing a stain, the entire area of the trim should be cleaned.

As many volatile cleaners are toxic and harmful, certain precautions should always be taken. Always use in a well-ventilated area, and the car windows and garage doors must be open when such cleaners are used.

Avoid prolonged or repeated breathing of the vapors from the cleaner and also repeated contact with the skin. Keep the volatile cleaner away from eyes and mouth. In addition, remember that many cleaners are flammable and should not be used where there is a naked flame.

When using a detergent to clean the trim, first make a solution in luke warm water working up thick frothy suds. Then with a clean cloth or sponge, dampened with lukewarm water, apply suds only to the surface of the upholstery using light to medium pressure. Repeat several times, applying more suds with a clean portion of the cloth or sponge.

With a second clean cloth, dampened with lukewarm water, rub over the area with medium pressure to remove excess detergent and loose material. Wipe off all excess moisture with a clean dry cloth, or a vacuum cleaner.

Allow the upholstery to dry, then repeat the above treatment if necessary to remove the stain.

Solutions containing water are not recommended for general cleaning of broadcloth. Water has great destructive powers on the high face or high gloss finish of broadcloth, causing the nap to curl and roughen to such an extent that the finish is destroyed or made very unsightly. Use a broom or vacuum cleaner to remove dirt and dust from the upholstery or floor covering. Vinyl and woven plastic trim that is dusty can usually be cleaned with a damp cloth.

In case battery acid gets on the upholstery, immediately apply ordinary household ammonia, saturating the area thoroughly, permitting the ammonia to remain on the spot so that it will have ample time to neutralize the acid. Then rinse the spot by rubbing with a clean cloth, saturated with cold water.

Body Service

To remove chewing gum from the upholstery, first harden the gum with an ice cube and then scrape off the particles with a dull knife. If the gum cannot be removed completely by this method, moisten it with benzine or carbon tetrachloride and work it from the fabric with a dull knife while the gum is still moist.

Fruit stains and stains from liquor can usually be removed with very hot water. Wet the stain well by applying hot water to the spot with a clean cloth. If the spot and stain is an old one, it may be necessary to pour very hot water directly on the spot and then follow by scraping and rubbing. However, care must be exercised, as hot water in many cases will discolor the fabric.

To remove blood stains, wash the stain with a clean cloth saturated with cold water until no more of the stain can be removed. Then, if necessary, apply a small amount of household ammonia, using a brush or cloth. Rub the stain again with a clean cloth saturated with water. Do not use hot water or soap on blood stains as they will tend to set the stain, thereby making it practically impossible to remove.

Candy stains, other than stains made from chocolate candy, can be removed by rubbing the surface with a cloth saturated with very hot water. This, if necessary, can be followed with a volatile type of cleaner. In the case of stains made from chocolate candy, use a cloth soaked in lukewarm soap suds and scrape while wet with a dull knife.

If grease or oil has been spilled on the material, as much as possible should be removed by scraping with a dull knife before further treatment is attempted. Grease and oil stains may be removed by rubbing lightly with a clean cloth saturated with volatile cleaner. Be sure all motions are toward the center of the stained area, to decrease the possiblility of spreading the stain. Use a clean white blotter, blot area to remove excess cleaner and loosen grease or oil.

To remove the stains made by paste or wax type shoe polishes, a volatile cleaner is usually needed. Rub the stain gently with a cloth wet with a volatile cleaner until the polish is removed. Use a clean portion of the cloth for each scrubbing operation, and rub the stained area from the outside to the center.

If tar gets on the upholstery, first remove as much as possible with a dull knife. Moisten the spot lightly with a volatile cleaner and again remove as much of the tar as possible with a dull knife. Follow this operation by rubbing the spot lightly with a cloth wet with a cleaner until the stain is removed.

The compositions of different brands of lipsticks vary, making the stains very difficult to remove. In some instances, a volatile cleaner may remove the stain. If some stain remains after repeated applications of the volatile cleaner, it is best to let it dry and try other measures.

Sponge urine stains with clean cloth saturated with lukewarm soap suds (mild neutral soap) and then rinse well by rubbing the stain with a clean cloth dipped in cold water. Then saturate a clean cloth with a solution of one part of household ammonia and five parts water. Apply the cloth to the stain and allow solution to remain on the affected area for one minute, then rinse by rubbing with a clean wet cloth.

Sponge nausea spots with a clean cloth dipped in clear cold water. After most of the stain has been removed by that method, wash lightly with soap (mild neutral) using a clean cloth and lukewarm water. Then rub with another clean cloth dipped in cold water. Household ammonia can also be used in many cases.

WHAT TO DO ABOUT RATTLES

Most squeaks and rattles can be eliminated by carefully going over the car once or twice a year and tightening all the bolts, screws and nuts. This applies particularly to the bolts, nuts and sheet metal screws joining the various panels and shrouds under the hood. Pay particular attention to the bolts attaching the bumper to the frame. Also make sure the door latches and striker plates are tight and correctly adjusted. Rattles and squeaks are sometimes caused by weather stripping and antisqueak material that has slipped out of position. When such a condition exists, apply additional cement or other adhesives and install the material in the proper location to eliminate this difficulty. If necessary, obtain new weather stripping and antisqueak material and install it with a proper type of cement.

HOW TO KEEP THE BODY FROM RUSTING

Whenever possible, the car should be stored in a closed garage so it is protected from the sun rays and snow. When cars are driven in areas where salt is used on icy roads, care should be taken to wash the car as frequently as possible. Be sure to wash all accumulations from the underside of the fenders.

One of the major causes of car bodies rusting is failure to keep open the drain holes located on the underside of each rocker panel, quarter panel and door, Fig. W-1. These drain holes are provided so that the water will not accumulate within the panels. When the drain holes are not open water will accumulate which will soon rust the panels from the inside. The drain holes become clogged with road dirt and will not drain the water from the interior of the panels.

The door bottom and drain hole sealing strip is attached to the door inner panel over the drain holes by a snap-on fastener at each end of the strip, Fig. W-1. To prevent the strip from adhering from the door inner panel and blocking the drain hole, apply a sparing amount of silicone rubber lubricant on the center section of the sealing strip.

FIXING DUST AND WATER LEAKS

Any unsealed crevice or small opening in the body will permit dust and water to enter the interior. The actual location of the point of entry is often difficult to locate, but by removing the interior trim panel, the source of the leak can usually be found. In many cases dust and rain will leave a trail on the body panel. Water testing a car should be done in sections by spraying water on small areas at a time. In that way, it is possible to locate the points which require sealing. The correct method of water testing is to start at the bottom and work up.

All panel seams, screws, hose and grommets should be carefully closed with body sealer. Check the various openings around the cowl and windshield openings, and apply body sealer where needed. In addition, raise the hood and make sure that there are no openings in the dash panel, which will permit leakage into the driver compartment. Also check the sealer on the door hinges. The body sealer should be filled flush with the pillar post.

Door openings contribute to water leaks in two ways: First, there may be leaks at metal joint seams; and, secondly, the roughness of the door opening metal may not provide a good sealing contact surface for the weatherstrip. Leaks around the weather stripping can be located by the water test, or by using carpenter's blue chalk blown from a testing bulb.

Faulty weather stripping should always be removed and replaced with new. When installing weather stripping, follow the instructions applying to that particular cement. If necessary, build up low areas of the weather stripping by means of rubber shim stock.

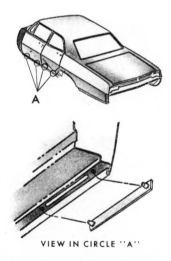

VIEW IN CIRCLE "A"

Fig. W-1. Details of sealing strips on bottom of doors. Drain holes must be kept free to prevent accumulation of water within the panels.

In the case of water leaks around the windshield weather strip, seal the weather strip against the body opening by carefully working a thin coating of windshield rubber sealer between the body edge and the rubber molding. Or, lift the lip of the rubber strip where it contacts the body and use a nozzle type of applicator.

If faulty sealing of the glass to the windshield has caused the leak, apply sealer as far down as possible between the inner weather strip and the glass, for a considerable distance at each side of the leaking point.

To determine the exact location of a dust leak, remove the following trim from inside the vehicle: Floor mats, dash and toe panel pad, and kick pads. Dust leaks should be evident when these pads and mats are removed. Leaks can be sometimes located by putting a bright light under the vehicle body, or checking the interior of the body at joints and weld lines. Light will show through where leaks exist.

Seal all leaks and road test the vehicle on a dusty road to make sure all leaks are sealed. Check for indication of dust leaks around the doors.

Openings that allow dust leaks will also provide water leaks. When checking for water leaks, a helper should be used on the inside of the car to locate the entrance of water while it is applied on the outside.

Water leaks do not always enter the body in the location where they show up. Therefore, back tracking the path of water may be required to show the true entrance of the leak.

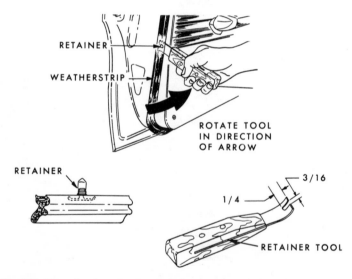

Fig. W-2. Type of tool used and method of removing weatherstrip from doors.

FRONT AND REAR DOOR WEATHER STRIPS

On recent models, both front and rear doors use nylon fasteners to retain the door weather strips. The fasteners are a component part of the weather strip and secure the weather strip to the door by engaging piercings in the door panels. Serrations of the fastener retain the fastener in the piercing and also seal the openings from water entry, Fig. W-2. On certain body styles, the nylon fasteners are used all around the entire perimeter of the door. On other style bodies, the nylon fasteners are used below the belt line only. Weather strip adhesive retains the weather strip around the door upper frame from above the belt line on such bodies, Fig. W-3.

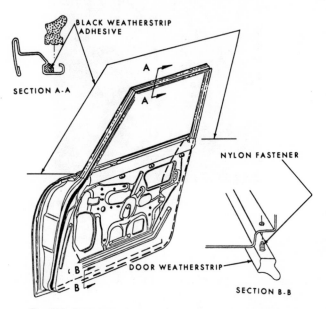

Fig. W-3. Location and type of weatherstrip used on doors.

To disengage nylon fasteners from door panel piercings, use a tool as indicated in Fig. W-2, which permits removal of the weather strip without damaging the serrations on the fasteners so that the weather strip can be reinstalled if desired.

Although a replacement door weather strip will include the nylon fasteners, individual fasteners are available as a service part.

The flat blade tool such as a putty knife can be used to break the cement bond between the door and weather strip.

When installing weather strip, make sure that the nylon fasteners are not damaged and replace those which have been damaged. Also clean off all weather strip and adhesive from the door.

On body styles without door upper frames, position weather strip to door and install plastic fasteners at front and rear end of weather strip.

On sedan styles with door upper frames, position color coded section of weather strip to the door as follows: On front doors, color code should be located at rear upper corner of door upper frame. On rear doors, color coded sections should begin at belt line of door lock pillar and extend upward.

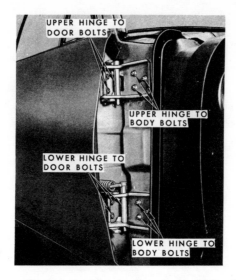

Fig. W-4. Front door hinge attachment. (Typical)

Tap nylon fasteners into door piercings using a hammer and blunt caulking tool.

On Chevelle and Nova sedan styles, apply a bead of black weather strip adhesive to gutter of door frame, Fig. W-3. Allow adhesive to become tacky and then install weather strip.

After all fasteners have been installed on sedan styles, apply weather strip adhesive between door and weather strip outboard surface as needed.

On 1962 and 1963 models, the need for sealing the weather strip clips along the bottom facing is eliminated. On previous models the weather strip clips are also cemented along the bottom and up a short distance on each pillar.

ADJUSTING DOORS

Door hinges are adjustable so as to correctly position the door in the body. There should be approximately 1/8 in. between the edge of the door and the body or body pillar.

On recent models, the front hinges are adjusted through the use of floating anchor plates in the door and front body hinge pillars, Fig. W-4.

Up-and-down and fore-and-aft adjustments are provided at the body hinge pillars. And in-and-out adjustments are provided at the door hinge pillars.

On rear doors, in-or-out and up-or-down adjustment is provided at the door side hinge attaching screws. Fore-or-aft and a slight up-or-down adjustment is available at body side (center pillar) hinge attaching screws, Fig. W-5.

Body Service

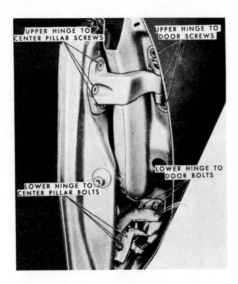

Fig. W-5. Rear door hinge attachment. (Typical)

Before removing any door, use a pencil and mark location of hinges on door or center pillar. On styles equipped with window regulators, or vacuum operated locks, proceed as follows: Remove door trim assembly and inner panel water deflector. Disconnect wire harness connector from regulator motor and/or vacuum hoses from the lock actuator. Remove electric conduit from door, and remove wire harness and/or vacuum hoses from door to conduit access hole.

With door properly supported, loosen upper and lower hinge attaching screws or bolts from the door or center pillar and remove door from the body.

REMOVING DOOR INSIDE HANDLES

Door inside handles are retained by either screws or spring clips. On styles with screw retained handles, the screws are either exposed or covered only with an applied type arm rest that can be removed by the removal of several screws.

On styles with clip retained handles, the clip is either exposed when the arm rest is removed, or else is hidden by the handle, Fig. W-6. Exposed clips can be disengaged from the remote control spindle with a screwdriver. Clips hidden by the handle can be disengaged as follows:

Depress door trim assembly sufficiently to permit inserting tool, Fig. W-6, between handle and plastic bearing plate. With tool in same plane as handle, push tool as indicated to disengage clip. Pull handle inboard to remove from spindle.

To install, engage retaining clip on handle. On ventilator and window

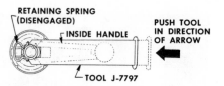

Fig. W-6. Type of tool designed to remove window control handles.

regulator spindles, position handle at same angle as opposite side handle and press handle outboard until clip engages spindle. On remote control spindles, put handle in horizontal position.

REAR DECK LID ADJUSTMENT

To adjust rear compartment lid forward or rearward, or from side-to-side, in the body opening, loosen both hinge strap attaching bolts, Fig. W-7. Adjust lid as required and then tighten bolts. To adjust compartment lid at hinge area up or down, install shims between lid inner panel and hinge straps.

HOOD ADJUSTMENT

The hood is adjusted forward or rearward, or from side to side in the body opening, as follows: Loosen the hinge strap to hood attaching bolts at each hinge, adjust the hood as required, then tighten the bolts.

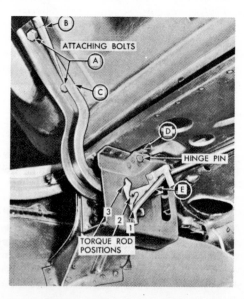

Fig. W-7. Rear compartment hinge and torque rod.

Fig. W-8. Lock to striker engagement.

To adjust the hood up or down, loosen the hinge to body attaching bolts, then shift hood to required position and tighten bolts.

ADJUSTING STRIKER PLATE

To adjust striker up or down, or in or out, loosen striker bolt, and shift striker as required, then tighten striker.

To determine if striker fore-or-aft adjustment is required, proceed as follows: First make sure door is properly aligned. Then apply modeling clay caulking compound to lock bolt opening, as shown in Fig. W-8. Close door only as far as necessary for striker bolt to form an impression in the clay. Do not close door completely as that will make the clay difficult to remove.

Measure striker impression as follows: Striker edge should be centered fore-and-aft as shown, however some tolerances are allowed. In any alignment, it is important that minimum dimensions as outlined in Fig. W-8 are strictly maintained. Spacers are available as service parts and can be used individually or in combination to achieve the desired alignment.

REMOVING TRIM ASSEMBLY

The front and rear door trim assemblies are attached by means of retaining nails attached to the back side of the door trim assembly. To remove the trim, apply masking tape to the door inner panel at trim assembly locations to avoid paint damage when pad is removed. With a clean rubber mallet, tap around entire edge of trim assembly to free trim nails from plastic retainers. Insert a flat blade tool between inner panel and door trim assembly, and carefully loosen trim assembly nails from retainers until trim can be removed from the door.

POWER WINDOW SERVICE

Generally most common failure of power windows to open are "Open" and "Short" circuits. An open circuit is one in which the circuit cannot be completed, due to a broken wire, poor terminal contact or improper ground. A short circuit is one in which the current is grounding before it reaches the operating unit. This creates an overload and actuates the circuit breaker or blows the fuse.

When a short circuit exists in a given circuit, the circuit breaker will be actuated or fuse will blow. However, if the short is located between a switch and an operating unit, the circuit breaker will actuate or the fuse will blow only when the switch is actuated. If the short occurs between the circuit breaker (or fuse) and the switch, the circuit will be inoperative all the time. This will continue until the short is repaired or the battery runs down.

In every case, first check to make sure that the fuse is not blown, and then make sure that the current is reaching the motor. If no current is reaching the motor when the switch is closed, examine the entire circuit for loose or dirty connections, or a broken wire. If none of the windows will operate with the ignition switch on, the probable cause is a short or open circuit in the power feed circuit.

If the right rear door window does not operate from master control switch on left door, or from control switches on right rear door, but the left door window operates, check for an open or short circuit between the right rear door harness and the power window front harness. Also check for a short or open circuit in affected window control switch, or window motor circuit. Also check for possible mechanical failure or bind in window channels. There is also a possibility that the window motor may be defective.

If right door windows will operate from left door master control switch, but will not operate from right door control switches, but left door windows operate, check for open or short circuit in front harness feed wire circuit.

GLASS POLISHING

Minor glass scratches can be effectively removed or substantially reduced by special polishing methods. A low speed (600 to 1300 rpm) rotary polisher is needed together with a wool felt rotary type polishing pad and powered cerium oxide (Glass-Nu or its equivalent) and a wide mouth jar to hold the polish.

The polish is mixed with sufficient water to obtain a creamy consistency. The mixture must be agitated frequently to keep the cerium oxide from settling out. Draw a circle around the scratches on the opposite side of the glass with marking crayon. Also use masking paper where needed to catch drippings or spattered splash.

Saturate the pad with the polish and use a moderate but steady pressure against the surface. Excessive pressure will cause the glass to heat. Should it become heated, allow it to air dry. Do not apply cold water. With a feathering out motion polish the affected area. Never hold the tool in one spot any longer than 30 to 45 seconds. When polishing the windshield glass, care must be taken to avoid excessive polishing, as the optical qualities may be distorted and affect the vision.

WOOD GRAIN TRANSFER

Two types of vinyl grain transfer are used on station wagons. The two types of transfer are not to be used on the same vehicle.

Transfers should not be replaced at temperatures below 65 deg. F. or over 90 deg. F.

Instructions covering the removal and application of such transfer material are included with the material.

Bill Hielscher with his 327 cu. in. Corvette in which he set a record of 170.69 mph at Bonneville Flats for the B/GT class cars. Co-driver Lee Kelley is on the left.
(Holley Carburetor Co.)

MORE SPEED
AND POWER

Stock Chevrolet engines are now available which provide terrific performance. For example, the 427 cu. in. V-8 engine with special carburetion, cams and other refinements develops 435 hp @ 5800 rpm. That is exactly 100 hp more than with standard cams and carburetion. The 396 cu. in. V-8 engine will develop 325 hp @ 4800 rpm, 350 hp @ 5200 rpm and 375 hp @ 5600 rpm depending on the equipment selected. As a result, many men who formerly developed their own engines are using such stock engines instead.

For those who wish to improve the performance of their own engines, there is a large variety of special equipment available which is readily obtainable from specialists in the field. Such special equipment includes:

Special camshafts	Stroked crankshaft
Special intake manifolds	Special exhaust manifold
High lift rocker arms	Magnetoes
Superchargers	Race type spark plugs
Injectors	Carburetors
Lightweight flywheels	Lightweight connecting rods
Roller type valve lifters	High pressure valve springs

FIRST STEPS IN BETTER PERFORMANCE

The basis of improved performance, better acceleration and higher top speed is precision workmanship. Every effort must be made to reduce friction and step up power. It must be remembered that extreme accuracy in setting ignition and carburetion, together with a good valve job, will give better than usual performance.

Contributing largely to stepped-up performance is precision balancing of crankshaft, together with piston and ring assemblies. Special equipment is used for balancing the piston and rod assemblies so that they are all the same weight, Fig. X-1. When they are balanced, their equivalent in weight is attached to the crankshaft, which is then balanced on a crankshaft balancer, Fig. X-2. Such equipment will detect any unbalance of .002 ounce. This far exceeds the 1/2 ounce that is used as a standard on many conventional passenger car engines. Balancing of the crankshaft is so critical and precise that allowance is even made for the weight of the oil in the crank throws.

Such precision balancing permits greatly increased speed and what is equally important it reduces the load on the bearings. As a result, the engine will have many more miles of useful life. When used in normal service, a precision balanced engine will easily deliver in excess of 300,000 miles of trouble-free service. This has been demonstrated many times in the commercial vehicle field.

Fig. X-1. Note special weighing scales in background for weighing pistons and connecting rods, also the set of special rods and pistons in foreground left.

The clearance of bearings and pistons must receive special attention. For street use, main and rod bearing clearance should range from .0025 to .003 in. for most engines. For drag strip operation, a slightly greater clearance should be given. Usually .003 in. has been found to be satisfactory. Side clearance of the rods should be increased to about .003 in.

Intake valves with hollow stems are preferred because of their lighter weight. Sodium filled exhaust valves are considered a must because they can better withstand the higher operating temperatures.

The cylinder block should be "boiled out" to remove all traces of rust and scale from the water jacket and should also be checked with a Magnaflux tester for cracks. Particular attention should be paid to the webbing, main bearing caps, cap bolts and the cylinder head area around the head bolts for stress and cracks. Nicks and scratches should be smoothed away from all surfaces. Grind away any casting flashes.

If a new cylinder block is used, it should also be "boiled out" to be sure there is no casting sand in the waterjacket. New or old, all parts should be checked with a Magnaflux type tester.

Fig. X-2. One type of special equipment used to balance crankshafts.

HINTS ON RAISING COMPRESSION

The answer to the question, how high should compression be raised, depends largely on the compression ratio of the original engine, on the fuel that is to be used, and the type of racing or driving in which the car is to be used. In general, it is seldom advisable to use a compression ratio of over 11 to 1. The usual method of increasing the compression ratio is to plane the gasket surface of the cylinder block, or the cylinder head. In most cases with Chevrolet overhead valve engines, race mechanics prefer to plane the cylinder head. The reason is that the piston, when it comes to the top of its stroke, is flush with the top of the cylinder block and therefore the combustion chamber is in the cylinder head.

When raising compression be sure to check the clearance between the valves in their open position and the top of the piston. If this is not done, the piston may strike the valve with severe damage to the engine.

In the case of the pistons in the 409 cu. in. Chevrolet V-8 engine, these have recessed marks on top to provide the necessary clearance for the valve.

In order to calculate how much the volume of the combustion chamber should be reduced, in order to obtain the desired compression ratio, use is made of the following formula:

$$A = \frac{B}{C-1}$$

Where A is the volume of the combustion chamber, B is the displacement of the cylinder, and C is the desired compression ratio. For example, if it is an eight cylinder engine, with a total displacement of 320 cu. in. (40 cu. in. per cylinder) and the desired compression ratio is 11 to 1, then

$$A = \frac{40}{11-1} = \frac{40}{10} = 4 \text{ cu. in.}$$

the volume of the combustion chamber should then be 4 cu. in. In the case of a flat top piston, which at the top of its stroke is flush with the top of the cylinder block, all the combustion chamber will be in the cylinder head. To measure the volume of the combustion chamber, place the cylinder head on a work bench with the combustion chamber up. Using a spirit level, make sure the gasket surface is perfectly level. Using a chemist's graduate calibrated in tenths of an inch, see how much fluid is required to fill the combustion chamber. The job will be simplified if a piece of clear plastic is clamped firmly to the top of the combustion chamber. Fluid such as brake fluid or kerosene is then poured through a hole in the sheet of plastic.

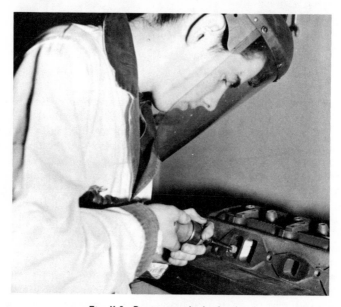

Fig. X-3. Porting a cylinder head.

Boring the cylinders will also increase the compression ratio. In the case of cylinders of about 3-1/2 in. in diameter, when the diameter is increased .060 in. the compression ratio will be increased approximately .2. In general, .060 in. is about the maximum the cylinder can be rebored without danger of breaking through into the water jacket, or at least seriously weakening it.

While working on the combustion chambers, it is important to check the volume of each to be sure they are identical. Any variation in volume will result in a rough running engine, and accompaning vibration and loss of power. Usually, all that is necessary can be accomplished by carefully polishing the surface of the combustion chamber, including the top of the piston. Before deciding on raising the compression of an engine, it is important to decide on what fuel is to be used. Commercial high test gasoline can be used in engines up to approximately 11 to 1. For higher compression ratios it is usually necessary to use special racing fuels.

POINTER ON PORTING

On older engines considerable improvement in performance can be obtained by "porting" the cylinder head, Fig. X-3. That process increases the diameter of the exhaust and intake valve ports in the cylinder head, together with larger diameter valve heads. On more recent models, the factory has used that method of improving the performance of their engine. While the valve ports on stock engines of recent model engines are about as large as possible, some work can still be done on the ports. This is in the form of polishing and making sure that the ports are as much alike as possible.

Special care must be taken so all ports are the same size. A fine emery wheel is used in an electric drill. The wheel must be a fine grit, as the object is to polish rather than to remove metal. Most mechanics use a pair of inside calipers to check the size of the ports to make sure all intake ports are of equal size and that all exhaust ports are of the same size. In some instances, a mechanic will fashion a plug type gauge for checking the size of the ports.

Closely associated with porting is work done on the manifolds, both intake and exhaust. Because of its complex shape, there is not much that can be done to polish the interior of a manifold. The important point is to check to see how the openings in the manifold line up with the openings in the cylinder head. To do this, coat the gasket surface of the manifold with a light coating of Prussian blue and then bolt it in position. When the manifold is removed, some of the blue will have been transferred to the cylinder block, clearly indicating any offset. If the ports do not match up, it will be necessary to enlarge the bolt holes in the manifold so it can be shifted to the desired position. In some cases it may be more desirable to grind the edges of the ports on the manifold so that there will be no overlapping with the ports in the cylinder head. Further in connection with manifolds, many mechanics take advantage of the special speed manifold that has been designed by speed specialists, especially for Chevrolet engines. Fig. X-4 shows Bobby Unser setting a new record in the Pike's Peak climb. Note the four carburetor air intakes. Fig. X-5 shows an Offenhauser dual quad intake manifold.

TIPS ON CARBURETION

Some experimentation with carburetor jets is necessary to obtain the best air-fuel ratio. When running without an air cleaner, it usually takes an increase of three to four sizes over standard to get a good mixture. However, the exact mixture will vary with air temperature, altitude, humidity, etc.

When using a 348 cu. in. or a 409 cu. in. Chevrolet engine for the road and dragster work, many mechanics will raise the compression ratio from 1 to 1-1/2 points over stock, and a three carburetor intake manifold with 1-3/16 in. venturi, two-barrel carburetor. A broad recommendation is

Fig. X-4. Bobby Unser used a Chevrolet engine equipped with Perfect Circle piston rings and valve seals to crack the Pike's Peak record and win his ninth championship class title.

1 sq. in. of venturi area for every 40 cu. in. displacement. However, detailed carburetor specifications have to be worked out on a trial testing of each engine.

Some experimentation with carburetion is necessary to obtain the best air-fuel ratio. When running without an air cleaner, an increase of three to four sizes over standard jet size is often required. However, this will vary with different engines and carburetors. It must be remembered that the mixture ratio will also vary with air temperature, altitude and humidity. So it pays to make frequent checks, noting carefully which jet size gives the best performance for each particular weather condition.

Fig. X-5. Special Offenhauser dual quad intake manifold.

With multiple carburetor installations, great care must be taken in the adjustment of the throttle rods so that the opening and closing of the carburetor throttles are correctly synchronized. If this is not done, some cylinders will tend to lag and full power will not be produced.

Fig. X-6. Installing a Chevrolet engine in a rail job at a speed shop in Elk Grove, Illinois. The dragster is owned by the Automotive Parts Division of Borg-Warner Corp.

WHAT TO DO ABOUT RODS AND PISTONS

Lightweight aluminum connecting rods, accurately balanced, are available from race parts specialists. However, those not wishing to go to the expense of aluminum connecting rods, should carefully polish and balance connecting rods that are standard equipment with the engine. Pistons must also be accurately balanced, as any variation in the weights of the pistons and rod assemblies will result in vibration and stepped-up bearing loads, Fig. X-1.

Special lightweight pistons are also available. For higher engine speeds, it is necessary to increase the clearance of the pistons in the engines.

Remember that on V-type engines, when replacing pistons and rods, they must weigh the same as the original parts in order to maintain the balance. If the replacement piston and rod assemblies are different weights than the originals, the crankshaft and the reciprocating assemblies will then have to be rebalanced.

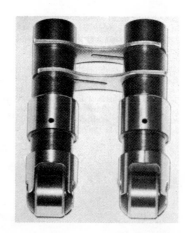

Fig. X-7. Special roller type valve lifters.

VALVES, SPRINGS, CAMS

Valves, springs and cams play an important part in speed and performance.

Valve head diameter should be as large as possible, and in older engines particularly, great improvement in performance can be obtained by cutting larger diameter seats in the cylinder heads and installing larger diameter valves. On more recent model engines, the design has been changed so that larger valves are already incorporated in the design and not much more can be gained in that respect. However, heavier valve springs which will reduce the tendency of valves to bounce at high speeds, are used extensively. Care must be taken that the valve spring height is the same throughout the engine.

It is always important to make sure that the valve head will not strike the piston when the piston is at the top of the stroke. The absolute minimum piston to valve head clearance is .125 in. To check this clearance without dismantling the engine, have the valve lash to the .125 in. clearance. For example, if the valve lash is .025 in. and the piston to valve clearance is .125 in., the total is .150 in. Use a feeler gauge of that thickness and insert it between the valve stem and the rocker arm. Manually turn the engine over twice and if the piston does not hit the valve, you have the proper minimum clearance. Check all eight cylinders. In some cases the pistons may have to be fly cut to provide adequate clearance.

Solid, adjustable valve lifters are used in place of hydraulic lifters and many mechanics prefer lifters of the roller type, Fig. X-7. The rollers are especially heat treated to withstand the higher load of stiffer valve springs and higher speeds. Along with stiffer springs, special heavy-duty valve spring retainers are also used.

In order to get greater valve opening, rocker arms with increased ratios such as 1.5 to 1, or 1.75 to 1, are available.

Installation of a special camshaft is important if increased performance is to be obtained. Racing cams lift the valves higher and hold them open longer than stock camshafts. In that way more air-fuel mixture is drawn into the cylinder. In addition, a larger portion of the burned gases will be expelled from the engine. However, the installation of such a camshaft results in extreme rough idling. There are several different types of cams, each designed for a specific type of operation. No one particular cam provides all the desirable characteristics. The generally recognized types of cams include road or semi-race, three-quarter grind, full race and super. The road or semi-race provides good acceleration with fair idling. In fact such cams are virtually standard stock design on present passenger cars. The three-quarter grind will not idle as well as the semi-race, but will provide better acceleration and more top speed.

The full-race cam gives more top speed and acceleration, while the super cam is still more of the same, but both idle very poorly. Naturally, as valves are kept open longer, improved carburetion is a must in order to take full advantage of the faster cam. Also different rear axle ratios are needed to take advantage of the higher engine speeds. If the car is to be used for conventional transportation, as well as speed, the road or semi-cam should be used.

WHAT TO DO ABOUT IGNITION

For sustained high speed driving, many mechanics prefer the use of a magneto. Such magnetos are available in a type that can be substituted directly for the original equipment, Fig. X-8. If the decision is made to stick with battery ignition, a double breaker arm distributor with two ignition coils is preferred.

The correct type of spark plugs for sustained high speed driving is critical. The standard equipment spark plugs are usually too hot for such work. As compression is increased and higher speeds maintained, the use of a colder running plug is essential. The best way to determine which is the correct type of spark plug to use is to operate the engine under race conditions, and try spark plugs of different heat range until the correct one is discovered.

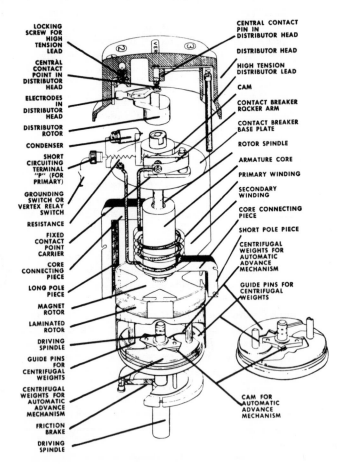

LOCKING SCREW FOR HIGH TENSION LEAD

CENTRAL CONTACT POINT IN DISTRIBUTOR HEAD

ELECTRODES IN DISTRIBUTOR HEAD

DISTRIBUTOR ROTOR

CONDENSER

SHORT CIRCUITING TERMINAL "P" (FOR PRIMARY)

GROUNDING SWITCH OR VERTEX RELAY SWITCH

RESISTANCE

FIXED CONTACT POINT CARRIER

CORE CONNECTING PIECE

LONG POLE PIECE

MAGNET ROTOR

LAMINATED ROTOR

DRIVING SPINDLE

GUIDE PINS FOR CENTRIFUGAL WEIGHTS

CENTRIFUGAL WEIGHTS FOR AUTOMATIC ADVANCE MECHANISM

FRICTION BRAKE

DRIVING SPINDLE

CENTRAL CONTACT PIN IN DISTRIBUTOR HEAD

DISTRIBUTOR HEAD

HIGH TENSION DISTRIBUTOR LEAD

CAM

CONTACT BREAKER ROCKER ARM

CONTACT BREAKER BASE PLATE

ROTOR SPINDLE

ARMATURE CORE

PRIMARY WINDING

SECONDARY WINDING

CORE CONNECTING PIECE

SHORT POLE PIECE

CENTRIFUGAL WEIGHTS FOR AUTOMATIC ADVANCE MECHANISM

GUIDE PINS FOR CENTRIFUGAL WEIGHTS

CAM FOR AUTOMATIC ADVANCE MECHANISM

Fig. X-8. Special magneto designed to be substituted for conventional distributor.

Examination of the spark plug insulator after the plug has been in operation will disclose whether it is of the correct heat range. If the insulator is white to a light amber in color, it is correct for that engine and that particular type of work. However, if the insulator has blistered or is pockmarked, a colder running plug should be substituted.

TURNING DOWN FLYWHEELS

The flywheels used on conventional passenger cars are designed to provide smooth low speed idling. As a result they are made relatively heavy. However, the greater inertia reduces acceleration. To overcome this condition, race car mechanics usually reface the flywheel in order to reduce its weight. The amount of metal to be removed depends largely on how much of the smooth idling the owner wishes to sacrifice. In general, the

Fig. X-9. Lightweight flywheel.

maximum that is removed is about one-third of the total weight. However, many mechanics will remove approximately one-quarter of the weight. When refacing a flywheel the metal should be removed from the forward face, in order not to change the surface contacted by the clutch plate. Metal should not be removed from the area of the flywheel contacting the crankshaft flange, as this would affect clutch operation. The starter ring gear should also be left intact. Fig. X-9 shows a special lightweight flywheel designed by race specialists for use on Chevrolet cars.

MORE HIGH SPEED TIPS

The cooling fan consumes a lot of power. At high speeds, up to 5 hp is requred to drive a fan. At road speeds above 35 miles per hour, the fan is not needed to cool the radiator. Consequently, fan blades can be removed unless the car is to be driven in traffic.

Additional savings in power can be made by reducing the battery charging rate to a minimum if the car is fitted with a magneto. If the car is to be used for racing only the battery and generator can be removed. Anything that can be done to reduce the weight of the car will aid materially in improving acceleration, top speed and fuel economy. In this connection, some mechanics will drill 1 in. holes in the frame. Spare tires and wheels are eliminated. Magnesium wheels are also available.

Shock absorbers are of extreme importance, both from the standpoint

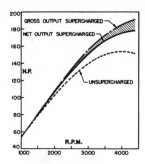

Fig. X-10. Comparison of power developed by supercharged and nonsupercharged engine.

of speed and control of the car. Leaks or defective shock absorbers will permit the driving wheels to spin and increase steering difficulties. For high speed work, different shock absorbers are therefore used. On race cars it is customary to install additional shock absorbers to get the amount of control desired.

SUPERCHARGERS AND TURBOCHARGERS

Superchargers and turbochargers are designed to force more of the air fuel mixture into the combustion chamber than would be drawn in by the normal suction of the pistons. In that way the performance of the engine is

Fig. X-11. Note timing belt for driving the supercharger on this 327 cu. in. Chevrolet engine on exhibition at parts show.

increased, Fig. X-10. Both devices are essentially blowers. The super-charger is driven mechanically by gears or chains, while the turbocharger is driven by the force of exhaust gases. Superchargers have been used for many years, while the turbocharger is a more recent development. The supercharger frequently used on stock engines is the unit developed by General Motors Diesel and is of the Rootes type, Fig. X-11. When used on the Chevrolet V-8 engines it is usually mounted between the banks of cylinders and driven by a chain belt from a sprocket at the front end of the crankshaft.

One of the disadvantages of the supercharger is the power required to drive the unit, Fig. X-10. This naturally cuts down the power available to drive the car. The turbocharger does not have this difficulty as it uses the pressure of the exhaust gases to rotate the veins of the blower.

Fig. X-12. Type of turbocharger being used to step up performance.

One type of turbocharger developed for passenger car engines is shown in Fig. X-12. Exhaust gases drive the turbine wheel which turns the compressor fan, up to 90,000 rpm at maximum engine speed. With increased compression, pressures resulting from the supercharging effect of the turbocharger, there is a tendency to detonate. To overcome this condition, the Chevrolet design also includes an alcohol injector. When alcohol is injected into the manifold, the octane rating of the fuel mixture is increased, and detonation is thereby reduced.

FUEL INJECTION

The Chevrolet type fuel injection system, Fig. X-13, comprises three basic assemblies: The intake manifold, the air meter, and the fuel meter-injector nozzle assembly.

In operation, the accelerator pedal controls the volume of air, and the volume of air in turn determines the amount of gas delivered to the fuel injection nozzles. A high pressure pump, submerged in a fuel reservoir,

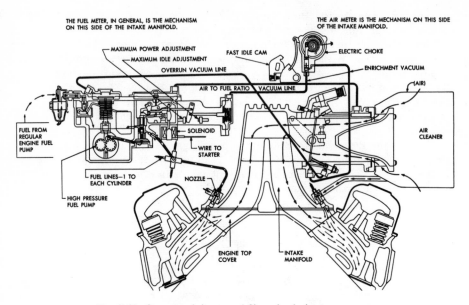

THE FUEL METER, IN GENERAL, IS THE MECHANISM ON THIS SIDE OF THE INTAKE MANIFOLD.

THE AIR METER IS THE MECHANISM ON THIS SIDE OF THE INTAKE MANIFOLD.

MAXIMUM POWER ADJUSTMENT

MAXIMUM IDLE ADJUSTMENT

OVERRUN VACUUM LINE

FAST IDLE CAM

ELECTRIC CHOKE

ENRICHMENT VACUUM

AIR TO FUEL RATIO VACUUM LINE

(AIR)

FUEL FROM REGULAR ENGINE FUEL PUMP

SOLENOID

WIRE TO STARTER

AIR CLEANER

FUEL LINES—1 TO EACH CYLINDER

NOZZLE

HIGH PRESSURE FUEL PUMP

ENGINE TOP COVER

INTAKE MANIFOLD

Fig. X-13. Operational diagram of Chevrolet fuel injector system.

and driven by the distributor, delivers the fuel to a metering chamber from which there are two outlets. The lower outlet leads to the nozzle, and the upper to an overflow line.

A plunger sensitive to the flow of air in the system meters the amount of fuel directed toward the cylinders. Pressure at the .011 in. orifices of the nozzle measures up to 20 lb. per sq. in. The spray from these nozzles is so fine it cannot be seen by the naked eye, and is directed into the intake ports, immediately before the intake valves. The fuel-air mixture is ignited in the usual way by the spark plug.

YEAR AND MODEL	Displacement	Number of Cylinders, Bore and Stroke	Brake Horsepower	Compression Ratio	Compression Pressure	AC Spark Plug Model	Spark Plug Gap	Location of Timing Mark	Breaker Point Open Deg. BTDC	Breaker Point Gap Used Points	Valve Lash Intake	Valve Lash Exhaust
1960	235	6-3.56x3.94	135	8.25	130	44	.035	F	5B	.016	hy 1-1/2 t	hy 1-1/2 t
1960 Hi-Thrift	235	6-3.56x3.940	135	8.25	130	44	.035	F	5	.016	1-1/2 t	1-1/2 t
1960 Turbo Fire 2 BBL.	283	V8-3.875x3.000	185	8.50	140	44	.035	V	8	.016	3/4 t	3/4 t
1960 Turbo Fire 4 BBL.	283	V8-3.875x3.000	230	9.50	150	44	.035	V	8	.016	3/4 t	3/4 t
1960 Turbo Thrust	348	V8-4.125x3.250	250	9.50	150	44N	.035	V	8	.016	3/4 t	3/4 t
1960 Turbo T. Spe. Cam	348	V8-4.125x3.250	300	11.10	150	44N	.035	V	8	.016	.008H	.018H
1960 3x2 Carb.	348	V8-4.125x3.250	280	11.00	150	44N	.035	V	12	.016	.008H	.018H
1960 3x2 Carb. Spe. Cam	348	V8-4.125x3.250	315	11.25	150	44N	.035	V	12	.016	.008H	.018H
1961 L6	235	6-3.56x3.940	135	8.25	145	44	.035	F	5	.016	1-1/2 t	1-1/2 t
1961 2 BBL.	283	V8-3.875x3.000	170	8.50	150	45	.035	V	4	.016	3/4 t	3/4 t
1961 4 BBL.	283	V8-3.875x3.000	230	9.50	150	45	.035	V	4	.016	3/4 t	3/4 t
1961 4 BBL.	348	V8-4.125x3.250	250	9.50	150	44N	.035	V	8	.016	1-1/2 t	1-1/2 t
1961 4 BBL. Spe. Cam	348	V8-4.125x3.250	305	11.25	150	43N	.035	V	12	.016	.008H	.018H
1961 4 BBL. Spe. Cam	348	V8-4.125x3.250	320	11.25	150	43N	.035	V	12	.016	.008H	.018H
1961 3x2 Carb.	348	V8-4.125x3.250	280	11.00	150	44N	.035	V	8	.016	.008H	.018H
1961 3x2 Spe. Cam	348	V8-4.125x3.250	335	11.25	150	43N	.035	V	12	.016	.008H	.018H
1962 Chevy II Four	153	4-3.876x3.25	90	8.50	140	46N	.035	V	4	.016	1 t	1 t
1962 Chevy II Six	194	6-3.564x3.25	120	8.50	140	46N	.035	V	8	.016	1 t	1 t
1962 L-6	235	6-3.560x3.940	135	8.25	145	46	.035	F	5	.016	1 t	1 t
1962	283	V8-3.875x3.000	170	8.50	150	46	.035	V	4	.016	1 t	1 t
1962 4 BBL.	327	V8-4.00x3.25	250	10.50	150	44	.035	V	4	.016	1 t	1 t
1962 4 BBL. ALUM	327	V8-4.00x3.25	300	10.50	150	44	.035	V	8	.016	1 t	1 t
1962 4 BBL.	409	V8-4.312x3.50	380	11.00	200	43N	.035	V	12	.016	.008H	.018H
1962 4 BBL.Dual	409	V8-4.312x3.50	409	11.00	200	43N	.035	V	12	.016	.008H	.018H
1963 Chevy II Four	153	4-3.876x3.250	90	8.50	140	46N	.035	V	4	.016	1 t	1 t
1963 Chevy II Six	194	6-3.564x3.250	120	8.50	140	46N	.035	V	8	.016	1 t	1 t
1963	230	6-3.875x3.250	140	8.50	130	46	.035	V	4	.016	1 t	1 t
1963 2 GC	283	V8-3.875x3.000	195	9.50	150	46N	.035	V	4	.016	1 t	1 t
1963 4 GC	327	V8-4.00x3.250	250	10.50	160	45	.035	V	4	.016	1 t	1 t
1963 AFB	327	V8-4.00x3.250	300	10.50	160	44	.035	V	8	.016	1 t	1 t
1963 4 GC	409	V8-4.313x3.500	340	10.50	150	43N	.035	V	10	.016	1 t	1 t
1963 AFB, Spe. Cam	409	V8-4.313x3.500	400	11.00	150	43N	.035	V	12	.016	.012S	.020S
1963 2 AFB, Spe. Cam	409	V8-4.313x3.500	425	11.00	150	43N	.035	V	12	.016	.012S	.020S
1964 Chevy II Four	153	4-3.875x3.250	90	8.50	130	46N	.035	V	4	.016	1 t	1 t
1964 Chevy II Six	194	6-3.564x3.250	120	8.50	130	46N	.035	V	8	.016	1 t	1 t
1964 L6	230	6-3.875x3.250	140	8.50	130	46N	.035	V	4	.016	1 t	1 t
1964 2 BBL.	283	V8-3.875x3.000	195	9.25	150	45	.035	V	4	.016	1 t	1 t
1964 4 BBL.	283	V8-3.875x3.000	220	9.25	150	45	.035	V	4	.016	1 t	1 t
1964 4 BBL.	327	V8-4.000x3.250	250	10.50	160	44	.035	V	4	.016	1 t	1 t
1964 AFB, Spe. Cam	327	V8-4.000x3.250	300	10.50	160	44	.035	V	8	.016	1 t	1 t
1964 4 BBL.	409	V8-4.313x3.500	340	10.00	150	43N	.035	V	6	.016	1 t	1 t
1964 AFB, Spe. Cam	409	V8-4.313x3.500	400	11.00	150	43N	.035	V	12	.016	.012S	.020S
1964 2 AFB	409	V8-4.313x3.500	425	11.00	150	43N	.035	V	12	.016	.012S	.020S
1965 L4	153	4-3.87x3.250	90	8.50	130	46N	.035	V	4	.016	1 t	1 t
1965 L6	194	6-3.563x3.250	120	8.50	130	46N	.035	V	8	.016	1 t	1 t
1965 L6	230	6-3.875x3.250	125	8.50	130	46N	.035	V	4	.016	1 t	1 t
1965 L6	230	6-3.875x3.250	140	8.50	130	46N	.035	V	4	.016	1 t	1 t
1965 2 BBL.	283	V8-3.875x3.000	195	9.25	150	45	.035	V	4	.016	1 t	1 t
1965	327	V8-4.000x3.250	250	10.50	160	44	.035	V	4	.016	1 t	1 t
1965	327	V8-4.000x3.250	300	10.50	160	44	.035	V	8	.016	1 t	1 t
1965	327	V8-4.000x3.250	350	11.00	160	44	.035	V	8	.016	1 t	1 t
1965	327	V8-4.000x3.250	365	11.00	150	44	.035	V	10	.016	.030	.030
1965	409	V8-4.313x3.500	340	10.00	150	43N	.035	V	6	.016	hy	hy
1965	409	V8-4.313x3.500	400	11.00	150	43N	.035	V	12	.016	.025	.025
1966	153	4-3.875x3.250	90	8.50	130	46N	.035	V	4	.016	1 t	1 t
1966	194	6-3.563x3.250	120	8.50	130	46N	.035	V	8	.016	1 t	1 t
1966	230	6-3.875x3.250	140	8.50	130	46N	.035	V	4	.016	1 t	1 t
1966	250	6-3.875x3.530	150	8.50	130	46N	.035	V	6	.016	1 t	1 t
1966	283	V8-3.875x3.000	195	9.25	150	45	.035	V	4	.016	1 t	1 t
1966	283	V8-3.875x3.000	220	9.25	150	45	.035	V	4	.016	1 t	1 t
1966	327	V8-4.000x3.250	275	10.50	160	44	.035	V	8	.016	1 t	1 t
1966	327	V8-4.000x3.250	300	10.50	160	44	.035	V	6	.016	1 t	1 t
1966	327	V8-4.000x3.250	350	11.00	150	44	.035	V	10	.016	1 t	1 t
1966	396	V8-4.094x3.760	325	10.25	160	43N	.035	V	4	.016	1 t	1 t

For explanations of abbreviations see page 345.

343

YEAR AND MODEL	Displacement	Number of Cylinders, Bore and Stroke	Brake Horsepower	Compression Ratio	Compression Pressure	AC Spark Plug Model	Spark Plug Gap	Location of Timing Mark	Breaker Point Open Deg. BTDC	Breaker Point Gap Used Points	Valve Lash	
											Intake	Exhaust
1966	396	V8-4.094x3.760	360	10.25	160	43N	.035	V	4	.016	1 t	1 t
1966	427	V8-4.250x3.760	390	10.25	160	43N	.035	V	4	.016	1 t	1 t
1966	427	V8-4.250x3.760	425	11.00	150	43N	.035	V	8	.016	.020	.024
1967	153	4-3.875x3.250	90	8.50	130	46N	.035	V	4	.016	1 t	1 t
1967	194	6-3.563x3.250	120	8.50	130	46N	.035	V	4	.016	1 t	1 t
1967	230	6-3.875x3.250	140	8.50	130	46N	.035	V	4	.016	1 t	1 t
1967	250	6-3.875x3.530	155	8.50	130	46N	.035	V	4	.016	1 t	1 t
1967	283	V8-3.875x3.000	195	9.25	150	45	.035	V	4	.016	1 t	1 t
1967	327	V8-4.000x3.250	210	8.75	160	44	.035	V	2	.016	1 t	1 t
1967	327	V8-4.00x3.250	275	10.00	160	44	.035	V	8	.016	1 t	1 t
1967	327	V8-4.00x3.250	300	10.00	160	44	.035	V	6	.016	1 t	1 t
1967	327	V8-4.00x3.250	325	11.00	150	44	.035	V	10	.016	1 t	1 t
1967	327	V8-4.00x3.250	350	11.00	150	44	.035	V	10	.016	1 t	1 t
1967	350	V8-4.00x3.480	295	10.25	160	44	.035	V	4	.016	1 t	1 t
1967	396	V8-4.094x3.760	325	10.25	160	43N	.035	V	4	.016	1 t	1 t
1967	396	V8-4.094x3.760	350	10.25	160	43N	.035	V	4	.016	1 t	1 t
1967	427	V8-4.250x3.760	385	10.25	160	43N	.035	V	4	.016	1 t	1 t
1967	427	V8-4.250x3.760	390	10.25	160	43N	.035	V	4	.016	1 t	1 t
1967	427	V8-4.250x3.760	400	10.25	160	43N	.035	V	4	.016	1 t	1 t
1967	427	V8-4.250x3.760	425	10.25	150	43N	.035	V	10	.016	.022	.024
1967	427	V8-4.250x3.760	435	11.00	150	43N	.035	V	5	.016	.024	.028
1968	153	4-3.875x3.250	90	8.50	130	46N	.035	V	Od	.016	1 t	1 t
1968	230	6-3.875x3.250	140	8.50	130	46N	.035	V	Od	.016	1 t	1 t
1968	250	6-3.875x3.530	155	8.50	130	46N	.035	V	Od	.016	1 t	1 t
1968	302	V8-4.000x3.000	290	11.00	190	43	.035	V	4	.016	.030	.030
1968	307	V8-3.85x3.250	200	9.00	150	43S	.035	V	2	.016	1 t	1 t
1968	327	V8-4.00x3.250	210	8.75	160	44	.035	V	2g	.016	1 t	1 t
1968	327	V8-4.000x3.250	250	8.75	160	44S	.035	V	4	.016	1 t	1 t
1968	327	V8-4.000x3.250	275	10.00	160	44	.035	V	Od	.016	1 t	1 t
1968	327	V8-4.000x3.250	300	10.00	160	44	.035	V	4	.016	1 t	1 t
1968	327	V8-4.000x3.250	325	11.00	150	44	.035	V	4	.016	1 t	1 t
1968	327	V8-4.000x3.250	350	11.00	150	44	.035	V	4	.016	1 t	1 t
1968	350	V8-4.000x3.480	295	10.25	160	44	.035	V	0	.016	1 t	1 t
1968	396	V8-4.094x3.760	325	10.25	160	43N	.035	V	4	.016	1 t	1 t
1968	396	V8-4.094x3.760	350	10.25	160	43N	.035	V	TC	.016	1 t	1 t
1968	396	V8-4.094x3.760	375	11.00	160	43N	.035	V	4	.016	1 t	1 t
1968	427	V8-4.250x3.760	385	10.25	160	43N	.035	V	4	.016	1 t	1 t
1968	427	V8-4.250x3.760	390	10.25	160	43N	.035	V	4	.016	1 t	1 t
1968	427	V8-4.250x3.760	400	10.25	160	43N	.035	V	4	.016	1 t	1 t
1968	427	V8-4.250x3.760	425	11.00	150	43N	.035	V	4	.016	.024	.028
1968	427	V8-4.250x3.760	430	12.00	150	43XL	.035	V	12	.016	.022	.022
1968	427	V8-4.250x3.760	435	11.00	150	43N	.035	V	4	.016	.024	.028
1969-1970	153	4-3.87x3.25	90	8.50	130	R46N	.035	V	TCd	.016	1 t	1 t
1969-1970	230	6-3.87x3.25	140	8.50	130	R46N	.035	V	TCd	.016	1 t	1 t
1969-1970	250	6-3.87x3.53	155	8.50	130	R46N	.035	V	TCd	.016	1 t	1 t
1969-1970	302	V8-4.00x3.00	290	11.00	190	R43	.035	V	4B	.016	.030	.030
1969-1970	307	V8-3.87x3.25	200	9.00	150	R45S	.035	V	2B	.016	1 t	1 t
1969	327	V8-4.00x3.25	210	9.00	160	R45S	.035	V	2Ae	.016	1 t	1 t
1969	327	V8-4.00x3.25	235	9.00	160	45S	.035	V	2Ae	.016	1 t	1 t
1969-1970	350	V8-4.00x3.48	255	9.00	160	R44	.035	V	TCd	.016	1 t	1 t
1969-1970	350	V8-4.00x3.48	300	10.25	160	R44	.035	V	TCd	.016	1 t	1 t
1969-1970	350	V8-4.00x3.48	350	11.00	160	R44	.035	V	4B	.016	1 t	1 t
1969-1970	350	V8-4.00x3.48	370	11.00	190	R43	.035	V	4B	.016	1 t	1 t
1969	396	V8-4.09x3.76	265	9.00	160	R44N	.035	V	TCd	.016	1 t	1 t
1969	396	V8-4.09x3.76	325	10.25	160	R44N	.035	V	4B	.016	1 t	1 t
1969-1970	396	V8-4.09x3.76	350	10.25	160	R43N	.035	V	TCd	.016	1 t	1 t
1969-1970	396	V8-4.09x3.76	375	11.00	160	R43N	.035	V	4B	.016	.024	.028
1970	400	V8-4.12x3.75	265	9.00	160	R44T	.035	V	4Bj	.016	1 t	1 t
1970	400	V8-4.12x3.75	330	10.25	160	R44T	.035	V	4B	.016	1 t	1 t
1969	427	V8-4.25x3.76	335	10.25	160	R44N	.035	V	4B	.016	1 t	1 t
1969-1970	427	V8-4.25x3.76	390	10.25	160	R43N	.035	V	4B	.016	1 t	1 t
1969-1970	427	V8-4.25x3.76	400	10.25	160	R43N	.035	V	4B	.016	1 t	1 t
1969	427	V8-4.25x3.76	425	11.00	150	R43N	.035	V	4B	.016	.024	.028
1969-1970	427	V8-4.25x3.76	430	12.00	150	R43XL	.035	V	12B	.016	.022	.024
1969-1970	427	V8-4.25x3.76	435	11.00	150	R43N	.035	V	4B	.016	.024	.028

For explanation of abbreviations see next page.

CHEVROLET TUNE-UP SPECIFICATIONS (Continued)

YEAR AND MODEL	Displacement	Number of Cylinders, Bore and Stroke	Brake Horsepower	Compression Ratio	Compression Pressure	AC Spark Plug Model	Spark Plug Gap	Location of Timing Mark	Breaker Point Open Deg. BTDC	Breaker Point Gap Used Points	Valve Lash Intake	Valve Lash Exhaust
1971	250	6-3.87x3.53	145	8.50	130	R46TS	.035	V	4B	.016	1 t	1 t
1971	307	V8-3.87x3.25	200	8.50	150	R45TS	.035	V	4Bj	.016	1 t	1 t
1971	350	V8-4.00x3.48	245	8.50	160	R45TS	.035	V	2Bk	.016	1 t	1 t
1971	350	V8-4.00x3.48	270	8.50	160	R45TS	.035	V	4Bj	.016	1 t	1 t
1971	350	V8-4.00x3.48	330	9.00	150	R44TS	.035	V	8Bm	.016	.024	.030
1971	400	V8-4.12x3.75	255	8.50	160	R44TS	.035	V	4Bj	.016	1 t	1 t
1971	402	V8-4.12x3.76	300	8.50	160	R44TS	.035	V	8B	.016	1 t	1 t
1971	454	V8-4.25x4.00	365	8.50	160	R42TS	.035	V	8B	.016	1 t	1 t
1971	454	V8-4.25x4.00	425	9.00	150	R42TS	.035	V	8Bm	.016	.024	.028
1972	140	4-3.50x3.625	80 #	8.00	140	R42TS	.035	V	6N	.016	.015	.030
1972	140	4-3.50x3.625	90 #	8.00	140	R42TS	.035	V	6N	.016	.015	.030
1972	250	6-3.87x3.53	110 #	8.50	130	R46T	.035	V	4B	.016	1 t	1 t
1972	307	V8-3.87x3.25	130 #	8.50	150	R44T	.035	V	4BJ	.016	1 t	1 t
1972	307	V8-3.87x3.25	135 #	8.50	150	R44T	.035	V	4BJ	.016	1 t	1 t
1972	350	V8-4.00x3.48	155 #	8.50	160	R44T	.035	V	6B	.016	1 t	1 t
1972	350	V8-4.00x3.48	165 #	8.50	160	R44T	.035	V	6B	.016	1 t	1 t
1972	350	V8-4.00x3.48	175 #	8.50	160	R44T	.035	V	4BJ	.016	1 t	1 t
1972	350	V8-4.00x3.48	255 #	9.00	150	R44T	.035	V	4BJ	.016	.024	.030
1972	402	V8-4.12x3.76	170 #	8.50	160	R44T	.035	V	2Bk	.016	1 t	1 t
1972	402	V8-4.12x3.76	210 #	8.50	160	R44T	.035	. V	8B	.016	1 t	1 t
1972	402	V8-4.12x3.76	240 #	8.50	160	R44T	.035	V	8B	.016	1 t	1 t
1972	454	V8-4.25x4.00	270 #	8.50	160	R44T	.035	V	8B	.016	1 t	1 t

ABBREVIATIONS APPLICABLE TO TUNE-UP SPECIFICATIONS
Pages 343 and 344

A - After top dead center.
B - Before top dead center.
d - Applies to cars with manual shift transmissions. Set timing at 4 deg. BTDC on cars with automatic transmission.
e - Applies to cars with manual transmission. Set timing 2 deg. BTDC on cars with automatic transmission.
F - Flywheel.
f - Applies to cars without A.I.R. Cars with A.I.R. set timing 6 deg. BTDC.
g - Applies to cars with automatic transmission. Set timing at 2 deg. after top dead center on cars with manual transmission.
H - Adjust valve lash with engine hot.
hy - Hydraulic lifters.
j - Applies to cars with manual transmissions. On cars with automatic transmissions set timing at 8B.

J - 6 deg. for California registration.
k - Applies to cars with manual transmission. On cars with automatic transmission set timing at 6 deg. B.
m - Applies to cars with manual transmission. On cars with automatic transmission set timing at 12 deg. B.
N - 4 deg. BTDC for California vehicles.
P - Set with engine stopped.
R - 0 deg. K20 Suburban models for California only.
S - For sustained high speeds adjust valve lash to .018 in. for intake and .030 in. for exhaust valves.
t - Number of turns from zero lash with hydraulic lifters.
TC - Top dead center.
V - Timing mark on vibration damper or on crankshaft pulley.
- Net or as-installed horsepower ratings.

Wheel Alignment Specifications

YEAR	Caster Degrees	Camber Degrees	Toe-In Inches	Steering Axis Inclination Degrees
Chevrolet				
1960	0	+1/2	1/8 to 1/4	7-1/4
1961	0	+1/2	1/16 to 1/8	7-1/4
1962-1963	0	+1/2	1/8 to 1/4	7-1/4
1964	0	+1/2	1/16 to 3/16	7-1/4
1965-1966	+1/4	+1/4	1/8 to 1/4	7-1/2
1967-1970	+3/4	+1/4	1/8 to 1/4	7-1/2
1971	-1	+1/2	1/8 to 1/4	...
1972	+1	+1/2	3/16	...
Chevelle				
1964	+1/4	+3/4	0 to 1/8	8-1/4
1965-1970	-1 m	+1/2	1/8 to 1/4	8-1/4
1971	-1	+3/4	1/8 to 1/4	...
Chevy II				
1962-1967	+1	+1/2	1/4 to 3/8	7
1968	+1/2	+1/4	1/8 to 1/4	8-3/4
Corvette				
1960	+2	0	0 to 1/8	4
1961-1962	+2	0	1/8 to 3/8	4
1963	+1/2	+2-1/2	1/8 to 1/4	7
1964	+1-1/2	+3/4	3/16 to 5/16	7
1965	+1-1/2	+3/4	7/32 to 11/32	7
1966-1969	+1	+3/4	3/16 to 5/16	7
1971-1972	#	#	#	...
Camaro				
1967-1969	+1/2	+1/4	1/8 to 1/4	8-3/4
1971-1972	0	+1	1/8 to 1/4	...
Nova				
1969-1970	+1/2	+1/4	1/8 to 1/4	8-3/4
1971-1972	+1/2	+1/4	1/8 to 1/4	...
Monte Carlo				
1972	0	+3/4	3/16	...
Vega				
1971	-3/4	+1/4	1/4	...
1972	-3/4	+1/4	1/4	...

m - Applies to all except El Camino, SS and Monte Carlo which are 1/2
- Caster manual steering +1. Caster power steering 2-1/4. Camber 3/4. Toe-in 3/16 to 5/16 in.

ENGINE TIGHTENING SPECIFICATIONS

ENGINE MODEL	Cylinder Head Bolt Torque ft. lb.	Main Bearing Bolt Torque ft. lb.	Connecting Rod Bolt Torque ft. lb.
1950-1952, 216, Six	70-80	100-110	35-45
1950-1962, 235, Six	80-95	100-110	35-45
1963-1965, 230, Six	90-100	60-70	30-35
1955-1957, 265, V-8	60-70	60-70	30-35
1957-1965, 283, V-8	60-70	60-70	30-35
1962-1965, 327, V-8	60-70	60-70	30-35
1958-1961, 348, V-8	60-70	95-105	35-45
1962-1965, 409, V-8	60-70	90-100	35-45
1962-1965, 153, Four	90-100	60-70	30-35
1962-1965, 194, Six	90-100	60-70	30-35
1960-1964, Corvair	27-33	....	20-26
1965-1967, Corvair	32-38	....	20-26
1966-1970, 153	95	65	35
1966-1967, 194	95	65	35
1966-1970, 230	95	65	35
1966-1972, 250	95	65	35
1966-1967, 283	65	80	35
1966-1968, 327	65	80	35
1966-1968, 396	80	80	50
1966-1968, 427	80	80	50
1967-1968, 350	65	80	35
1968, 302	65	80	50
1968, 307	65	80	50
1969-1970, 302	65	75	45
1969-1972, 307	65	75a	45
1969, 327	65	75	45
1969-1972, 350	65	75a	45
1969-1970, 396	80	105	50
1969-1970, 427	80	105	50
1970, 400	65	75a	45
1971-1972, 402	80	75	50
1971-1972, 454	80	75	50

a - Outer bolts on engines with 4 bolt caps 65 lb. ft.

Torque specifications are for clean, undamaged and lightly lubricated threads only. Dry, dirty and damaged threads produce friction which prevents accurate measurement of tightening torque.

COOLING SYSTEM AND CRANKCASE SPECIFICATIONS

CAR AND MODEL	Cooling System With Heater Capacity Quarts	Radiator Cap Relief Pressure lb.	Engine Crankcase Refill Capacity Qt.
Chevrolet			
1952 Six	16	3-1/2 - 4-1/2	5
1953 Six	17	3-1/2 - 4-1/2	5
1954 Six	17	6-1/4 - 7-1/2	5
1955-1957 Six	17	6-1/4 - 7-1/2	5
1955-1957 V-8	17	6-1/4 - 7-1/2	4
1958 Six	17-1/2	13	5
1958-1960, 283, V-8	17	13	4
1958-1960, 348, V-8	23	13	4
1959-1961, Six	17	13	5
1961-1965, 283, V-8	18-1/2	13	4
1961, 348, V-8	22	13	4
1962, 235, Six	18	13	5
1962-1965, 327, V-8	18-1/2	13	4
1962, 409, V-8	18-1/2	13	7
1963-1965, 230, Six	12	13	4
1963, 409, V-8	18-1/2	13	5
1964-1965, 409, V-8	22	13	5
1962-1965, 153, Four	9	13	4
1962-1965, 194, Six	12	13	5
1966-1968, 153	9	15	4
1966-1967, 194	12	15	4
1966-1968, 230	12	15	4
1966-1968, 250	13	15	4
1966-1967, 283	18-1/2	15	4
1966-1967, 327	18-1/2	15	4
1966-1968, 396	23	15	4
1966-1968, 427	22	15	4
1967, 350	18	15	4
1968-1970, 302	17	15	4
1968, 307	17	15	4
1968, 427 Corvette	22	15	5
1968, 350 Camaro	18	15	4
1968, 396 Camaro	23	15	4
1968, 327 Camaro	18	15	4
1969-1970, 153	9	15	4
1969-1970, 230	13	15	4
1969-1972, 307 Chevelle	17	15	4
1969, 327	17	15	4
1969-1970, 396	23	15	4
1969-1970, 250 Camaro	13	15	4
1969-1972, 250 Chevelle	13	15	4
1969-1970, 250 Nova	13	15	4
1969-1972, 250 Chevrolet	12	15	4
1969-1972, 350 Camaro	16	15	4
1969-1972, 350 Chevelle	16	15	4
1969-1972, 350 Nova	16	15	4
1969-1972, 350 Chevrolet	16	15	4
1970-1972, 400	17	15	4
1969-1970, 427 Chevrolet	22	15	4
1969-1970, 427 Corvette	22	15	5
1971-1972, 402	. .	15	4
1971-1972, 454	22	15	4

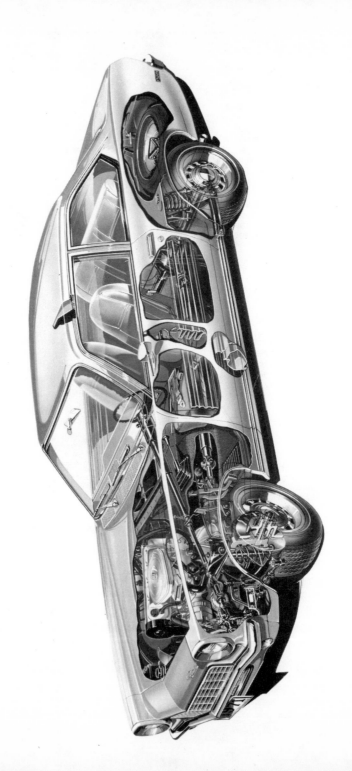

Cutaway view of *Chevrolet Vega 2300.*

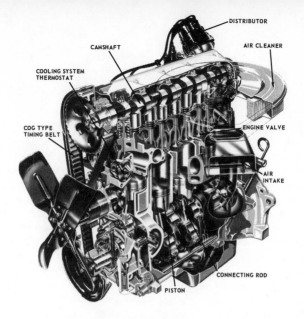

Fig. 1. Details of Vega 140 cu. in. engine.

SERVICING THE VEGA

Service information pertaining to the Vega has been placed in this special section of Fix Your Chevrolet. Every effort has been made to supply as complete information as is possible on those phases of maintenance which are most frequently encountered. Special emphasis has been placed on such operations as tune-up, ignition, brakes, carburetion, valve lash, cooling system, and shock absorbers.

Many basic service procedures are similar to those used on the larger Chevrolet cars, therefore, it is recommended that the reader study those sections of this book for such information which may not be contained in these special pages. This applies particularly to such areas as trouble shooting and reconditioning of parts after they have been removed from the vehicle.

The Vega engine is a 3.50 x 3.625 in., 140 cu. in. four cylinder vertical engine with die cast cylinders of aluminum with silicon evenly distributed throughout to provide a proper bore surface. In addition, the bores are electrochemically treated. Pistons are electroplated with successive coatings of zincate, copper, iron and tin. Cylinder head is cast iron. See Fig. 1.

Two versions of the engine are available. One with a single barrel carburetor developing 90 hp @ 4800 rpm, and the other with a two barrel carburetor developing 110 hp @ 5000 rpm. Compression ratio is 8.5 to 1.

IGNITION TUNE-UP

When ignition breaker points become worn and pitted they must be replaced. See Fig. 2. The procedure is as follows: Release the distributor cap hold-down screws and remove the cap. Remove rotor. Pull the primary and condenser lead wires from the contact point quick disconnect terminal. Remove the contact point set attaching screw. Lift contact point set from the breaker plate. Clean breaker plate of oil smudge and dirt. Install a new set of breaker points by reversing the procedure. Note pilot on contact set must engage matching hole in breaker plate. Check breaker points for proper alignment. See Fig. B-19, page 29. If necessary, bend fixed contact support to obtain alignment of points.

Breaker point gap of new points is 0.019 in. and for used points in good condition is 0.016 in. To set point gap, turn distributor shaft until breaker arm rubbing block is on high point of cam. This provides maximum point gap. Use a screwdriver to move point support to obtain desired gap, Fig. B-20, page 30. Then tighten lock screw. If dwell meter is available, set dwell to 31 - 34 deg.

CONDENSER REPLACEMENT

Normally a new condenser is installed when the ignition breaker points are replaced. The procedure is to first remove the distributor cap and rotor. Disconnect the condenser lead from the contact point quick disconnect terminal, Fig. 2. Remove the condenser attaching screw and lift the condenser from the breaker plate. The new condenser is installed by reversing the procedure.

REMOVING THE DISTRIBUTOR

First remove the distributor cap. If necessary, remove the secondary lead wires from the cap after first marking the cap tower for No. 1 cylinder. Disconnect the distributor lead from the coil terminal. Scratch a realignment mark on the distributor bowl and engine in line with rotor segment. Remove the distributor hold-down bolt and clamp, and remove the distributor from the engine. Note position of vacuum advance mechanism relative to the engine. Avoid rotating crankshaft while the distributor is removed from the engine.

DISTRIBUTOR CHECKS

Check the distributor centrifugal advance mechanism by turning the distributor rotor in a clockwise direction as far as possible. Then release the rotor to see if it returns quickly to the retard position. Any stiffness in the operation of the spark control will affect ignition timing.

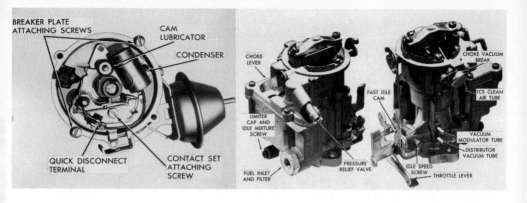

BREAKER PLATE
ATTACHING SCREWS
CAM
LUBRICATOR
CONDENSER
CHOKE
LEVER
CHOKE VACUUM
BREAK
FAST IDLE
CAM
TCS CLEAN
AIR TUBE
LIMITER
CAP AND
IDLE MIXTURE
SCREW
VACUUM
MODULATOR TUBE
DISTRIBUTOR
VACUUM TUBE
QUICK DISCONNECT
TERMINAL
CONTACT SET
ATTACHING
SCREW
FUEL INLET
AND FILTER
PRESSURE
RELIEF VALVE
IDLE SPEED
SCREW
THROTTLE LEVER

Fig. 2. Left. Note quick disconnect terminal and contact set attaching screw on Vega distributor. Fig. 3. Right. Adjusting Rochester MV carburetor.

To lubricate the distributor, remove the distributor cap and rotate the lubricator, Fig. 2, one-half turn at 12,000 mile intervals. Replace lubricator after 24,000 miles.

TIMING THE IGNITION

Make all adjustments with engine at operating temperature (choke valve and air cleaner damper door fully open), air conditioner on, vehicle drive wheels blocked and parking brake on. Note: Carburetor idle mixture is preset and "locked in" by the limiter caps. No attempt should be made to adjust the mixture. Do not remove mixture screw caps.

Disconnect fuel tank line from the vapor canister. Disconnect distributor spark advance hose and plug vacuum source opening. Disconnect electrical connection at anti-dieseling solenoid located on carburetor. Operate engine at idling speed of 850 rpm for cars with three speed transmission, 1200 rpm for cars with four speed transmission and 650 rpm on cars with automatic transmission. The markings on the timing tab by the crankshaft pulley are in two degree increments with the greatest number of markings on the BEFORE side of the 0. The 0 marking indicates top dead center and all before top dead center settings fall on the BEFORE (advance) side of the 0.

Adjust the ignition timing by loosening the distributor clamp and rotating the distributor body until the spark occurs at 6 deg. BTDC. If a timing light is not available, remove the distributor cap and turn the crankshaft until No. 1 piston is on compression stroke. Ignition breaker points should just start to open 6 deg. before top center as indicated by the timing tab.

Firing order of the Vega four cylinder engine is 1-3-4-2.

Whenever the engine is cranked remotely at the starter, with a special jumper cable or other means, the distributor primary lead must be disconnected from the negative pole on the coil and the ignition switch must be in the ON position. Failure to do this will result in a damaged grounding circuit in the ignition switch.

ADJUSTING THE SPARK PLUGS

When disconnecting the spark plugs, pull only on the boot; as pulling on the wire may cause separation of the conducting core of the cable. Use a 5/8 in. deep socket to remove the spark plugs. Inspect insulators for cracks and electrodes for wear and erosion. In general, spark plugs which have been in operation for 10,000 miles should be replaced if maximum economy is desired. Use AC R42TS plugs for normal driving conditions, or AC R41TS when colder plugs are required. Set plug gap to 0.035 in. by bending the center electrode. Before adjusting gap, file top of center electrode flat.

CARBURETOR TUNE-UP

Two service carburetors are available for the Vega cars. The basic carburetors are the Rochester Monojet, Fig. 3, and the Rochester 2GV,

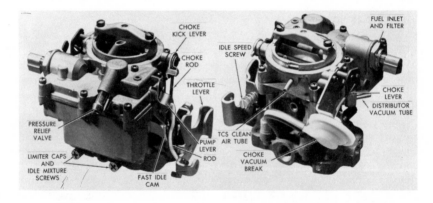

Fig. 4. Details of the model 2GV carburetor used on the 110 hp engine.

Fig. 4. However, there are two models of each of these carburetors, one for manual and one for automatic transmission cars.

PRELIMINARY CHECKS

Thoroughly warm up engine. If engine is cold, allow to run for at least fifteen minutes. Inspect torque of carburetor-to-intake manifold bolts and intake-to-cylinder head bolts to exclude possibility of air leaks. Inspect manifold heat control valve (if used) for freedom of action and correct spring tension. Check and adjust choke as required.

Note: Do not tamper with the idle mixture needle with the black limiter cap. This has been sealed by the manufacturer and must not be removed unless carburetor rebuilding becomes necessary.

Servicing the Vega

Fast idle adjustment must be set with the electrical lead to the Transmission Controlled Spark (TCS) solenoid disconnected and the transmission in Neutral. Make slow idle speed and mixture adjustments with the engine at normal operating temperature and transmission in Drive. If necessary to remove carburetor for rebuilding, install red plastic limiter cap after idle adjustment. Place fast idle cam so that cam follower tang is on highest step of the fast idle cam. Fast idle speed should be 2400 rpm with TCS disconnected and full spark to distributor. If not, insert screwdriver in slot on cam follower tang and bend tang as required to obtain specified speed.

FLOAT ADJUSTMENTS

Float level on MV carburetor is 1/16 in. and on the 2GV carburetor 21/32 in. Float drop on the 2GV carburetor is 1 3/4 in.

FUEL PUMP

The Vega is equipped with an electric fuel pump which is mounted in the fuel tank. Whenever this fuel pump becomes inoperative or does not supply an adequate supply of fuel, it is caused by one of the following reasons: 1. Mechanical defect (pump runs but does not pump adequately). 2. Open circuit (fuses OK but pump will not run). 3. Short circuit (fuse or fuses blown). First check for blown fuses and possibly defective ground. The fuel pump ground is located on the right side of the rear deck lid lock striker. Make sure ground is securely attached and making a good electrical contact. The electric fuel pump is fused both by the

Fig. 5. Left. Timing marks on camshaft and crankshaft sprockets.
Fig. 6. Right. Crankshaft sprocket alignment marks.

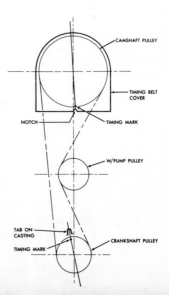

ALLEN WRENCH

Fig. 7. Left. Method of adjusting belt tension. Fig. 8. Right. Valve lash is adjusted by means of an Allen setscrew in the side of the valve lifter.

electric fuel pump 20 amp. fuse and the 10 amp. gauge fuse. Both fuses are located in the fuse panel.

FUEL FILTER MAINTENANCE

Disconnect fuel line connection at inlet fuel filter nut. Remove fuel filter nut from carburetor. Remove filter element and spring. Replace with new filter every 12,000 miles or 12 months, which ever comes first. Bronze or paper filter element should also be replaced if plugged or if flooding occurs.

THE VEGA ENGINE

TIMING BELT REPLACEMENT

Remove engine front cover and accessory drive. Drain engine coolant and loosen water pump bolts to relieve tension on timing belt. Remove timing belt lower cover, then remove timing belt from camshaft and crankshaft sprockets. Remove water pump. When reinstalling timing belt, first apply anti-seize compound to water pump retaining bolts and install water pump, but do not tighten bolts. Align timing mark on camshaft sprocket with notch on timing belt upper cover, Fig. 5. Align crankshaft sprocket timing mark with cast rib on oil pump cover, Fig. 6. Install timing belt on crankshaft sprocket - position back of belt in water pump track - then install belt to camshaft sprocket, making sure that both timing sprockets maintain their indexed positions. Install timing belt lower cover and adjust belt tension as follows: Place torque wrench with special extension in gauge hole adjacent to left side of water pump, Fig. 7. Apply 15 ft. lbs. torque to the water pump. Tighten water pump bolts while maintaining torque on side of pump. Replace remaining parts and refill cooling system.

ADJUSTING VALVE LASH

Valve lash should be adjusted with the engine cold. Intake clearance is 0.014 to 0.016 in. and the exhaust is 0.029 to 0.031 in. Valve lash adjustment is provided by a threaded Allen head screw in the side of the tappet, Fig. 8. This screw has a ground tapered ramp on one surface and is threaded through the tappet at a 5 deg. angle. The flat tapered ramp on the screw is square to the tappet axis and parallel to the valve stem tip which contacts the screw. Valve lash is adjusted with tappet on base circle of camshaft lobe and is adjusted in one turn increments. It is mandatory that the screw be turned a complete revolution each time so that the flat surface of the ramp is always in contact with the tip of the valve stem. Each revolution will change valve lash 0.003 in.

OIL PAN REMOVAL

To remove the oil pan, raise the vehicle and drain the oil. Support front of engine and remove front cross member and both frame cross member braces. Disconnect steering idler arm at frame side rail. On air conditioned vehicles, disconnect idler arm at relay rod. Mark re-

Fig. 9. Sequence to be followed when tightening cylinder head bolts.

lationship of steering linkage pitman arm to steering gear pitman shaft and remove pitman arm. Do not rotate steering gear pitman shaft while steering arm is disconnected as this will change steering wheel alignment. Remove flywheel cover or converter underpan as applicable. Remove pan-to-cylinder retaining screws, tap pan lightly to break sealing bond and remove oil pan from vehicle. Replacement tappet adjusting screws are available in three range sizes.

CYLINDER HEAD REMOVAL

Remove engine front cover, camshaft cover, timing belt and camshaft timing sprocket. Remove intake and exhaust manifolds. Disconnect coolant hose at thermostat housing. Remove cylinder head bolts and remove cylinder head. When replacing cylinder head, first install cylinder head gasket over dowel pins with smooth side of gasket up. Then, with the aid of an assistant, carefully guide cylinder head into place over dowel pins and gasket. Use anti-seize compound on cylinder head bolts. Cylinder head bolts on spark plug side are approximately 5 5/8 in. long and those on the manifold side are 6 3/8 in. long. First install bolts finger tight and then torque in sequence, shown in Fig. 9, to 60 ft. lbs.

EMISSION CONTROL SYSTEMS

Emission control systems on the Vega include: 1-Positive Crankcase Ventilation System. 2-Controlled Combustion System. 3-Evaporative Emission Control. 4-Transmission Controlled Spark. In addition the 1972 models have the Air Injector Reactor System.

Every 24,000 miles or 24 months the Positive Crankcase Ventilation Valve should be replaced and hoses and fittings cleaned. The system should be checked at every oil change for proper function. Make sure vacuum is drawing vapors from crankcase.

The Controlled Combustion System is designed to increase combustion efficiency through leaner carburetor adjustments and revised distributor calibration. In addition, on the majority of installations, special thermostatically controlled air cleaners are used. Basic servicing of these units is covered in the carburetor and ignition sections.

The Evaporative Emission Control System is designed to reduce fuel vapor emissions that normally vent to the atmosphere from the fuel tank and carburetor fuel bowl. The filter mounted at the bottom of the canister requires replacement every 12,000 miles. Care must be taken that the fuel tank cap is not damaged.

In the Transmission Controlled Spark system, the distributor vacuum advance has been eliminated in the low forward speeds. The control of the vacuum advance is accomplished by means of a solenoid vacuum switch which is energized in the low gears by a grounding switch at the transmission. The TCS system also incorporates a temperature override system which provides full vacuum in all gears when the engine is cold. A thermostatic water temperature switch provides the signal which energizes a normally closed relay, opening the circuit to the solenoid switch, thus providing full vacuum. The system may be checked for proper function by connecting a vacuum gauge between the solenoid and the distributor. Full vacuum should be obtained when the automatic transmission is in second speed; in the four speed transmission, full vacuum should be obtained in third and fourth speeds; and in the case of a three speed transmission, full vacuum should be obtained in third speed only.

COOLING SYSTEM

The cooling system of the Vega is of the pressurized type. The radiator cap is the 15 lb. type which permits engine operation at cooling temperatures up to 247 deg. F.

Coolant level in the cross-flow radiator should be maintained three inches below the bottom of the filler neck when the system is cold. Regardless of whether freezing temperatures are expected, cooling system protection should be maintained at least to zero degrees F to provide adequate corrosion protection and proper temperature indicating light operation. Flush system every two years with plain water and then refill with a new solution of antifreeze and water. Antifreeze must be of the permanent glycol base type. Do not use alcohol or methanol base antifreeze.

The thermostat is of the 195 deg. type. Cooling system capacity with heater and air conditioning is 6.5 quarts.

ELECTRICAL SYSTEM

GENERATOR

The 10-SI series Delcotron generator is similar to that shown in Fig. K-2a, page 149. This unit has a solid state regulator that is mounted inside the generator slip ring end frame. The regulator voltage setting never needs adjusting and no provision for adjustment is provided.

STARTING MOTOR

The starting motor used on the Vega is shown in Fig. L-1, page 164. No periodic lubrication of the starting motor solenoid is required. Since the starting motor and brushes cannot be inspected without disassembling the unit, no service is required between overhaul periods.

WIRING HARNESS

There are two basic wiring harnesses under the instrument panel. They are the instrument panel wiring harness and the instrument cluster wiring harness. The harnesses have their blocks bolted together, to the left of the steering column.

All instruments and gauges are removed from the front of the cluster.

The speedometer cable is also removed from the front of the instrument cluster.

BRAKES

Disc front brakes are standard equipment on the Vega and the rear brakes are of the drum type with leading-trailing shoe design. Rear brake adjustment is not automatic. Adjustment takes place, if needed, when the parking brake is applied.

SERVICING THE DISC BRAKES

It is not necessary to remove the hydraulic line to the caliper when removing the caliper. However, do not let the caliper hang from the suspension by the hydraulic line. Lay the caliper on the suspension members for support, or hang it from a wire.

To remove caliper and replace shoes: Raise the vehicle on a hoist and remove the front wheels. Remove the two mounting pin stamped nuts. See Fig. 10. Discard the nuts. Remove the two mounting pins and lift the

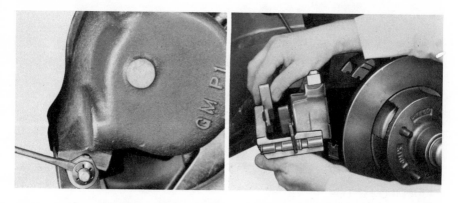

Fig. 10. Left. Removing caliper retainers. Fig. 11. Right. Removing or installing brake shoes on disc type brakes.

caliper from the disc. Remove the inboard and outboard shoes by sliding the shoes to the mounting sleeve opening, Fig. 11. Remove the mounting sleeves and bushing assemblies. Clean the inside of the caliper and exterior of the dust boot.

When reassembling, install new sleeves with bushings on the caliper grooves. The shouldered end of the sleeve must be installed toward the outside. Install the new inner shoe on the caliper and slide the shoe ears over the sleeve. Install the outer shoe in the same manner. Mount the caliper on the vehicle. It may be necessary to remove 1/2 in. of brake fluid from the main cylinder before installing the shoes. Install the mounting pins in a direction from inside to outside. Install the stamped nuts. Nuts should be pressed on as far as possible using a socket of suitable size. The stamped nuts must be pressed on with a socket that "just" seats on the outer edge of the nut. Replace the front wheels.

REAR BRAKE SERVICING

If rear brake drums cannot be removed, it will be necessary to remove the brake adjustment assembly. To gain access to the adjuster, knock out the lanced area in the web of the drum. See Fig. 12.

Release the rod assembly from the trailing shoe by pushing in on the rod until it is clear of the shoe. The pull back spring will pull the shoes

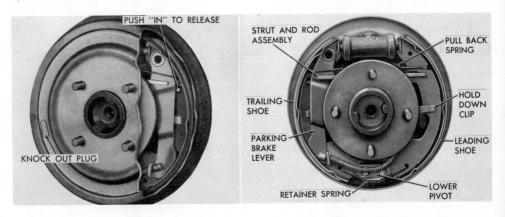

Fig. 12. Left. Location of knock-out-plug (lanced area) and release button on rear brakes of the Vega. Fig. 13. Right. Details of rear brakes.

toward each other and the drum may be removed. Be sure to remove the lanced piece of metal from the interior of the brake.

After removing the brake drum, completely release all tension from the parking brake equalizer. Remove the parking brake cable from the parking brake lever. Do not allow the lever to swing forward as the movement would "adjust" the brakes. Using pliers, remove the pull back spring, Fig. 13. Pull the leading and trailing shoes from under the hold-down clips and remove the shoes with the strut and adjuster assembly attached. Separate the shoes and remove the strut and adjuster assembly from the trailing shoe. Remove the parking brake lever.

New brake shoes can be installed by reversing the procedure. Note that the trailing shoe has a hole to accept the parking brake lever and an oblong hole to accept the adjuster rod. Also, the pull back spring must be installed so as to be in a position that is over the parking brake lever and engaging the trailing shoe.

HYDRAULIC SERVICE

Servicing the hydraulic system of the Vega brakes is the same as that described in the chapter QUICK SERVICE ON BRAKES in this text.

CLUTCH

The single plate diaphragm spring clutch, Fig. 14, in the Vega is cable operated. Adjustment for normal clutch wear is accomplished by turning the clutch fork ball stud counterclockwise to give 0.90 ± 0.25 in. lash at clutch pedal. To make adjustment, remove ball stud cap and loosen lock nut on ball stud end located to the right of the transmission on the clutch housing. Adjust ball stud to obtain specified free travel. Tighten lock nut to 25 ft. lbs. torque, being careful not to change adjustment. Install ball stud cap. Check operation.

MANUAL TRANSMISSION

The Vega is equipped with either of two manual transmissions. One is a three speed unit and the other a four speed unit. Both are fully synchronized in all forward speeds and have floor mounted shift controls.

To replace extension oil seal: Raise vehicle on a hoist. Remove propeller shaft and disconnect any items to obtain necessary clearance. Pry seal out of extension. Wash counterbore with cleaning solvent and inspect for damage. Prelubricate sealing lips and coat new seal outside diameter

Fig. 14. Details of the cable operated disc clutch. 1—Clutch cover. 2—Fork ball stud. 3—Lock nut. 4—Ball stud cap. 5—Throwout bearing support. 6—Support gasket. 7—Throwout bearing. 8—Diaphragm spring. 9—Clutch fork. 10—Clutch cable lock pin. 11—Clutch cable. 12—Pressure plate. 13—Driven disc. 14—Pilot bearing. 15—Flywheel.

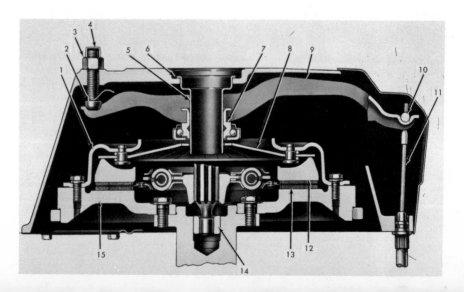

with Permatex or equivalent. Start straight in bore in case extension. Use round drift of appropriate diameter and tap seal into counterbore until flange bottoms against extension.

To remove manual shift transmission: Place shift lever in Neutral position and remove shift lever. Raise vehicle on hoist and drain lubricant. Remove propeller shaft assembly. Disconnect speedometer cable, TCS switch and back-up lamp switch. Remove cross member-to-transmission mount bolts. Support engine with jack stand and remove cross member-to-frame bolts. Remove cross member. Remove transmission-to-clutch housing upper retaining bolts and install guide pins in holes. Remove lower bolts and slide transmission rearward and remove from vehicle.

AUTOMATIC TRANSMISSION

The aluminum Powerglide transmission is similar to the one used on the larger Chevrolet models and is illustrated in Fig. P-12, pages 220 and 221. The manual shifting torque drive transmission is also available on the Vega. This transmission is similar to the aluminum Powerglide with the automatic shifting provisions removed. Lubrication, maintenance and service information are the same as that listed for the aluminum Powerglide.

REAR AXLE

The rear axle used on the Vega is similar to that illustrated in Fig. R-1, page 237. The procedure for removing axle shaft is also similar. The rear axle oil seal can be replaced by using the button end of the axle shaft. Insert the button end of the shaft behind the steel case of the oil seal. Then pry the seal out of the housing bore being careful not to damage the housing.

PROPELLER SHAFT

The propeller shaft and universal joints used on the Vega are similar to those shown in Fig. Q-1, page 233. To remove the propeller shaft, raise the vehicle on a hoist and mark the relationship of shaft to companion flange. Disconnect the rear universal joint by removing the trunnion bearing U bolts. Tape the bearing cups to trunnion to prevent dropping and loss of roller bearings. Withdraw propeller shaft front yoke from transmission by moving shaft rearward, passing it under the rear axle housing. Plug rear of transmission to prevent leakage of lubricant.

FRONT WHEEL ALIGNMENT

Camber and caster adjustments are made by the cam bolts which are

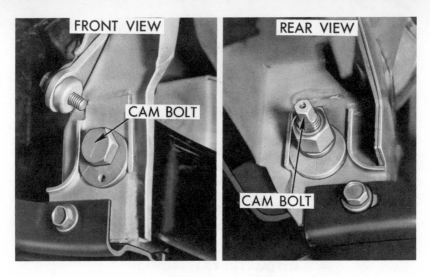

Fig. 15. Camber and caster adjustments.

the attachment for the lower control arm. Camber angle is adjusted first and is made by loosening the front lower control arm pivot nut and rotating the cam until proper setting is made. Caster is adjusted next, and is made by loosening the rear lower control arm pivot nut and rotating the cam until proper setting is reached. Fig. 15 shows the location of the adjustments. Toe-in is checked after making the camber and caster adjustments. Loosen the clamp bolt nut at each end of each tie rod and rotate the sleeve until the proper toe-in is obtained. The sleeve clamps must be positioned between the locating dimples at either end of the sleeve. The opening in the sleeve must not be covered by the clamp. Correct camber is +1/4 deg. and correct caster is - 3/4 deg. Toe-in is 3/16 in. to 5/16 in.

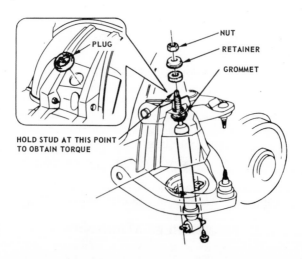

Fig. 16. Front shock absorber installation on the Vega.

SHOCK ABSORBER SERVICE

To remove the front shock absorbers: Hold the shock absorber stem and remove the nut, upper retainer and grommet, Fig. 16. Raise the vehicle on a hoist and remove the bolts from the lower end of the shock absorber. Lower the shock absorber from the vehicle. When installing new shock absorbers, place the lower retainer and rubber grommet in position. Extend the shock absorber stem and install the stem through the spring tower. Install the lower bolts and torque to 20 ft. lbs. Install the upper rubber grommet, retainer and nut on the shock absorber stem. Hold the stem and tighten nut to 120 ft. lbs.

To remove the rear shock absorbers: Raise vehicle on hoist and support rear axle assembly. Remove upper attaching bolts and lower attaching nut, retainer and cushion. Remove the shock absorber. To install a new shock absorber, reverse the procedure.

VEGA SPECIFICATIONS

Engine bore and stroke	3 1/2 x 3 5/8 in.
Engine displacement	140 cu. in.
Brake horsepower	90 @ 4800 rpm and 110 @ 5000 rpm
Brake horsepower, 1972	80 @ 4400 rpm and 90 @ 4800 rpm
Compression ratio	8.5 to 1
Compression	140 psi
Firing order	1-3-4-2
Spark plug, standard	AC R42TS
Spark plug, cold	AC R41TS
Spark plug gap	0.035 in.
Breaker point gap	0.016 in. (used)
Breaker point gap	0.019 in. (new)
Breaker point dwell	31 to 34 deg.
Ignition timing	6 deg. BTDC with vacuum disconnected
Valve lash with engine stopped	0.014 to 0.016 in. inlet
Valve lash with engine stopped	0.029 to 0.031 in. exhaust
Idle rpm, 3 speed trans.	850 rpm
Idle rpm, 4 speed trans.	1200 rpm
Idle rpm, automatic trans.	650 rpm in drive
Fuel pump volume	1 pint in 30 to 45 sec.
Crankcase vent	Service at 24,000 miles
Cooling system capacity with heater	6.5 qt.
Crankcase refill capacity with filter	4 qt.
Cooling thermostat opens at	195 deg.
Auto Transmission total capacity	8 1/2 qt.
Auto Transmission refill capacity	3 qt.

INDEX

Index